Race and Affect

in Early Modern English Literature

Race and Affect

in Early Modern English Literature

edited by

Carol Mejia LaPerle

Arizona State University
Tempe, Arizona
2022

Race and Affect in Early Modern English Literature was published in 2022 by ACMRS Press at Arizona State University in Tempe, Arizona.

This book is available online at https://asu.pressbooks.pub/race-and-affect/

Library of Congress Cataloging-in-Publication Data
Librarians will find the cataloging data for this book online. It was not available at the time of this printing.

Hardcover ISBN 978-0-86698-692-2
Paperback ISBN 978-0-86698-658-8
eISBN 978-0-86698-693-9

Hardcover and paperback editions are printed in the United States of America.

Contents

Foreword

MARGO HENDRICKS

Nearly thirty years ago, a small group of Black, Indigenous, Brown, and Asian scholars working in "Renaissance English Literature" challenged the idea that race was unimportant before the "Enlightenment." The insertion of race, racism, and race-making as a defining element in constructing universalities based on whiteness, settler colonialist and colonialist ideologies, and anti-Blackness was deemed unnecessary and anachronistic. The construction of a *historical past* within and around early modern English history ignored the presence of non-white peoples or insisted the numbers were too negligible to matter. Of course, as we've come to learn, the *Past* is never as obvious as it may appear on the surface, especially when one is removed from said histories by centuries, geographic spaces, and a techno-global economy burdened by the ideologies and systems of racial capitalism.

It is not an understatement to say writing about "race" in relation to early modern English literature and its *Past* was a challenge. Yet, a theoretical and critical practice emerged that fundamentally altered twentieth-century scholarly writings about early modern English culture. Premodern Critical Race Studies (PCRS) insisted on the intersectionality of race-making, gender, sexuality, and class in the early modern English cultural representation of itself. From the start, PCRS concerned itself with the literary, visual, performative, social, and cultural moments of racism and recalibrations of race-making necessitated by the advent of early modern imperialism, early modern white settler colonialism, and the ideological use of anti-Blackness and anti-Indigenous representations. Indebted to Critical Race Theory and Black feminism for its theoretical foundations, PCRS recognized and continues to recognize the importance of attending to the usage and circulation of texts local to a specific culture and temporality while questioning the idea of their universality.

From this theoretical and critical intervention, the collection of essays in this anthology emerges as *next gen* PCRS. The authors strategically explore the relationship between "affect" and "race" in early modern texts such as William Shakespeare's *A Midsummer Night's Dream*, Thomas Heywood's *Fair Maid of the West*, Edmund Spenser's *The Faire Queene*, or Philip Massinger's *The Renegado* — texts that circulate in classrooms, on the stage, and in publications. In the aftermath of the murders of Black men in the United States, the rampant rise of fascism across the globe, the indifference on the part of white-centric governments primarily in Europe and the United States toward indigenous peoples around the world in the advent of the coronavirus, and deadly misogynist assaults on LGTBTIA people, these authors brilliantly demonstrate why, even in the twenty-first century, continued attention must be paid to early modern English literary texts and their role in race-making.

Often, we cannot be sure a book will have an impact beyond a small coterie. Can and will *Race and Affect in Early Modern English Literature* have an effect? The answer is yes. The authorial voices here represent a fundamental sea change. These are the descendants of that small band of intrepid scholars who insisted on the study of race, racism, and race-making in early modern English culture. These voices complement and carry forward the need for critique, interrogation, and revolutionary thinking about the *Past* and its histories — both as affect and effect. *Race and Affect in Early Modern English Literature* is the collective resistance of an emerging generation of Premodern Critical Race scholars and scholarship to a field rooted in racism, homophobia, misogyny, and classism. With these profound and intuitive readings, this collection reminds us that *affect* is central to race-making.

Introduction

CAROL MEJIA LAPERLE

> How does it feel to be a problem?
> ~ W.E.B. Du Bois, *The Souls of Black Folk* (1903)
>
> How does it feel to be the problem of feeling?
> ~ Fred Moten, *In the Break* (2003)
>
> To be a problem is the being-ness of blackness
> ~ Calvin L. Warren, *Ontological Terror* (2018)

In W.E.B. Du Bois's development of the concept of double consciousness in *The Souls of Black Folk*, he evokes the metaphor of the color-line to critique the obstacles to African American civic engagement, economic prosperity, and social standing. In this landmark analysis of early twentieth-century racial politics, he poses a distinctly intimate question: "How does it feel to be a problem?"[1] In his provocation, *feeling* is simultaneously an experience and an attribution. He articulates a social categorization embedded in the accusation that the individual is disjointed from or disruptive of the dominant ideology, that the individual is a "problem." But beyond this attribution, the syntax (as a question) extracts from the subject's position an articulation of affect. "How does it feel" is an invitation to put into words the nexus of relations, dispositions, and sensations that constitute the racialized subject's lived experience. Fred Moten conjures this sentiment when he asks: "How does it feel to be the problem of feeling?" indicating not just the affective experience of a divided self, but also a nonnormative phenomenology characterized as the sense of error or erasure in relation to feeling itself.[2] For Moten, to be "the problem of feeling" is to dwell on a condition manifested as both a disruption of order and

1. W.E.B. Du Bois, *The Souls of Black Folk* (New York: Millennium Publications, 2014), 4.
2. Fred Moten, *In the Break: The Aesthetics of the Black Radical Tradition* (Minneapolis: University of Minnesota Press, 2003), 77.

the source of creative potential. Building on these philosophical considerations, Calvin L. Warren locates in Blackness the disturbance, the contradiction, and yet the very foundation of racial subjectivity. "To be a problem is the being-ness of blackness" signals a metaphysical claim to selfhood marked by its own alterity.[3] It is a complaint about the epistemological grounds for being-ness itself, locating in metaphysics the imbrication of subjugation and erasure within doctrines of autonomy. But Warren's statement is also, in a less lofty, philosophical sense, a truism. The troubles, the struggles, the questions — the problems — of racialized subjectivity are disclosed by Black intellectuals as entrenched in feeling.

In its investigation of plays, poetry, letters, travel accounts, medical treatises, social documents, and performances, this collection connects modern Black scholars' insights to a much longer history. It does so by building on the foundation established by early modern race scholarship, such as the ground-breaking collection *Women, "Race," and Writing in the Early Modern Period*.[4] The editors, Margo Hendricks and Patricia Parker, stress the scare quotes around race in order to make apparent the institutionally sanctioned suppression of research on race in early modernity. From accusations of anachronism to outright denial of the existence of Black subjects in England, the critical status quo represented by those scare quotes determined not just whose findings were published, but also the influence and impact afforded them. The significance of racial thinking to early moderns had to be justified repeatedly, despite evidence and analyses to prove not only the presence of this thinking, but also the widespread social impact of English engagements with, and representations of, racial difference. The process played out something akin to Joyce Green MacDonald's investigation of racialized women in *Women and Race in Early Modern Texts*.[5] MacDonald brilliantly demonstrates that the com-

3. Calvin L. Warren, *Ontological Terror: Blackness, Nihilism, and Emancipation* (Durham, NC: Duke University Press, 2018), 29.
4. Margo Hendricks and Patricia Parker, eds., *Women, "Race" and Writing in the Early Modern Period* (London: Routledge, 1994).
5. Joyce Green Macdonald, *Women and Race in Early Modern Texts* (Cambridge: Cambridge University Press, 2002).

pulsion of early modern authors to appropriate dynamic representations of non-white identity nonetheless Europeanized, and attempted to elide, racial difference. This form of gaslighting, as it were, is replicated in the field's compulsion to undermine race scholarship by insisting that the presence of racialized characters in literature was not indicative of the formations and operations of racial thinking.

Inevitably and permanently, the efforts of premodern critical race scholars shattered the scare quotes around race. [6] Hendricks, Parker, and MacDonald prevail as crucial arbiters for reading the intersections of race and gender in early modern English literature and culture. The painstaking archival work of Imtiaz Habib, the critique of humanist education and Renaissance rhetoric by Ian Smith, the connections between sexuality and racial formation by Arthur L. Little Jr., the innovative methodologies and performance analyses of Ayanna Thompson — these represent a portion of the substantial contributions to understanding how race influences social attitudes, political investments, interpersonal engagements, economic interests, and self-fashioning, then and now.[7] An anthology of primary texts on race compiled and edited by Ania Loomba and Jonathan Burton, *Race in Early Modern England*, offers a crucial resource for teachers to share previously inaccessible materials with students.[8] Decades of premodern critical race scholarship, employed in the study of genealogy, language, economics, religion, clothing, behavior, skin color, and ethnicity expanded the materials and the methods through which Englishness,

6. For the state of the field, see Ayanna Thompson, ed., *The Cambridge Companion to Shakespeare and Race* (Cambridge: Cambridge University Press, 2021).
7. Imtiaz Habib, *Black Lives in the English Archives, 1500–1677: Imprints of the Invisible* (London: Routledge, 2008); Ian Smith, *Race and Rhetoric in the Renaissance: Barbarian Errors* (New York: Palgrave Macmillan, 2009); Arthur L. Little Jr., *Shakespeare Jungle Fever: National-Imperial Re-Visions of Race, Rape, and Sacrifice* (Stanford, CA: Stanford University Press, 2002); Ayanna Thompson, *Performing Race and Torture on the Early Modern Stage* (London: Routledge, 2009); *Passing Strange: Shakespeare, Race, and Contemporary America* (Oxford: Oxford University Press, 2013).
8. Jonathan Burton and Ania Loomba, eds., *Race in Early Modern England: A Documentary Companion* (New York: Palgrave Macmillan, 2007).

and its investments in racial formation, are analyzed.[9] For instance, Patricia Akhimie's *Shakespeare and the Cultivation of Difference* is a milestone in bridging the visual and the nonvisual markers of race by showing how conduct literature, and the modes of surveillance and discipline it codifies, inflict the painful physical marks and ascribe the intellectual defects that racial subjects are accused of being born with.[10] Notably, the revolutionary examination of colonialism and empire in Kim F. Hall's *Things of Darkness* models an intersectional lens for examining race, gender, and class across a wide range of literary texts and visual artifacts. Many of the chapters in this collection are profoundly indebted to Hall's inimitable scholarship.[11] Racial thinking influences the reading, performance, and experience of literature today, and fundamentally shapes the future

9. Many scholars consider historical contexts alongside their analyses of literature to investigate ideologies of power and iterations of racial identity. Beyond scholarship previously cited, see also Bernadette Andrea, *Women and Islam in Early Modern English Literature* (Cambridge: Cambridge University Press, 2007); Lara Bovilsky, *Barbarous Play: Race on the English Renaissance Stage* (Minneapolis: University of Minnesota Press, 2008); Dennis Austin Britton, *Becoming Christian: Race, Reformation, and Early Modern Romance* (New York: Fordham University Press, 2014); Jonathan Burton, *Traffic and Turning: Islam and English Drama, 1579–1624* (Newark, NJ: University of Delaware Press, 2005); Kimberly Anne Coles, *Bad Humor: Race and Religious Essentialism in Early Modern England* (Philadelphia: University of Pennsylvania Press, forthcoming); Mary Floyd-Wilson, *English Ethnicity and Race in Early Modern Drama* (Cambridge: Cambridge University Press, 2003); Sujata Iyengar, *Shades of Difference: Mythologies of Skin Color in Early Modern England* (Cambridge: Cambridge University Press, 2004); Barbara Fuchs, *Mimesis and Empire: The New World, Islam, and European Identities* (Cambridge: Cambridge University Press, 2001); Elizabeth Spiller, *Reading and the History of Race* (Cambridge: Cambridge University Press, 2011). These are some of the monographs that have shaped the discussion of race in the Renaissance in enduring and influential ways by focusing on genealogy, language, rhetoric, economics, religion, clothing, skin coloring, and comportment. Understanding racial formation based on ethnic, physical, religious, or behavioral differences is essential to historicizing and critiquing the colonial projects and formative narratives of early modern race ideology.
10. Patricia Akhimie, *Shakespeare and the Cultivation of Difference: Race and Conduct in the Early Modern World* (London: Routledge, 2018).
11. Kim F. Hall, *Things of Darkness: Economies of Race and Gender in Early Modern England* (Ithaca, NY: Cornell University Press, 1995).

of our discipline. In the inspiring words of Thompson, whose RaceB4Race initiatives and symposiums have challenged the racism endemic to the field, "Race is not a niche subfield. Wake up academy. *We're here.*"[12]

Not a subfield, indeed, since Premodern Critical Race Theory (PCRS) draws from scholarship in the social sciences, law, and humanities in order to expose the violence attending racialization in the archives and our classrooms, from metaphysics to economics, writ in law and widespread in popular culture.[13] In its dedication to social justice and opposition to white supremacy, Critical Race Theory exposes the histories and legacies of slavery.[14] These histories and legacies continue to create racial hierarchies, facilitate social oppression, and obscure the mechanisms of racism in everyday life. Literature is part of this legacy, but it is not enough to simply point that out. Beyond recognizing the operations of race formation and racism in texts, PCRS amplifies resistance and empowerment by employing what bell hooks calls "the right to gaze" at what is deemed normal or beyond inquiry: "an overwhelming longing to look, a rebellious desire, an oppositional gaze. By courageously looking, we defiantly declared: 'Not only will I stare. I want my look to change real-

12. Ayanna Thompson et al., "To Protect and Serve: A RaceB4Race Roundtable" (roundtable, Arizona Center for Medieval and Renaissance Studies, Arizona State University, 23 July 2020), recording posted by ACMRS on YouTube, https://www.youtube.com/watch?v=AYnmcBu0b-8.
13. For an introduction to Critical Race Theory, see Richard Delgado, Jean Stefancic, and Angela P. Harris, eds., *Critical Race Theory: An Introduction*, 3rd ed. (New York: New York University Press, 2017); Kimberlé Williams Crenshaw, Luke Charles Harris, Daniel Martinez HoSang, and George Lipsitz, eds., *Seeing Race Again: Countering Colorblindness across the Disciplines* (Oakland: University of California Press, 2019).The following scholars, many of whom are cited throughout this collection, constitute an important body of scholarship in Critical Race Theory: Derrick Bell, James Baldwin, Kimberlé Crenshaw, Jennifer L. Morgan, bell hooks, Achille Mbembe, Kwame Anthony Appiah, Patricia Hill Collins, Saidiya Hartman, Sylvia Wynter, Patricia Holland, Toni Morrison, and Fred Moten.
14. The impact and outcome of enslavement as a sociopolitical order that Hortense J. Spiller articulates as "human sequence written in blood," as "a scene of actual mutilation, dismemberment, and exile" cannot be overstated. ("Mama's Baby, Papa's Maybe: An American Grammar Book," *Diacritics* 17, no. 2 [1987]: 67).

ity.'"[15] Many of the chapters here begin with an unflinching look at the operations of race mobilizing whiteness in the formation of an English commonwealth. Ruth Frankenberg's definition articulates how whiteness is not simply a matter of representation, but rather, central to the politics of domination:

> [Whiteness is] a set of locations that are historically, socially, politically, and culturally produced, and, moreover, are intrinsically linked to unfolding relations of domination. Naming "whiteness" displaces it from the unmarked, unnamed status that is itself an effect of its dominance. Among the effects of white people both of race privilege and of the dominance of whiteness are their seeming normativity, their structured invisibility ... To look at the construction of whiteness, then, is to look head-on at a site of dominance.[16]

While sites of dominance in early modern English literature comprise a portion of our findings, they are only part of the antiracist orientation of this collection. Critical Race Theory, as it informs the study of premodern literature and culture, necessitates a different relationship with scholarship.

To this, the chapters abide by hooks's defiant "oppositional gaze" as a posture of skeptical discontent, as a troubling of one's relationship with the text, as a challenge to normative methods of inquiry, and as an apprehensive disposition towards Western epistemology. All of which is meant to lay the groundwork for change in how we read, research, teach, and experience early modern texts. As Marissa J. Fuentes points out in her study of enslaved women whose lived experiences must be culled from the documents of slavery, "How do we critically confront or reproduce these accounts to open up possibilities for historicizing, mourn-

15. bell hooks, "The Oppositional Gaze: Black Female Spectators," in *The Feminine and Visual Culture Reader*, ed. Amelia Jones (London: Routledge, 2003), 94.
16. Ruth Frankenberg, *White Women, Race Matters: The Social Construction of Whiteness* (Minneapolis: University of Minnesota Press, 1993), 6.

ing, remembering, and listening to the condition of enslaved women?"[17] Borrowing Fuentes's formulation, this collection historicizes, mourns, remembers, and listens with attentiveness to feelings and impressions that forgo adherence to established forms of knowledge building. To demonstrate this point in a deceptively simple manner, I ask readers to notice the range of approaches essayists have taken to tackle key racial terms. Instead of insisting on uniformity, the collection offers authors a chance to elaborate on their choices. It might seem like a trivial point to decide whether or not "Black" should be capitalized or to insist on lower case "east," but in fact the choice, as well as the controversies and debates that choice evokes, is a demonstration of a kind of relationship to discourse — one that is self-reflexive and attentive to the moment. This is not a matter of being politically correct. It is safe to say that many authors in this collection are productively controversial. Instead, troubling key concepts reflects skepticism about the stability of racial terms and the concepts they are meant to capture; it demonstrates a willingness to critically interrogate foundational premises; it resists the reproduction of normative methodologies which have historically been used to serve white supremacy. We are not interested, in other words, in making the use of these terms easier for ourselves or for anyone else.

Additionally, engagement with Critical Race Theory includes questioning our premises about what is worthy of investigation.[18] Which subject positions are privileged and which are, by violent design, erased or distorted? How do we reckon with the incomplete traces left by this violence? Part of reckoning includes acknowledging the ephemerality and contradictions accompanying this kind of work. Critiquing the conven-

17. Marisa J. Fuentes, *Dispossessed Lives: Enslaved Women, Violence, and the Archives* (Philadelphia: University of Pennsylvania Press, 2016), 1.
18. Importantly, this change builds on, rather the obscures, the work of critical race scholars. Margo Hendrick calls out the "white settler colonizing" of a particular kind of analysis that obscures the mechanisms of racism by neglecting, erasing, or appropriating the decades long work of critical race scholars ("Coloring the Past, Rewriting our Future: RaceB4Race" [lecture, "Race and Periodization" symposium, Folger Institute, Washington, DC, September 2019], https://www.folger.edu/institute/scholarly-programs/race-periodization/margo-hendricks).

tional heuristics that underwrite humanist agendas, Alexander G. Weheliye asks, "what different modalities of the human come to light if we do not take the liberal humanist figure of Man as the master-subject but focus on how humanity has been imagined and lived by those subjects excluded from this domain?"[19] To this important question, *Race and Affect* adds – what are the feelings, dispositions, and senses that accompany the representation of racialized subjectivities beyond the "liberal humanist figure"? For those "excluded from this domain," how does race feel?

In its application of transdisciplinary methodologies to the study of intersubjective experiences, responses, dispositions, and emotions, affect studies is invaluable to literary analysis.[20] To early modern English literary scholarship specifically, affect studies has offered explanatory vocabulary and theoretical interventions for investigating the history of passions, querying the ecology of a performance space, and exploring the affective communities formed out of shared or diverging dispositions.[21] A char-

19. Alexander G. Weheliye, *Habeas Viscus: Racializing Assemblages, Biopolitics, and Black Feminist Theories of the Human* (Durham, NC: Duke University Press, 2014), 8. In Denise Ferreira da Silva's formulation of Sylvia Wynter's challenge to ontology, she traces how Wynter "focuses on the ways in which the architectures of colonial juridical-economic power are encoded, and thus sustain, what it means to be human while also offering a *refiguring* of humanness that is produced *in relation to* the monumental history of race itself" ("Before *Man*: Sylvia Wynter's Rewriting of the Modern Episteme," in *Sylvia Wynter: On Being Human as Praxis*, ed. Katherine McKittrick [Durham, NC: Duke University Press, 2015], 93 original emphases).
20. Emotions and affect are not synonymous, but they occasionally overlap in that the "specific physiological responses that then give rise to various effects ... may or may not translate into emotions" (Elizabeth Wissinger, "Always on Display: Affective Production in the Modeling Industry," in *The Affective Turn: Theorizing the Social*, ed. Patricia Ticineto Clough and Jean Halley [Durham, NC: Duke University Press, 2007], 232).
21. Early modern scholarship drawing from affect's versatile "relatedness" to investigate audience/actor performances, to examine the history of passions, and to explore the networks of feeling informing early modern culture include Ronda Arab, Michelle M. Dowd, and Adam Zucker, eds., *Historical Affects and Early Modern Theater* (London: Routledge, 2015); Gail Kern Paster, Katherine Rowe, and Mary Floyd-Wilson, eds., *Reading the Early Modern Passions: Essays in the Cultural History of Emotion* (Philadelphia:

acteristically broad and often abstract application does not hinder usefulness, as conveyed by Gregory J. Seigworth and Melissa Gregg's explication: "Because affect emerges out of muddy, unmediated relatedness and not in some dialectical reconciliation of cleanly oppositional elements or primary units, it makes easy compartmentalisms give way to thresholds and tensions, blends and blurs."[22] In other words, feelings, responses, dispositions, arousals, intensities, sentiments, and the sensorium — some of the traces of affect that comprise this collection's inquiries — are explored in their contradictory, messy, precognitive, linguistically elusive forms.[23]Affect's circuitous and ubiquitous characteristics have been described by scholars as an unthinking reaction to stimuli. Eric Shouse explains that "At any moment, hundreds, perhaps thousands of stimuli impinge upon the human body and the body responds by infolding them all at once and registering them as an intensity. Affect is this intensity."[24] Reaction to stimuli might take the form of a prickle of fear, or a stab of recognition, or a charge in the air. These are reactions to one's

University of Pennsylvania Press, 2004); Robert Cockcroft, *Rhetorical Affect in Early Modern Writing: Renaissance Passions Reconsidered* (New York: Palgrave Macmillan, 2003); Drew Daniel, *The Melancholy Assemblage: Affect and Epistemology in the English Renaissance* (New York: Fordham University Press, 2013); Jeffrey Masten *Queer Philologies: Sex, Language, and Affect in Shakespeare's Time* (Philadelphia: University of Pennsylvania Press, 2016); Amanda Bailey and Mario DiGangi, eds., *Affect Theory and Early Modern Texts: Politics, Ecologies, and Form* (New York: Palgrave Macmillan, 2017). While these monographs and collections address the transdisciplinary potential of affect theory in discussing representation and performance in the Renaissance, affects are not explored in relation to the structurality of race.

22. Gregory J. Seigworth and Melissa Gregg, "An Inventory of Shimmers," in *The Affect Theory Reader*, ed. Melissa Gregg and Gregory J. Seigworth (Durham, NC: Duke University Press, 2010), 4.
23. Sara Ahmed, *Queer Phenomenology: Orientations, Objects, Others* (Durham, NC: Duke University Press, 2006); Brian Massumi, *Politics of Affect* (Cambridge: Polity, 2015); José Esteban Muñoz, "Feeling Brown, Feeling Down: Latina Affect, the Performativity of Race, and the Depressive Position," *Signs: Journal of Women in Culture and Society* 31, no. 3 (2006): 676–88.
24. Eric Shouse, "Feeling, Emotion, Affect," *M/C Journal* 8, no. 6 (2005): https://doi.org/10.5204/mcj.2443.

external environment but intensely felt *as if from inside*, so to speak. Affect as intensity mobilizes, transfers, and gets under the skin, which is Teresa Brennan's point when she claims that "The 'atmosphere' or the environment literally gets into the individual."[25] It is precisely the autonomous, ambient features of affect that interest many contributors in this collection: the ways affects belong to no one, but is experienced by, and with, everyone.[26]

Yet to point out the blurring and blending of affect between individuals, to study what Seigworth and Gregg call the "*in-between-ness* [that] resides as accumulative *beside-ness*,"[27] is incomplete if it fails to account for how appositions influence group dynamics as these, in turn, shape individual experiences. Lauren Berlant reminds that "affective atmospheres are shared, not solitary," and that "bodies are continuously busy judging their environments and responding to the atmospheres in which they find themselves."[28] Building on Berlant's point, it is worth noting that judgments are rarely neutral and that ephemerality is not innocuous. Kathleen Stewart captures this point in her study of the sensorium, claiming that "power is a thing of the senses."[29] Individual experiences of intersubjectivity – for instance, a disposition towards certain smells, or a

25. Theresa Brennan, *The Transmission of Affect* (Ithaca, NY: Cornell University Press, 2014), 1. "The transmission of affect, whether it is grief, anxiety, or anger, is social and psychological in origin. But the transmission is also responsible for bodily changes; some are brief changes, as in a whiff of the room's atmosphere, some longer lasting. In other words, the transmission of affect, if only for an instant, alters the biochemistry and neurology of the subject. The 'atmosphere' or the environment literally gets into the individual. Physically and biologically, something is present that was not there before, but it did not originate sui generis: it was not generated solely or sometimes even in part by the individual organism or its genes" (1).
26. "Affect is autonomous to the degree to which it escapes confinement in the particular body whose vitality, or potential for interaction, it is. Formed, qualified, situated perceptions and cognitions fulfilling functions of actual connection or blockage are the *capture* and closure of affect" (Brian Massumi, "The Autonomy of Affect," *Cultural Critique* 31 [1995]: 96 original emphasis).
27. Seigworth and Gregg, "An Inventory of Shimmers," 2 original emphases.
28. Lauren Berlant, *Cruel Optimism* (Durham, NC: Duke University Press, 2011), 15.
29. Kathleen Stewart, *Ordinary Affects* (Durham, NC: Duke University Press, 2007), 84.

reaction towards another's facial expression, or sensing that you are, or are not, welcome in the room you just walked into — are embroiled in ideologies, narratives, and forms underwritten by socially stratified power structures. The world affects always, but not equally.

Affects do not just transmit through bodies, they also influence, attribute, and categorize in ways that reflect and reinforce unequal power structures. In her study of spectacles of animated bodies and the nasty, bestiary affects they convey, Sianne Ngai illustrates how "emotional qualities slide into corporeal qualities in the case of racialized subjects, reinforcing the notion of race itself as a truth located, quite naturally, in the always obvious, highly visible body."[30] Such demarcations not only render the raced body highly visible, easily manipulated, and sentience depleted (in Ngai's words, "inert" or "mechanical"), they also serve a disciplinary function. Oppression and marginalization are inflicted on those represented and perceived as highly visible, easily manipulated, and sentience depleted subjects. In other words, the people of color targeted with the attribution of "emotional qualities [that] slide into corporeal qualities" are the very people often beleaguered by the disciplinary force of racialized, affective experiences.[31] It also goes the other way: whiteness is indexed by the affects that attend and enable its privileges. José Esteban Muñoz makes this point when he criticizes "a cultural logic that prescribes and regulates national feelings and comportment. White is thus an affective gauge that helps us understand some modes of emotional countenance and comportment as good or bad."[32] Race informs affective experiences and vice versa: the intensities, sentiments, dispositions, and states that constitute affects have a long history of contributing to racial formation. Still, affect's power to cultivate and intensify belonging or exclusion, its ability to render visceral and thus naturalize machinations of control

30. Sianne Ngai, "'A Foul Lump Started Making Promises in My Voice': Race, Affect, and the Animated Subject," *American Literature* 74, no. 3 (2002): 573.
31. For biopolitics of affects of sentimentality and impressibility, and hierarchies emerging from it, see Kyla Schuller, *The Biopolitics of Feeling: Race Sex, and Science in the Nineteenth Century* (Durham, NC: Duke University Press, 2017).
32. Muñoz, "Feeling Brown, Feeling Down," 680.

enacted on bodies, its influential yet unthinking priming towards how we treat people, in other words, affect's contributions to racial subjectivity and race relations, are as formidable as they are understudied.

This collection seeks to intervene by drawing from affect theory to understand the relational, interpersonal, and ambient operations of race-making in the early modern period. *Race and Affect* not only addresses racial formations and racist ideologies through affect theory, it also premises that race formation is connected to intersubjective experiences, responses, and dispositions in ways cultivated by and reflected in early modern English literature. Whether through plays or poems, letters or medical treatises, literature does something to those who consume it. Affiliations with or dissonance from the world represented on the page, impressions that lodge in the mind long after reading, the senses evoked by descriptions both alluring and disgusting, a ripple in the audience at a poignant moment in performance, sympathy with or rejection of a character's suffering — these affective experiences inform our interpretation of, and interaction with, the world. Affects depicted in early modern English literature are not only *available to* racializing regimes, they also mobilize the experience and the attribution of race and racism.

Race is not a coherent ideology, or a stable experience, or an innate characteristic; rather, its operations and expressions are repeated, reiterated, reinvented in the context of social and cultural histories. Yet the insidiousness of race is precisely that it can *feel* coherent, stable, and innate at an immediate and visceral level, rendering spontaneous what is instead a complex network of ideological pressures. What is the role of early modern English literature in this phenomenon of the visceral components of racialized experience? The visceral denotes that which is "affecting the viscera or bowels regarded as the seat of emotion; pertaining to, or touching deeply, inward feelings." Additionally, the visceral resides in both physiological and anatomical domains, existing in "internal organs" and "those parts of the brain which mediate bodily activity."[33] The visceral blurs what is felt and what is embodied, and as such prompts the following questions with regards to race and affect: What are the vis-

33. *OED Online*, s.v., "visceral," adj. 1.a.; 2; 5.c.

ceral experiences of racial formation and racist ideologies as these shape the contours of affective communities? How do modalities of affect — through the sensorium, or via emotions, or in sexual encounters — come to signify race? What is the affective register of anti-Blackness woven into the production and reception of literature and how do its harms pervade scholarly practice? Peter Erickson and Kim F. Hall assert, in the Introduction to their 2016 *Shakespeare Quarterly* special issue, that "race, as an ideology that organizes human difference and power, is always protean and sticky, attaching to a range of ideologies, narratives, and vocabularies in ways both familiar and strange."[34] The visceral aspects of race take their cue from the "familiar and strange" in the circulation of affective relations, reactions, and resonances. Race and affect are embroiled in how we read, perform, research, and teach. The chapters to follow identify and analyze moments through which feelings experienced and responses encountered, sensations intensified and dispositions aroused, signify racial formation and mobilize the racism at its wake.

The first section, "Racial Formations of Affective Communities," investigates how affect and race are foundational to group categorizations and the communities that emerge. These chapters tarry over moments of conflicted, concentrated, and affectively charged encounters that, on the one hand, provide the signs and the opportunities for belonging and, on the other hand, become catalysts for race-based exclusions. Preceding any coherent strategy for global engagement or a stable conception of nation-building, affectively charged encounters and imaginings in these texts nonetheless establish borders along racial lines. Ambereen Dadabhoy's "Imagining Islamicate Worlds: Race and Affect in the Contact Zone" interrogates Islamophobic demonizations on the pages of early modern texts. Dadabhoy scrutinizes what this overdetermined affective register does to the reader who is excluded from an English, European, and white identity and who therefore identifies with the very subject who is demo-

34. Peter Erickson and Kim Hall, "A New Scholarly Song: Rereading Early Modern Race," *Shakespeare Quarterly* 67, no. 1 (2016): 12. This special issue features innovative race scholarship that bridges historical and presentist work while providing a re-vision of our engagement with the past.

nized. Dadabhoy foregrounds the racialized subject's vexed relationship with her scholarship by providing insights on the historical and contemporary affects of Islamophobia in Philip Massinger's *The Renegado*, thus revealing the limits of a universalized, white subject. Troubling the universality of whiteness by exploring foreign queens in "Desire, Disgust, and the Perils of Strange Queenship in Edmund Spenser's *The Faerie Queene*," Mira Assaf Kafantaris examines state power and racial reproduction in allegory. As a groundbreaking intervention in Spenser studies, Kafantaris investigates "a racial logic that embeds miscegenation within the framework of allegory and its moral and apocalyptic concerns."[35] Feelings of disgust and sentimentality are powerful nation-building forces, mobilized through the foreign queen whose role in the English commonwealth destabilizes the political, sexual, and religious foundations on which that commonwealth rests. Departing from the England allegorized in Spenser's epic poetry, the next chapter considers the letters sent from the outposts of colonial expansion. In "New World Encounters and the Racial Limits of Friendship in Early Quaker Life Writing," Meghan E. Hall innovatively examines the archives of white female voices in New World encounters. Hall provides an investigation of the expansionist missionary project of 17th century Quakers through an analysis of the affects of disorientation and disconnection emerging from such correspondences. A focused reading of Alice Curwen's letters outlines the communities and affiliations that ultimately rest on exclusions and denunciations, thus illuminating the complicities of white femininity, particularly white female fear, in the race-making tactics unique to religious expansionism. The final chapter in this section enhances our understanding of affect and race by critiquing exclusionary technologies employed through the sensorium. Querying the circulation of prejudice in "Early Modern Affect Theory, Racialized Aversion, and the Strange Case of *Foetor Judaicus*," Drew Daniel contextualizes anti-Semitism through an imagined and anticipated disgust. *Foetor Judaicus*, the allegation that Jews have a distinctive, unpleasant odor,

35. An important call to amplify research on race and Spenser is made by Dennis Austin Britton and Kimberly Anne Coles, "Beyond the Pale," *Spenser Review* 50, no. 1 (2020): http://www.english.cam.ac.uk/spenseronline/review/item/50.1.5.

conveys early indications of what will later be part of natural philosophy's justification for racist differentiations. Daniel explores how affect anticipates exclusion and inclusion through the sensorium by asking how the senses "express, enact, and translate race into feelings, actions, and outcomes." This chapter implicates the viscerality of the sensorium in establishing racial prejudice, as well as anticipates the next section wherein the expression, enactment, and translation of race intersect with early modern representations of gender and sexuality.

How these shaping views of inclusion and exclusion intersect with various forms of sexuality, from legitimate procreation to deviant longings, is the topic of the second section, "Racialized Affects of Sex and Gender." In "Conversion Interrupted: Shame and the Demarcation of Jewish Women's Difference in The *Merchant of Venice*," Sara Coodin theorizes the internalization of shame as part of the racialized and gendered experience of self-loathing. The convertibility of the passing fair Jew, in plays like *The Merchant of Venice*, conveys how race thinking has the power to direct negative emotions inward. Shame and self-loathing, Coodin proves, are bound up with the processes that attend the racial othering of the fair Jewish woman, despite her ostensible inclusion into the fold of Christianity. Contrastingly, Kirsten Mendoza's analysis of a female character whose claim to belonging is beyond reproach traces the racialization of gendered affects through the kiss of a white woman. In "Navigating a Kiss in the Racialized Geopolitical Landscape of Thomas Heywood's *The Fair Maid of the West*," Mendoza troubles the erotic politics of Heywood's play by illustrating its cultural investment in white womanhood and racialized masculinity. Tracking how "the play validates xenophobic feelings in the process of cultivating racism," Mendoza outlines the ways global encounters are rife with the intensified feelings and affective reactions that incorporate idealized Englishness abroad. Continuing the examination of assemblages of desire in erotic, commercial, and political realms, in "Branded with Baseness: Bastardy and Race in *King Lear*" Mario DiGangi locates in bastardy the problems of masculine racial formation. DiGangi's attentiveness to Edmund's famous soliloquy demonstrates that sexual transgressions attribute dispositions and emotions that constitute racialized affects. DiGangi outlines how the categorization and broadening of hegemonic power, as crucial features of racial formation, are problematized by the bastard because he disrupts indexes of sexuality in performance, virility, and procreative futures.

While the essays in the first two sections innovatively bring into dialogue the fields of affect studies and Critical Race Theory, this methodology is urgently needed for the study of anti-Blackness in early modern English literature. In his investigation of racialized subjectivity in the period, Matthieu Chapman demonstrates how the "staging of black flesh on the English stage [was] part of a continuum of anti-Black thought in the English psyche."[36] The third section, "Feelings and Forms of Anti-Blackness," investigates the emergence of an English psyche fundamentally invested in the negation and denial of Black personhood. The chapters analyze the corporeal, psychological, and emotional vectors in representations of anti-Blackness. These vectors cultivate the racialized affects that are later mobilized as justification for enslavement and its atrocities. The chapters also premise that what is felt and what is embodied in racist operations unleashed on Black subjects is unique and needs to be understood as such. In Frank B. Wilderson III's terms, the extractive and dehumanizing violence that is the condition of enslavement and the foundation of Black suffering needs to be understood unfettered by the "ruse of analogy": "because analogy *mystifies*, rather than clarifies, Black suffering. Analogy mystifies Black peoples' relationship to other people of color. Afropessimism labors to throw this mystification into relief — without fear of the faults and fissures that are revealed in the process."[37] Afropessimism outlines the exclusion of Black subjects from the identifications and privileges of humanity and, furthermore, argues that this exclusion is the very foundation of humanity.[38] As Sharon Patricia Holland reminds, "our examples of racial being and racist targets are often grounded in black

36. Matthieu Chapman, *Anti-Black Racism in Early Modern English Drama: The Other "Other"* (London: Routledge, 2017), 33.

37. Frank B. Wilderson III, *Afropessimism* (New York: Liveright Publishing, 2020), 228 original emphasis.

38. "What civil society needs from Black people is confirmation of Human existence" (Wilderson, *Afropessimism*, 219). The "confirmation of Human existence" hinges on the negation of the Black experience in relation to the privileges granted to full personhood within the commonweal.

matter(s). In this instance, the black body is the quintessential sign for subjection, for a particular experience that it must inhabit and own all by itself."[39] Early modern English literature contributed to the feelings, dispositions, and senses that made the enslavement and subjection of Black people possible. To deny the canon's complicity is to continue that subjection today.

The chapters in this final section show how early modern English texts participated in the formation of racial slavery and its attending affects in various ways, from material production to theatrical performance to literary form. What is the affective register of anti-Blackness mobilized by the early modern English canon? In "Black Ink, White Feelings: Early Modern Print Technology and Anti-Black Racism," Averyl Dietering answers this question by scrutinizing print history. With specific attention to medical treatises, Dietering demonstrates how anatomical woodcuts convey the formation of feelings through the visual and textual codification of bodily difference. Whose bodies are afforded interiority and emotion versus whose bodies are the surfaces on which villainization and dehumanization are read, is recorded in the materials and ideologies generated by the technologies and artifacts of book history. Anti-Blackness in performance is the topic of Matthieu Chapman's "Away, You Ethiop!": A *Midsummer Night's Dream* and the Denial of Black Affect — A Song to Underscore the Burning of Police Stations." Chapman conveys the limits of affect in relation to the valuation of Black lives and the recognition of their suffering. Racist modalities in theatre go unnoticed because Black death is so integral to public entertainment. Chapman reveals how Shakespearean production, with its history of challenging the prejudices of sexual and gender difference, nevertheless remains complicit in normalizing racist language. Cora Fox considers the affects of anti-Blackness in the history of emotion in "Othello's Unfortunate Happiness." Fox probes the intertextual relevance of happiness to illustrate that Othello insistently and self-consciously challenges the "irregular and doomed circulation of joy" that attends the racialization of emotion. Contextualizing the appeal of happi-

39. Sharon Patricia Holland, *The Erotic Life of Racism* (Durham, NC: Duke University Press, 2012), 4.

ness in the early modern period – from an outcome of good fortune to a *mood* – Fox challenges narratives of happiness and exhibits the exclusionary mechanisms embedded in "the hue of Othello's joy." Exclusion from positive affects is likewise formative in Shakespeare's sonnets. In "The Racialized Affects of Ill-Will in the Dark Lady Sonnets," I theorize ill-will as a racializing affect that problematizes kinship and kindness within the stylized, erotic persuasions delineating the poet's fair and virtuous friend from the ruthless dark mistress who seduces both men. Rendered kinless and unkind, the dark lady's consequent exclusions from the privileges of kin and the designations of kind underwrite the anti-Black violence embedded in the genre's sexual politics.

Investigating the affective economies that contribute to the depictions and performances of race, this collection offers new ways of reading and interpreting literary traditions, religious beliefs, gendered experiences, class hierarchies, sexual knowledges, and social identities. The chapters pursue the overlapping questions relevant to book historians, theatre practitioners, early modern scholars of history, literature, and culture, as well as their students. But how relevant are these inquiries today? Why study race and affect now?

We struggled with this question during a pandemic, stalled by quarantine and paralyzed by uncertainty. *Race and Affect* was written while enduring the unprecedented anxiety and, at times, inconsolable grief, brought on by this extraordinary global event. In the course of completing this collection, some of our most visceral reactions, intense sensations, and profound feelings – our fears and confusions, certainly, but also loss and longing – were underscored by race and racism. And so it is just as important for this collection and its readers to ponder the racialized affects of millions of lives lost – many from the global south and, disproportionally in the United States, people of color on the front lines of 21st-century consumerism. Although far from being as important as documenting the loss of lives, it is also critical to dwell on what this collection could not bring to fruition. From the commencement of this project at the Shakespeare Association of America's 2019 conference to its final configuration in front of a reader, good work was lost. An antiracist revolution, in which this collection aims to participate, remains unrealized partly because the labor of pursuing social justice and racial equity are laden on the backs of scholars of color. In rethinking our relationship to scholarship, it is worth considering the costs borne by the most vulnerable in our field and how much we all lose when their scholarly work is unrealized. The pandemic exacerbated inequities and enmities already directed at Black, Indigenous, and people of color scholars. This fact should be an impetus to action, in the form of eradicating biased gatekeeping in the profession, combating macro- and microaggressions in academia, and instituting measurable changes in hiring, publication, and funding.[40]

Race and affect, intertwined in circuits of feeling and identity, reveal something fundamental about contemporary lived experience. Beginning in summer 2020, a surge of righteous anger swept the globe. Protestors exacted reckoning for the deaths of innocent Black people, tore down statues of slave owners, and demanded the legislation of antiracist policies. Revolutionary awakening to the vestiges of slavery, as these played out in social media, in the news, in diversity statements, and in the streets, made apparent the burden of emotional and physical labor of advocacy and activism. But it did little to alleviate this burden for those most affected by the slings and arrows and bullets of white supremacy. Because, unlike the alt-white, fully armed radicals who, with minimal consequence, stormed government buildings and launched a traitorous insurrection, antiracist protestors — mostly unarmed and peacefully marching on public streets — were pepper-sprayed, hosed down, pushed away, kidnapped, beaten, and intimidated into disbursement by a militarized police force. And so the dire consequences of a global health crisis, and the racial injustices woven into the fabric of democratic life, are viscerally experienced — *felt* — by racialized subjects on the body and under the skin. The inexorable toll of COVID-19, as it sacrifices lives and lungs to assuage global capitalism from its own fragilities and flaws, reveals the glaring racial chasm between who bears the brunt of these crises, and

40. See Kimberly Anne Coles, Kim F. Hall, and Ayanna Thompson, "BlacKKKShakespearean: A Call to Action for Medieval and Early Modern Studies," MLA *Profession*, November 2019, https://profession.mla.org/blackkkshakespearean-a-call-to-action-for-medieval-and-early-modern-studies/.

who is spared.[41] The crushing omnipresence of systemic racism, funneled through a police officer's knee bearing down on the neck of George Floyd, puts on display the targeted brutality unleashed on Black lives for centuries. Race and affect are in the breath taken in, and in the breath taken away.

41. For an explanation of the disproportionate health risks of/to minority populations, start with "Risk of Exposure to COVID-19: Racial and Ethnic Health Disparities," Centers for Disease Control and Prevention, updated 10 December 202, accessed July 2021, https://www.cdc.gov/coronavirus/2019-ncov/community/health-equity/racial-ethnic-disparities/increased-risk-exposure.html.

Section I

Racial Formations of Affective Communities

1. Imagining Islamicate Worlds: Race and Affect in the Contact Zone

AMBEREEN DADABHOY

Embodied Affects

Reading is an affective relation. In reading the canon, the reader's subjectivity and embodiment come into contact and conflict with the normative identity on which that canon builds and in which it has material investments. What happens when you read texts for whom you are not the intended audience, by writers who could not have imagined you as a reader? I experience the stigma of demonization because I embody the identity of the antagonist in almost everything I read, study, and analyze.[1] My identity challenges the canon's universalism. Steeped in centuries of authority, canons are constructed bodies of texts from a very specific culture, geography, nation, and language. They overcome their local particularity and are transcendent, seemingly able to speak to and for all humanity, as vessels for articulating the universal human condition. I, then, must stand apart – or more accurately – be prohibited from the universal. My identity, however, has been essential to its formation. I cannot be a universal subject because I experience harm from the can(n)on fire.[2] I am the detritus that results from its discharge; the waste, excess,

1. Shokoofeh Rajabzadeh, "The Depoliticized Saracen and Muslim Erasure," *Literature Compass* 16, nos. 9–10 (2019): e12548, https://doi-org.ccl.idm.oclc.org/10.1111/lic3.12548.
2. Toni Morrison, "Unspeakable Things Unspoken: The Afro-American Presence in American Literature," in *The Source of Self-Regard: Selected Essays, Speeches, and Meditations* (New York: Knopf, 2019), notes the homology between cannon and canon: "when the two words faced each other, the image became the shape of the cannon wielded on (or by) the body of the law. The boom of power announcing an 'officially recognized set of texts.' Cannon defending canon" (161). I employ her formulation in my construction here.

or abject; the requisite material necessary to its successful colonial trajectory; the ambit of its imperial aspirations.

These provocations haunt my work as a literary scholar, as I negotiate the field's mandates that I deny my-*self* in service of the universal, normative whiteness inscribed within the canon. I seek permission to assert my raced, sexed, gendered, classed self into my analysis and risk delegitimization because my interlocutors believe themselves to be none (or just one) of those. I presume to have a locus of enunciation even though my object of study could not even conceive of me as an audience, a reader and/or a critic. I risk the charge of anachronism by bringing my-*self* to my intellectual efforts despite knowing that the universal white subject can function in and out of time. I try to protect my being from the constant assault on my subjectivity because I am enveloped by structures of thought designed to teach me how to hate myself and my kind.[3]

My investigation into race, religion, and affect in the contact zone of the early modern Mediterranean interprets through these affective states because they signal my position as a literary critic and my dis/connection from/to the objects I examine. Who I am, my social and cultural identity, shapes how I interpret and analyze texts and cultures. Who I am in relation to my objects, determines not just their meaning but also the ways their meanings play in and on me, how they affect my being and subjectivity; how they construct their own narratives and logics about my identity; and how they enmesh me within a network of relations and significations over which I have little control. When I talk about race, religion,

3. Malcolm X, "Who Taught You to Hate Yourself," posted by Bihibindi News on 28 June 2016, YouTube video, 3:46, https://youtu.be/sCSOiN_38nE. Speech delivered on May 5, 1962 in Los Angeles, following the LAPD killing of Ronald Stokes. https://www.themelaninproject.org/tmpblog/2020/2/11/malcolm-x-may-20-1962-speech-on-police-brutality-in-los-angeles-california. I use Malcolm X, rather than el Hajj Malik el-Shabazz, because of its more familiar circulation within Anglo-American culture; however, I believe it is vital to recognize the multiple identity transformations he underwent, from Malcolm Little to Detroit Red to Malcolm X and finally to el Hajj Malik el-Shabazz. These different naming practices are suggestive of his conscription within and resistance to normative racist regimes of whiteness and his embrace of a global anti-racist Muslim identity.

and affect, who am I, if I am not the person–scholar who is raced, whose religion has been demonized through the US-led War on Terror, and who perceives how this demonization is not unrelated to the dangerous and derogatory constructions of Muslim identity in the early modern English imaginary. These bald facts, these reflections, and the rhetorical and ideological violence of these texts undergird the study I attempt here. They accompany my readings, my focus on those identities labeled by the dominant culture as different, and hence other, that are constructed only to service that same culture and ideology. I reckon with the shame of identifying with the other and feeling that I, too, am coerced into service. If I must serve, then, I choose to serve my-*self*. I choose to love my being, my culture, and my kind by problematizing the false image of me that treads the boards of the early modern stage and continues to circulate in the canon. In doing so, I attend to that estranged other in whom I perceive a distorted reflection, a construction I can succor by illuminating the very many political, cultural, and ideological forces contouring her discursive being.

Deviating from previous investigations of the early modern Mediterranean and Islamic identity — which sought to foreground the real and material power of Islamicate and Ottoman regimes in the period, thereby obviating the need for analysis rooted in the kinds of racialized Orientalism in which these texts neatly trafficked — here, I foreground the constitutive role of race in constructing Muslim alterity.[4] Rather than arguing for the primacy of religious difference as the form of otherness *par excellence* in the period, particularly in relation to the circulation of Islamic identity in early modern English texts, I consider how religious difference must be racialized in order to be made legible on the English stage. Discursively racializing Islam serves to locate it within a specific geog-

4. See, for example, Nabil Matar, *Turks, Moors, and Englishmen in the Age of Discovery* (New York: Columbia University Press, 2000); Daniel J. Vitkus, *Turning Turk: English Theater and the Multicultural Mediterranean*, 1570–1630 (New York: Palgrave Macmillan, 2016); Jonathan Burton, *Traffic and Turning: Islam and English Drama*, 1579–1624 (Newark: University of Delaware Press, 2005); Matthew Dimmock, *New Turkes: Dramatizing Islam and the Ottomans in Early Modern England* (London: Routledge, 2017).

raphy and boundary, thereby ideologically diminishing its threat while simultaneously rendering Islam visible in non-white bodies. In this study, I examine the contact zone of the early modern Mediterranean, as it is constructed in the English imaginary, to argue that the traffic and intercourse it facilitates between European Christians and non-European Muslims create and sustain racial formations by establishing the modes and mores of normative whiteness.[5] Thus, I claim that the contact zone aids in the construction of a kind of hegemonic whiteness that relies on locating and stabilizing race as whiteness within Christianity and race as non-whiteness within non-Christian confessional traditions.

Affective Geographies

Perhaps the most important contact zone in the early modern period, the Mediterranean Sea connected Europe, Africa, and Asia. Its boundaries and borders cinched together different religious and imperial traditions, bringing into intimate proximity Christendom and Islam, the Hapsburgs and the Ottomans, and several other confessional cultures, ethnicities, and societies. The polyphony of the Mediterranean was signaled by the various competing interests that traversed its geography and who it served through its porous fluidity. In other words, the slippery boundaries of the Mediterranean allowed for all forms of movement and transformation. The many ways the Mediterranean became a site for various forms of border crossing, whether literal or symbolic, point to both the opportunities and dangers of the locale. The region could enrich or impoverish those who sought their fortunes in its waters; that fickleness emblematized the anxieties, fears, and desires inherent therein. Sustained English interest in the Mediterranean began in 1581 when Elizabeth I granted the

5. I use "European" here with full awareness of the way this term lacked any coherent logic in the period, and to distinguish the kind of Christianity of this locale and its differences from the forms of Christian identity within the broader Mediterranean, specifically Eastern Orthodox Christianity. The use of European is further complicated by the fact that the Ottoman Empire controlled much of Eastern Europe and yet there is a hesitancy in the discourse to refer to them as a European empire. These terms deserve further scrutiny and study.

Levant Company its charter and monopoly to explore and buoy trade in the east.[6] Moreover, the queen cultivated special relationships with Muslim potentates, such as the Moroccan king, Abd-el Malik, and the Ottoman sultan, Murad IV.[7] The ascension of James I in 1604, his rapprochement with Spain, and open hostility towards the Ottoman Empire (best manifested in his poem *Lepanto*, 1591) shifted England's ideological position vis-à-vis the Islamicate societies of the Mediterranean despite ongoing commercial exchange within that sphere.

Like the mercantile enthusiasm for Mediterranean exchanges, the early modern stage was attentive and vulnerable to the allure of that geography. Several English plays featured an imagined, discursive, and constructed Mediterranean, which allowed playwrights to experiment with the fears and desires generated by the contact zone, where peoples, cultures, languages, and goods mixed and mingled.[8] Moreover, this contact zone furnished the opportunity to represent various racial and religious identities, signaling thc multicultural and multiethnic composition of this space. The genre of the "staged Mediterranean," as I call it, allowed playwrights to bring home and domesticate the foreign through dramatic representation. England's shifting political alliances found ready and convenient analogues in the drama, so that "commercial activity was accompanied by corresponding ideological changes: the culture and literature of the time were profoundly affected by the intensified international circulation of people, goods, and texts."[9] As I have argued elsewhere, the polysemy of

6. I do not capitalize the east in order to signal the diversity of customs and cultures that comprise this geography. I want to deliberately undermine Orientalist framing that positions the east as a monolithic entity.
7. Nabil Matar, 'Queen Elizabeth I through Moroccan Eyes," *Journal of Early Modern History* 12, no. 1 (2008): 55–76; Bernadette Andrea, *Women and Islam in Early Modern English Literature* (Cambridge: Cambridge University Press, 2008), 13–14.
8. Louis Wann, "The Oriental in Elizabethan Drama," *Modern Philology* 12, no. 7 (1915): 423-447.
9. Daniel Vitkus, "'The Common Market of All the World': English Theater, the Global System, and the Ottoman Empire in the Early Modern Period," in *Global Traffic: Discourses and Practices of Trade in English Literature and Culture from 1550 to 1700*, ed. Barbara Sebek and Stephen Deng (New York: Palgrave Macmillan, 2008), 27.

the staged Mediterranean demonstrated its aptness as a site to interrogate the intimacies fostered by increased contact, exchange, conflict, and intercourse with the foreign other; furthermore, it positions the Mediterranean as "a space for experimenting with both the imperial project and national subjectivity."[10] This national subjectivity is rooted in forms of race-making, specifically in making whiteness paradoxically both visible and hegemonic. The geography of the Mediterranean assists in these efforts because it felicitously necessitates contact with the non-English and non-European.

Philip Massinger's *The Renegado* (1624) follows in the tradition of staged Mediterranean plays such as Christopher Marlowe's *The Jew of Malta* (1589), Thomas Kyd's *Soliman and Perseda* (1599), Thomas Heywood's *The Fair Maid of the West* (1597), William Shakespeare's *Othello* (1603), and Robert Daborne's *A Christian Turn'd Turk* (1612). These plays exhibit and instantiate topoi and tropes that become standard motifs of the staged Mediterranean: an interest in traffic and exchange; imperiled European Christian subjectivity; racial and religious variation; Islamic violence and tyranny; the allure and seductions of Muslim women; and, above all, European Christian triumph and primacy over the cultures and peoples of this geography. Thus, these plays contribute to the burgeoning desire for, and ideology of, empire. The very threats posed by the multiplicity of culture, custom, and identity in this geography are what facilitate the construction of a nationalist subjectivity. Expressions of normative and local subjectivity require forms of religious and racial difference in order to constitute and make themselves legible.

Massinger sets his tragicomedy, *The Renegado*, in the Ottoman-controlled suzerainty of Tunis. While the plot flirts with the very real possibility of altered identity, of the extreme early modern fear of "turning Turk," its ideological and political thrust is to turn "Turks," or Muslims, into Christians.[11] The plot involves the influx of European Christians into

10. Ambereen Dadabhoy, "The Other Woman: The Geography of Exclusion in *The Knight of Malta* (1618)," in *Remapping Travel Narratives, 1000–1700: To the East and Back Again*, ed. Montserrat Piera (York, UK: ARC Humanities Press, 2018), 237–38.

11. Vitkus, *Turning Turk*, 161.

Ottoman lands for the ostensible purposes of trade, but, we soon learn that these merchants are also on a mission to recover Paulina, a Venetian gentlewoman captured by the titular renegade, Grimaldi, and sold to the viceroy of Tunis, Asambeg. Paulina's rescuers are her brother Vitelli, who is disguised as a merchant, Gazet, his servant, and Francisco, a priest. On the whole, this group makes up the majority of the European Christian characters. The one exception is Carazie, a eunuch who serves the Sultan's niece, Donusa. A romance plot involving Vitelli and Donusa, her rejection of the Muslim suitor, Mustapha, sent to her by her uncle, the Ottoman Sultan, and the discovery of their illicit sexual escapades by the viceroy, fully encapsulate the dangers of cross-cultural intercourse. Donusa and Vitelli are summarily sentenced to death, yet before their executions, Donusa attempts to save them both by convincing Vitelli to convert to Islam. However, her scheme is foiled by Vitelli's Christian conviction, in the face of which *she* is moved to convert to Christianity. Meanwhile, Paulina pretends that she will "turn Turk" and succumb to Asambeg's advances, all the while strategizing with the priest Francisco and his new ally, the repentant and newly redeemed Grimaldi, to engineer their escape. The play ends not with death, but with the European Christians triumphing over the Muslims. Through these stratagems, Massinger emplots the precarious position and bodily danger faced by European Christians within the domain of the foreign other; moreover, the plot instrumentalizes religious and racial difference to construct and buttress European Christian cultural supremacy.

Through its many completed and aborted conversions, the play puts pressure on the overdetermined trope "turning Turk," which requires further investigation, particularly in its associations with the Mediterranean. A common phrase in early modern English drama, "turning Turk" indicates conversion to Islam, yet it is often glossed as a betrayal or a form of inconstancy, to abjure religion, culture, and nation.[12] In the geography of the staged Mediterranean, "turning Turk" operates on literal and symbolic registers: to become a Muslim — from the Christian perspective — means

12. Daniel J. Vitkus, "Turning Turk in *Othello*: The Conversion and Damnation of the Moor," *Shakespeare Quarterly* 48, no. 2 (1997): 145–76.

that one has enacted a betrayal against God and country. The phrase also subsumes religious identity within an ethnic or imperial one, and effects the erasure of a competing religion by elevating a distinct and different cultural identity. Islamic cultures were more diverse than is represented by the Ottoman Empire; yet through the mobilization of "turning Turk," Islam became synonymous with an ethnicity, and so its theology was circumscribed and diminished. Moreover, the term "turning Turk" locates Islam within racially marked bodies. Even though Ottoman identity in the early modern English imaginary was often void of somatic markers, certain symbolic accoutrement, such as turbans and scimitars, stood as proxy signs of its difference. Islam, then, served as the ultimate form of both racializing and differentiating Ottomans from other Europeans. Thus, racial formation in the Mediterranean relied on making religion visible via the body. A further meaning of "turning Turk," is its temporary or transient status: if one can "turn Turk," one can similarly turn back. In this capacity, "Turk" functions as an unstable marker of identity, but perhaps only for those who make that first turn. The possibility of becoming a "Turk" is open to any and all who enter the geography of the Mediterranean. However, *The Renegado* demonstrates that its opposite, to become Christian, is only available to a few. The logics of conversion that cohere around this term signal the flexibility of race within the marker of "Turk," but only for those discovered to be fit for Christian salvation and its attendant whiteness.

Set in the contact zone of the early modern Mediterranean, *The Renegado* mobilizes the vexed affects this geography elicits: fear, desire, and the precarious contingency of these emotional states. I borrow the term "contact zone" from Mary Louise Pratt, who defines these zones as "social spaces where disparate cultures meet, clash, and grapple with each other, often in highly asymmetrical relations of domination and subordination."[13] In fact, the contact zone "is the space of imperial encounters, the space in which peoples geographically and historically separated come into contact with each other and establish ongoing relations, usually involving

13. Mary Louise Pratt, *Imperial Eyes: Travel Writing and Transculturation*, 2nd ed. (London: Routledge, 2007), 7.

conditions of coercion, radical inequality, and intractable conflict."[14] Pratt's formulation attends to the operations of power and affect within this geography, especially if we consider the relational and enmeshed quality of affect that "marks the body's belonging to a world of encounters; or a world's belonging to a body of encounters but also in non-belonging."[15] The contact zone encodes hierarchies of power and subjectivity, the power inherent in some subjects, and the power of some bodies to be affected by and to affect their own subjectivities in this space. We must recall, however, that the staged Mediterranean is a particular kind of contact zone — a discursive one. As Edward W. Said cogently demonstrates in *Orientalism*, such discourses do not require any *real* corollary.[16] There obtains, then, a rupture between the staged Mediterranean and the political and imperial powers dominating the actual geography. The ideological function of the staged Mediterranean and the popularity of these plays reside in the tidy ways these scripts make England's imperial desires and designs legible for audiences at home.[17] They create, as Pratt argues, "in the imperial center of power an obsessive need to present and re-present its peripheries and its others continually to itself. It becomes dependent on its others to know itself."[18] While early modern England did not yet possess its full imperial power, these dramas collude in a discourse that imagines, consumes, and celebrates the desirability and availability of such power for their domestic public.

Racial Affects

If part of the ideology subtending *The Renegado* (and most staged Mediterranean plays) is to certify imperial power and logics, then it does

14. Pratt, *Imperial Eyes*, 8.
15. Gregory J. Seigworth and Melissa Gregg, "An Inventory of Shimmers," in *The Affect Theory Reader*, ed. Melissa Gregg and Gregory J. Seigworth (Durham, NC: Duke University Press, 2010), 2.
16. Edward W. Said, *Orientalism* (New York: Vintage, 2003), 5.
17. Kim F. Hall, *Things of Darkness: Economies of Race and Gender in Early Modern England* (Ithaca, NY: Cornell University Press, 1995), 59.
18. Pratt, *Imperial Eyes*, 4.

so, I argue, by simultaneously producing race, specifically through its construction of normative or hegemonic whiteness. Critical scholarship on *The Renegado* has tended to focus on its generic qualities and mercantile and religious arguments, prioritizing the ways the Mediterranean and its primary occupation, commercial traffic, contribute to anxieties about identity and subjectivity and its positive representation of Catholicism.[19] Given the Mediterranean's discursive positioning in the European imaginary as a site of contest between Islamicate and Christian powers, *The Renegado*'s emphasis on such religious conflict adroitly validates that enmity. Scholars have, therefore, focused on the surprising celebration of Catholic ritual and practice, particularly in light of prior English animus toward that confessional tradition. The greater threat of Islam, especially conversion to Islam — "turning Turk" — renders sectarian conflict redundant in this geography. Similarly, scholars have targeted their analyses of the play on the centrality of trade and the marketplace, tracing the anxieties contouring the fungibility of goods and people. The marketplace is, after all, the primary and public locale drawing all characters together, turning buyers into sellers, and destabilizing identity positions of rank, religion, and race. While some studies index race as a cognate to these anxieties, they have not tethered racial formation in the contact zone to imperial praxis that manifests and makes visible the normative power of whiteness. Following Kim F. Hall's powerful exegesis on the racialization of gender through the discourse of fairness in *Things of Darkness*, I demonstrate how whiteness materializes in affective relation to non-white,

19. Burton, *Traffic and Turning*; Benedict S. Robinson, *Islam and Early Modern English Literature: The Politics of Romance from Spenser to Milton* (New York: Palgrave Macmillan, 2007); Michael Neill, "Turn and Counterturn: Merchanting, Apostasy and Tragicomic Form in Massinger's *The Renegado*," in *Early Modern Tragicomedy*, ed. Subha Mukherji and Raphael Lyne (Cambridge: D. S. Brewer, 2007), 154–74; Jane Hwang Degenhardt, "Catholic Prophylactics and Islam's Sexual Threat: Preventing and Undoing Sexual Defilement in *The Renegado*," *Journal for Early Modern Cultural Studies* 9, no. 1 (2009): 62–92; Dennis Austin Britton, *Becoming Christian: Race, Reformation, and Early Modern Romance* (New York: Fordham University Press, 2014).

Ottoman, and Muslim identity.[20] Furthermore, I argue that this discourse makes race as non-whiteness visible in non-Europeans, facilitating asymmetric relations of power and domination while yoking to whiteness the hegemonic power of racial purity.

Charting the discourse of fairness within *The Renegado* exposes the term's malleability in service of white Christian identity. Fairness, as Hall argues, is both a moral and aesthetic category, implicated in tropes of beauty and race, and consequently in the imperial enterprise.[21] In *The Renegado*, the term is most often applied to the play's two female characters, the Ottoman princess and femme fatale, Donusa, and the virtuous Christian captive, Paulina. Although Paulina is also a femme fatale of a kind – because she orchestrates the destruction of the viceroy Asambeg – she is celebrated by the European cultural supremacist logic of the play. As applied to Donusa, fairness signals her beauty and desirability: she offers the seductive allure of the exotic, erotic east, in the face of which Christian masculinity becomes submissive and endangered. Her beauty points to an aggressive Muslim sexuality and to degeneracy because it signals her lack of chastity, which further demonstrates her religious alterity. Indeed, Francisco's caution to Vitelli expresses this specific danger:

> you are young
> And may be tempted, and these Turkish dames –
> Like English mastiffs that increase their fierceness
> By being chained up – from the restraint of freedom,
> If lust once fire their blood from a fair object,
> Will run a course the fields themselves would shake at
> To enjoy their wanton ends. (1.3.8–14)[22]

As depicted by Francisco's xenophobic screed, Muslim women are animalistic in their sexual appetites. Particularly because of the sex-segregated

20. Although the entire monograph works through this argument, I am particularly focused here on Chapter 3 (Hall, *Things of Darkness*, 123–76).
21. Hall, *Things of Darkness*, 3–9.
22. I cite throughout from Philip Massinger, *The Renegado*, ed. Michael Neill (London: Arden, 2010).

societies they inhabit, their perceived lack of liberty feeds their instinctive and bestial sexuality. By figuring Muslim women as demonically libidinous and licentious, Francisco creates and promotes a discursive othering that facilitates a relation of domination, whereby he attains power in a world where he ostensibly lacks it. He can define and represent, establishing an epistemic regime about Islam and Muslims that authorizes his racist comparison of "Turkish dames" to "English mastiffs." The essentializing difference of Muslim women that Francisco constructs is furthered by his claim about the fairness of the objects of their desire. His use of "fair" suggests beauty and desirability, but also whiteness in explicit contrast to the racialized animal imagery of Ottoman women. Positioned as a fair object, Vitelli is feminized by his relation to Donusa, which corresponds to his social position within Tunis. Here, whiteness and European Christian masculinity are imperiled because the contact zone makes inevitable intimate proximity to more powerful Muslim women who will "enjoy their wanton ends."

The Renegado counters Donusa's false fairness with Paulina's chaste, virtuous, Christian one. Paulina's position — as Vitelli's "fair sister" (1.1.127) and the "fair Christian virgin" (1.1.115) imprisoned by Asambeg and "mewed up in his seraglio and in danger / Not alone to lose her honor but her soul" (1.1.129–30) — reflects the common position of many early modern women who were taken captive by Mediterranean pirates and sold into Islamic slavery. Writing about the women in the Sultan's seraglio, George Sandys claims that the occupants of the harem "are his slaves, either taken in the wars, or from their Christian parents, and are indeed the choicest beauties of the Empire."[23] Similarly, Nicolas De Nicolay notes that in the seraglio

23. George Sandys, "*The Relation of a Journey Begun an: Dom:* 1610 (1615)," in *Race in Early Modern England: A Documentary Companion*, ed. Jonathan Burton and Ania Loomba (New York: Palgrave Macmillan, 2007), 196. The complete quote is: "His virgins, of whom there seldom are so few as five hundred, are kept in a seraglio by themselves, and attended on only by women, and eunuchs. They all of them are his slaves, either taken in the wars, or from their Christian parents, and are indeed the choicest beauties of the Empire."

> do dwell the wives and concubines of the great Turk, which in number are above 200 being the most part daughters of Christians, some being taken by courses on the seas or by land … some of the other are bought of merchants, and afterwards … presented unto the great Turk, who keepeth them within this Sarail, well appareled, nourished and entertained under straight keeping of … an eunuch.[24]

Joannes Leo Africanus, in his description of the King of Fez's harem, writes: "And yet his queen is always of a white skin. Likewise in the king of Fez his court are certain Christian captives, being partly Spanish, and partly Portugal women."[25] These historical examples all point to the common practice of Muslim rulers enslaving Christian women in their households, and more importantly, to the inherent appeal of fair, white, European Christian women. According to these narratives, white women were the most desirable objects that Muslim men could possess.

Paulina's captivity also reflects the commodification of white womanhood that occurs in historical accounts. Captured by pirates and sold in the slave markets of either the Ottoman regencies or in Istanbul — the foremost marketplace of the Ottoman Empire — these women were alienated from their identity, transformed into sexual objects, and exchanged for profit. The danger of the enslaved Christian woman or concubine is not just illicit sex with a Muslim man, but also the potential loss of religious identity through conversion. Looking at Sandys's account of the treatment of enslaved people betrays a concern regarding apostasy. He writes that slaves are chosen according to certain attributes:

> the women for their youths and beauties, who are set out in best becoming attires, and with their aspects of pity and affection,

24. Nicolas De Nicolay, "*The Navigations, Peregrinations and Voyages, Made into Turkie* (1585)," in *Race in Early Modern England: A Documentary Companion*, ed. Jonathan Burton and Ania Loomba (New York: Palgrave Macmillan, 2007), 116–17.
25. Joannes Leo Africanus, "*A Geographical Historie of Africa* (1600)," in *Race in Early Modern England: A Documentary Companion*, ed. Jonathan Burton and Ania Loomba (New York: Palgrave Macmillan, 2007), 157.

> endeavour to allure the Christians to buy them, as expecting from them a more easy servitude and continuance of religion: when being thrall to the Turk, they are more often enforced to renounce it for their better entertainment [...] *If any of their slaves will become Mahometans, they are discharged of their bondage.*[26]

Conversion to Islam results in immediate freedom for the enslaved person. The act, however, was condemned in European accounts because it was seen as emancipation at the expense of the captive's soul; consequently, the renegade "was the coward who deserved dire condemnation and judgment: he was the unheroic Christian unwilling to imitate Christ."[27] While *The Renegado* flirts with the issue of conversion for its male characters, that option is utterly denied to Paulina, even though her situation makes it a very real and perhaps necessary possibility. Paulina must remain immune to the allure of freedom offered by conversion, even though her captivity and the sexual advances of Asambeg conspire to endanger her body (with the threat of rape) and soul (through the possibility of apostasy). Her resolute Christian faith, her insistence on a fundamental difference between herself and the culture and religion of her captor, keeps her from slipping into the dangerous position occupied by the enslaved women in the historical narratives. Paulina's Christian ardor reinforces her virtue, signaling her fairness in body and mind.

Paulina's fairness is further yoked to her virginity, thus fetishizing whiteness in order to mobilize the discourse of color as race. She represents the white women who populate Islamicate harems who attest to, by their very confinement and enslaved status, the military, social, and cultural power of these empires. Their captivity points to the dominance and the hypermasculinity of Muslim potentates. The imperiled whiteness of

26. Sandys, "*The Relation of a Journey Begun an: Dom:* 1610 (1615)," 195 emphasis added. Sandys also relates how the virginity of the female slave is determined before the sale, and claims that a Christian is more likely to set a slave free if he has had sex with her and not sell her to someone else. The text remains ambivalent regarding the sex act itself between a Christian and his slave (195).
27. Nabil I. Matar, "'Turning Turk': Conversion to Islam in English Renaissance Thought," *Durham University Journal* 86, no. 1 (1994): 35.

these women, their personal vulnerability to sexual violence and aggression, establishes them as figures of sympathy. Their plight produces affective responses in the domestic audiences to whom these discourses are targeted. Endangered, fragile, chaste, and virtuous white femininity not only censures the regimes imprisoning these subjects, but also mobilizes European ideological and imperial aggression against those cultures. Paulina's virtue, chastity, and religious conviction shape her as the ideal fair woman, whose trajectory in *The Renegado* serves the interests of normative whiteness; therefore, Paulina's whiteness must remain inviolate and whole. The talismanic relic she wears offers her supernatural protection against Asambeg's sexual assault. It is, as Jane Hwang Degenhardt argues, an external manifestation of her unbroken hymen, her pristine chastity.[28] Moreover, the play's insistence on her somatic fairness secures her virginity, further inscribing her within the regime of white Christian identity by positioning her as endangered because of the desirability of her whiteness.

The play simultaneously reinforces the racial desirability of whiteness through Donusa's rejection of her Muslim suitor, Mustapha. While initially indifferent to Mustapha's romantic interest, Donusa turns cruel in her rejection after she has consummated her relationship with Vitelli. Her words repudiating his advances feature some of the play's most overtly racist language. Violently rebuffing Mustafa, Donusa exclaims:

> I have considered you from head to foot,
> And can find nothing in that wainscot face,
> That can teach me to dote, nor am I taken
> With your grim aspect, or tadpole-like complexion,
> Those scars you glory in, I fear to look on;
> And had much rather hear a merry tale
> Than all your battles won with blood and sweat,
> Though you belch forth the stink too, in the service,
> And swear by your mustachioes all is true.
> You are yet too rough for me, purge and take physic,

28. Degenhardt, "Catholic Prophylactics and Islam's Sexual Threat," 73.

> Purchase perfumers, get me some French tailor,
> To new create you; the first shape you were made with
> Is quite worn out, let your barber wash your face too,
> You look yet like a bugbear to fright children. (3.1.47–60)

Donusa initially rebuffs Mustafa on the grounds of his unhandsome and dark face, before swiftly turning to his hard military life, which has left his face marred with scars earned in battle. His aspect, in its purported darkness and his militarism, situate him outside the circuit of her desire. Michael Neill's editorial gloss on "wainscot face," notes that it could mean "hard, dark, and perhaps wrinkled or scarred"; and for "tadpole-like complexion," he similarly notes that it signifies color, this time "black."[29] From these textual clues, Neill suggests that Mustapha may have been performed in blackface.[30] If we follow Neill's hypothesis, Donusa's direction to "let your barber wash your face too," might seem an analogue to the proverbial white-washing of the Ethiope, another racially coded idiom, wherein non-whiteness, specifically Blackness, is constructed as dirty and unclean. Accepting Neill's interpretation of Mustafa's racialized representation, Donusa's criticism of him, specifically on his lack of desirability because of his color, confirms the beauty and allure of whiteness. Indeed, Mustafa's Blackness makes Vitelli's whiteness visible and underscores how the European merchant is a more enticing and valuable erotic object. Moreover, Mustafa's Blackness emphasizes the racialized composition of Islamicate societies. Grafted onto Muslim identity, Blackness or somatic non-whiteness symbolically others Islam to darken the religion and its adherents.

The Renegado's construction of Islam as a competing theology vis-à-vis Christianity, as embodied by the anxiety of conversion or "turning Turk," is managed through strategies of racial alterity and domination. Early on, Vitelli warns Gazet, his servant, not to trifle with the customs and conventions of the Ottomans, "Remember where you are too […] / Temper your tongue and meddle not with the Turks, / Their manners nor

29. Michael Neill, ed., The Renegado *by Philip Massinger* (London: Methuen, 2010), 153.
30. Neill, The Renegado *by Philip Massinger*, 153.

religion" (1.1.44–48). While the Ottomans grant outsiders the liberty to trade within their domains, this permission remains precarious and vulnerable to Ottoman political whims. The play fastens this cultural danger and allure onto anxieties about religious inconstancy: with Grimaldi, the renegade, serving as an example of the moral bankruptcy of conversion to Islam; Carazi, Donusa's eunuch, signaling the loss of European Christian vigor and masculinity; and Vitelli's sexual liaison with Donusa, indicating his abdication of Christian virtue. As the cause of these affective moments of shame and loss, Islam, its peoples, and societies, are positioned as materially alluring yet spiritually void. The fact that Francisco easily restores Vitelli's Christian fervor, which leads him to embrace martyrdom rather than convert to Islam, bolsters the claims of Christian superiority at the core of the play. Indeed, the temptation scene – initiated by Donusa to save both herself and Vitelli from the execution mandated by the Sultan for their illicit sexual relationship – affirms the spiritual truth of Christianity by further demonizing and denigrating Islam. Donusa begins her persuasions by highlighting the glories and riches of the Ottoman Empire: "Look on our flourishing empire – if the splendor, / The majesty and glory of it dim not / Your feeble sight – and then turn back and see / The narrow bounds of yours. [...] You must confess the deity you worship / Wants care or power to help you. (4.3.95–103). The generic and ideological logics of the play demand the failure of Donusa's arguments, which rely on worldly rather than spiritual rationales. In fact, the play has earlier pointed out the religious hypocrisy of the sexual charge against Donusa, because Islam allows Muslim men ultimate sexual freedom while limiting Muslim women's sexual agency:

> Indulgent Mahomet, do thy bloody laws
> Call my embraces with a Christian, death –
> Having my heat and May of youth to plead
> In my excuse – and yet want power to punish
> These that with scorn break through thy cobweb edicts
> And laugh at thy decrees? To tame their lusts
> There's no religious bit: let her be fair
> And pleasing to the eye, though Persian, Moor,

> Idolatress, Turk or Christian, you are privileged
> And freely may enjoy her. (4.2.128–33)

Massinger renders Donusa sympathetic through her attacks on Islamic sexual license and hypocrisy, a disposition that also fashions her as fit for conversion to Christianity. Her ability to expose the double standards at the root of Islamic law and prescription dissolves the bonds between her and the religion and culture of her birth. Moreover, her righteous complaints construct her as a victim of the tyranny of her religion.[31] She is transformed from the sexual aggressor of the earlier scenes into a victimized Muslim woman in need of saving by benevolent Christians.

Therefore, when Vitelli rejects Donusa's attempts at conversion, his appraisal of Islam similarly incriminates its materiality and venality, which corroborate its non-white racialization. Vitelli's language pays homage to common early modern stereotypes about Islam that rely on the supposed moral degeneracy of its prophet and therefore of his message.[32] Following the convention of staged Mediterranean plays, Vitelli is allowed an uninterrupted monologue that excoriates Islam and its prophet in front of an audience of shocked and immobile Muslims:

31. Britton points out that in early modern English Mediterranean plays featuring the "infidel-conversion motif [,] ... the religious identities of women are more malleable than those of men [and that] women who do convert are racial anomalies" (*Becoming Christian*, 171).

32. See for example, Richard Knolles, *The Generall Historie of the Turkes from the First Beginning of that Nation to the Rising of the Othoman Familie: With all the Notable Expeditions of the Christian Princes against Them. Together with the Liues and Conquests of the Othoman Kings and Emperours Faithfullie Collected out of the Best Histories, Both Auntient and Moderne, and Digested into one Continuat Historie Vntill this Present Yeare 1603* (London: Adam Islip, 1603); Paolo Giovio and Peter Aston, *A Short Treatise upon the Turkes Chronicles, Compyled by Paulus Paulus Iouius Byshop of Nucerne, and Dedicated to Charles the V. Emperour. Drawen oute of the Italyen Tong in to Latyne, by Franciscus Niger Bassianates. And Translated out of Latyne into Englysh by Peter Ashton* (Imprinted at London: In Fletestrete at the signe of the Sunne ouer agaynst the conduyte by Edvvarde VVhitchurche, 1546).

> Dare you bring
> Your juggling Prophet in comparison with
> The most inscrutable and infinite Essence
> That made this all and comprehends his work?
> […]
> Of your seducer, his base birth, his whoredoms,
> His strange impostures; nor deliver how
> He taught a pigeon to feed in his ear,
> Then made his credulous followers believe
> It was an angel that instructed him
> In the framing of his Alcoran. (4.3.114–31)

Vitelli's screed discredits the religion by demeaning Muhammad as a counterfeit and dishonest "juggler." His use of foul in relation to Muhammad's supposed sorceries accesses racialized tropes because it indicates corruption, staining, and darkening. His words depict Islam as a hoax full of false and "strange impostures," in contrast to Christian truth, transcendence, and salvation. By submitting to a fraudulent message, Muslims are also fouled — raced — by the degeneracy of their religion and enmeshed within a spiritual contest wherein the darkness of their belief must surrender to superior the light of the Christian faith. The scene mobilizes racial discourse by suturing spiritual and moral foulness onto the Muslims who would espouse and defend such a polluted doctrine.

Indeed, Donusa's subsequent conversion is punctuated by her violent rejection of Islam, making her a fit vessel to receive Christian truth. Moved by Vitelli's brazen Christian zeal, she exclaims, "I came here to take you, / But I perceive a yielding in myself / To be your prisoner, […] Then thus I spit at Mahomet," confirming the conflation of somatic markers of race with religious alliances (4.3.148–49; 158). This alignment depends upon the play's recurring deployment of the discourse of fairness. In preparation for his wedding and ensuing execution, Vitelli seeks Francisco's counsel on baptizing Donusa so that she may be redeemed by a Christian death: "Willing she is, / I know, to wear it as the choicest jewel / on her fair forehead" (5.1.24–26). Even though she has yet to be made fully Christian, the restoration of her fairness positions her as appropriate for conversion. Such scenes of female conversion are familiar topoi of early modern staged Mediterranean plays. As Ania Loomba notes, "the most common form of sexual transgression had in fact involved Christian men and Muslim women. In stories of Christians turning Turk that circulated in early modern times, Muslim women are temptresses who ensnare Christian men into a licentious faith. [...] But such fears are theatrically allayed by either the destruction of such women or their own conversions to Christianity and marriages to Christian men."[33] In addition to relieving the anxiety of such intimacies between European Christians and non-European Muslims, the discourse of race ensures that whiteness makes legible Donusa's fitness to enter the European Christian community even as that whiteness confirms Christian identity. Massinger emphasizes racial legibility and Christian whiteness during the actual baptism: tricking Asambeg into allowing the ceremony, Vitelli points out that the holy water "washes off / Stains and pollutions [...] / It hath power to purge those spots that cleave upon the mind" (5.3.112–15). The baptism transforms Donusa "I am another woman — till this minute / I never lived" (5.3.121–22); moreover, she once more rejects her former faith "False Prophet. / Impostor Mahomet" (5.3.132–33). Born again into whiteness, Donusa's curse functions as another sign of her newly acquired hegemonic position: the ability to perceive the theological emptiness and moral darkness of Islam.

Like other plays set in the Mediterranean contact zone, *The Renegado* ends with a well-timed rescue of the tragic lovers through the relentless plotting of Francisco, his newly re-Christianized henchman Grimaldi, and the intelligent schemes of Paulina. The intrepid Europeans happily evacuate the dangerous geography of Ottoman-controlled Tunis and leave the viceroy, Asambeg, to face the fatal fury of the Ottoman Sultan. *The Renegado*'s tidy ending confirms the cultural, religious, and racial superiority of the European Christian characters, thus conveying to its domestic audiences the appropriateness of their proto-imperial mission in the Mediterranean.

33. Ania Loomba, "'Delicious Traffick': Racial and Religious Difference on Early Modern Stages," in *Shakespeare and Race*, ed. Catherine M. S. Alexander and Stanley Wells (Cambridge: Cambridge University Press, 2000), 214.

Embodied Affects Redux

The Renegado is a deeply Islamophobic play. As a Muslim woman, the final acts of the play inflict violence upon me as a reader and scholar. The play, like so many other staged Mediterranean dramas of the period, denigrates my religion and suggests that the only way for my Muslim identity to be commensurate with normative identity is for me to abrogate my faith. Moreover, in its rehearsal of the "plight" of Muslim women, I encounter a familiar script, a mainstay of the United States' endless War on Terror. In the justifications for that conflict, Muslim women were constructed as victims of Islamic fundamentalism and in desperate need of Western liberation. Here I am not apologizing for extreme and cruel acts of violence attributed to religious extremists, but rather pointing to the historical links between these narratives and the insidious operations of an imperial feminism that licenses unlimited death and destruction in the morally hollow name of equality. The promise of freedom and liberty, of being seen as a full person rather than a dehumanized mass — as Muslims are often represented — comes with the steep price of rejecting and despising my identity, religion, and culture. The demands of white Christendom in *The Renegado* are the full and complete erasure and destruction of Muslim life. If we teach and study this play, we must recognize that for some members of its current and future audiences, its tragicomic message is neither a rhetorical exercise nor an intellectual pastime with which to wrestle. *The Renegado* traffics in their / my humanity.[34] To read this play is to experience the trauma of Islamophobia — it is part of an English literary can(n)on that contributed to our colonization and the degrading forms of imperial violence that accompanied it. When we pick up this play, we

34. The critical position I adopt here and throughout the section on embodied affects is influenced by bell hooks's theory of the "oppositional gaze" ("The Oppositional Gaze: Black Female Spectators," in *Black Looks: Race and Representation* [Boston: South End Press, 1992], 115–32) and Kim F. Hall's recent work on the trauma of the archive ("I Can't Love This the Way You Want Me to: Archival Blackness," *Postmedieval* 11, nos. 2–3 [2020]: 171–79). I am deeply indebted to the work of Black feminists who offer a mode of critique and activism attuned to intersectional forms of domination, violence, and erasure.

must consider who and what it serves, and who and what we serve with our engagement.

2. Desire, Disgust, and the Perils of Strange Queenship in Edmund Spenser's *The Faerie Queene*

MIRA 'ASSAF KAFANTARIS

In Edmund Spenser's courtly romance, *The Faerie Queene* (1590, 1596), the anxiety around queenship and power becomes a crucial site where racialization is produced through affect. While white womanhood secures the future of the Reformed realm, a foreign queen emblematizes the threat of infection, which can permeate the commonwealth religiously, culturally, or physiologically. At the point of contact, the strange woman's embodied difference evokes feelings of wonder and desire that inform early modern racialization. In this essay, I argue that *The Faerie Queene*'s affective constructions of racial identities provide a productive lens through which a foreign queen's racial otherness, namely her moral degeneration, sexual transgression, and religious idolatry, is made legible. This legibility is most vivid through the operative and disavowed component of disgust. By tracing how affective capacities shape the ideology of racial purity, I posit that boundaries of *feeling* operate as a coercive epistemological category in this sprawling allegory of hierarchy, difference, and power.

The threat of racialized foreign queens pervades *The Faerie Queene*. In Book 1, which celebrates Holiness, the Redcrosse Knight, a Saxon "sprung out of English race" (1.10.60), endures an ordeal that registers early modern anxieties with foreign contamination of white Reformed bodies.[1] Veering away from religious truth, Redcrosse dallies with Duessa, the allegorical Whore of Babylon. Once Duessa's real identity as "false truth" is uncovered, Redcrosse experiences feelings of utter disgust that lead him to despair. Ultimately, he is saved by Una, the figure of the One True Church, who restores his faith and fortitude in the House of Holiness.

1. All references (to book, canto, and stanza) are to Edmund Spenser, *The Faerie Queene*, ed. A. C. Hamilton (New York: Longman, 1977).

Certainly, erotic encounters with racialized others animate the generic conventions of chivalric romance, where the temporary slippage of virtuous characters into sin is restored through baptism and marriage.[2] However, as Dennis Austin Britton notes, the absence of the "infidel-conversion motif" in *The Faerie Queene* points to the formation of a new vocabulary of exclusion where religion figures as a racial category that is inherited.[3] By making Christianity into an inheritance passed genetically from parents to children, the performance of conversion via baptism becomes a moot point, since the children of Reformed parents are recipients of God's election in the womb. Following this logic, damnation is also considered a racial characteristic passed from non-Christian parents to their children. Therefore, in the poem's allegorized landscape, the godly commonwealth belongs to white, Christian-born bodies only.

Who will defend the godly commonwealth from the threat of contamination? Whose movement do fortified borders obstruct? As the reproductive agents in the circuit of monarchical succession and generation, foreign royal women embodied the biggest threat to white futurity. Spenser not only rejects the incorporation of non-white queens into the racially pure commonwealth, but also infuses his allegory with instructions on how to *feel* as a community of the faithful in the face of what a Protestant polemicist dubbed the threat of "unnatural mixing."[4] This

2. Spenser critics have long drawn the similarities between Armida's Garden in Torquato Tasso's *Gerusalemme liberata* (1581) and Acrasia's Bower of Bliss. See, for example, Jason Lawrence's recent *Tasso's Art and Afterlives: The* Gerusalemme Liberata *in England* (Manchester: Manchester University Press, 2017), esp. Chapter 2.
3. Dennis Austin Britton, *Becoming Christian: Race, Reformation, and Early Modern English Romance* (New York: Fordham University Press, 2014), 59–61.
4. See Mira Assaf Kafantaris, "Protestant Purity and the Anxieties of Cultural Mixing in William Shakespeare's and John Fletcher's *Henry VIII*," in *The Palgrave Handbook of Shakespeare Queens*, ed. Kavita Mudan Finn and Valerie Schutte (Cham, Switzerland: Palgrave Macmillan, 2018), 331–53, esp. 334–35. For an analysis of miscegenation as a plot that can only be understood through the frame of rape and white womanhood, see Arthur L. Little, Jr., *Shakespeare Jungle Fever: National-Imperial Re-Visions of Race, Rape, and Sacrifice* (Stanford, CA: Stanford University Press, 2000); Francesca T. Royster, "White-Limed Walls: Whiteness and Gothic Extremism in Shakespeare's *Titus Andronicus*," *Shakespeare Quarterly* 51, no. 4 (2000): 432–55, esp. 449–51; Kim F. Hall,

affective control animates racial formation in the famous erotic encounters between erring knights and Duessa, a hypervisible, oversexualized, and usurping foreign queen, who symbolizes the temptations of false religion and Protestantism's triumph over it. Affect figures as a semiotic and biopolitical border contouring the inside and outside of an ideal Protestant commonwealth. The poem's activation of feelings of wonder, desire, and disgust not only legitimates the expulsion of non-white, non-Christian queens from Spenser's Faerie Land, but more importantly, shapes and encodes the racial knowledge of its readers through affect.[5]

In recent years, Spenserians have grappled with allegory as a discursive space where racialization is tightly interlinked with other ideologies governing the poem, including Christian typology, aesthetic epistemology, and imperial violence.[6] In responding to the persistent claim that

Things of Darkness: Economies of Race and Gender in Early Modern England (Ithaca, NY: Cornell University Press, 1995), esp. Chapter 3, which analyzes the threat of miscegenation in *Antony and Cleopatra* and *The Tempest.*

5. Sylvia Wynter and Hortense J. Spillers' scholarship shed light on how biopolitics shape subjectivities and epistemologies as always in opposition to Blackness. See Sylvia Wynter, "Unsettling the Coloniality of Being/Power/Truth/Freedom: Towards the Human, After Man, Its Overrepresentation — An Argument," CR: *The New Centennial Review* 3, no. 3 (2003): 257–333; Hortense J. Spillers, "Mama's Baby, Papa's Maybe: An American Grammar Book," *Diacritics* 17, no. 2 (1987): 64–81.
6. For excellent investigations of Spenser's Irish experience and his knowledge of the colonial enterprise, see David J. Baker, *Between Nations: Shakespeare, Spenser, Marvell, and the Question of Britain* (Stanford, CA: Stanford University Press, 1997); Andrew Hadfield, *Edmund Spenser's Irish Experience: Wilde Fruit and Salvage Soyl* (Oxford: Oxford University Press, 1997); Christopher Highley, *Shakespeare, Spenser, and the Crisis in Ireland* (Cambridge: Cambridge University Press, 1997); Bradin Cormack, *A Power to Do Justice: Jurisdiction, English Literature, and the Rise of Common Law, 1509–1625* (Chicago: University of Chicago Press, 2007), especially Chapter 3. For an analysis of the racialization of Spenser's Indian fairies, see Margo Hendricks, "'Obscured by Dreams': Race, Empire, and Shakespeare's *A Midsummer Night's Dream*," *Shakespeare Quarterly* 47, no. 1 (1996): 37–60. See also Benedict S. Robinson's discussion of Islam in Spenser in "'Secret Faith,'" in *Islam and Early Modern English Literature: The Politics of Romance from Spenser to Milton* (New York: Palgrave Macmillan, 2007), 27–56. For allegorization of race in other contexts, see Barbara Fuchs, "Spanish Lessons: Spenser and the Irish Moriscos," *Studies in English Literature 1500–1900* 42, no. 1 (2002): 43–62; Jean

Spenser's epic should be read as a religious allegory only, Dennis Austin Britton and Kimberly Anne Coles have argued that allegory is not only a device through which ideology is transmitted, but is also composed of the same false stability that punctuates race. Spenser's allegory "both draw[s] from and produc[es] understandings of a racialized body."[7] While allegory helps orient readers along a relational map with both its sources and moral encoding, allegory cannot be separated from the anthropological contexts, cultural meanings, and political realities imposed on it.[8] I approach this lacuna by examining the ways the poem's affective mode physicalizes, exteriorizes, and amplifies the inner workings of power and difference housed in what Angus Fletcher calls "the hermeneutic walls of allegory."[9] In the movement between form and ideology, I see the production of race through affect, which previous readings of racialized allegory have not taken into account.

In other words, allegory is a medium that catalyzes the circuit between ideology and interpretation, form and meaning, narrative and context. The dynamic movement between a rich literary device and polyvocal cultural composition is, in itself, a racializing factor. The movement between form and ideology activates a network of connections between characters and feelings that has not been considered before. In relation to interracial contact and mixing, where human differences and feelings are sorted, dis-

E. Feerick, *Strangers in Blood: Relocating Race in the Renaissance* (Toronto: University of Toronto Press, 2010), especially Chapter 1; Melissa E. Sanchez, *Queer Faith: Reading Promiscuity and Race in Secular Love Tradition* (New York: New York University Press, 2019).

7. Dennis Austin Britton and Kimberly Anne Coles, "Beyond the Pale," *Spenser Review* 50, no. 1 (2020): http://www.english.cam.ac.uk/spenseronline/review/item/50.1.5, accessed 19 April 2020. They reiterate this point in Dennis Austin Britton and Kimberly Ann Coles, eds., "Spenser and Race: An Introduction," in "Spenser and Race," special issue, *Spenser Studies* 35 (2021):1–19.
8. Ross Lerner examines the "formal kinship" between race and allegory, drawing on the instability of both modes in "Allegorization and Racialization in *The Faerie Queene*," in "Spenser and Race," ed. Dennis Austin Britton and Kimberly Anne Coles, special issue, *Spenser Studies* 35 (2021): 107–35.
9. Angus Fletcher, "Allegory without Ideas," in *Thinking Allegory Otherwise*, ed. Brenda Machosky (Stanford, CA: Stanford University Press, 2009), 10.

ciplined, and hierarchized time and time again, how are feelings racialized? How does affective control operate as a coercive mode of hierarchy and difference? Spenser deploys affect, such as desire and disgust, to code racial formation. In what follows, I focus on the affects of racialization which, on the one hand, associate virtuous feelings such as sorrow, sadness, sympathy, and humility with true Englishness and, on the other, activate powerful feelings of disgust in response to the lustful, vilified Duessa. One signals generative sexuality that will sustain the poem's fictions of whiteness, while the other forecloses the foreign queen's humanity and paves the way to her containment.[10] In attending to the affective force of these two gendered constructs, I channel premodern critical race theorist Margo Hendricks's righteous call to "understand the immigrant [or foreign] woman's position in a world which symbolically exploits her 'otherness' as a literary and cultural foundation for the construction of a particular form of womanhood at the same time as it conceals her presence in Renaissance England."[11]

Central to the foreign woman's concealment is her subjection in relation to the ideal of white Protestant femininity. In Spenser, this takes the form of Una, who rides "Upon a lowly Asse more white than snow, / Yet she much whiter." Indeed, Una is described as a "louely lady" and "faire" (1.1.4); most importantly, her somatic whiteness and royal lineage reflect her inner virtues: "So pure an innocent, as that same lambe, / She was in

10. Early modern humoral theories, rooted in Hippocratic and Galenic medicine, understood the body to be porous and fluid, where the imagined imbrication of "the stuff of the outside world and the stuff of the body" influenced ideas about the emotions, according to Gail Kern Paster, *Humoring the Body: Emotions and the Shakespearean Stage* (Chicago: University of Chicago Press, 2004), 4. In this essay, I tie detectable emotions to racialized subjects, which are constructed as an inheritance, following Britton's work in *Becoming Christian*'s on infant baptism in Calvinist theology.
11. Even though Hendricks focuses on the invisibilization of women of African descent in white feminist historiography under the broad mantle of the "universal woman model," her theorization of a racialized, often vilified, foreign womanhood that throws in sharp relief white, upper-class, chaste womanhood helps my examination of foreign queens in this essay (Margo Hendricks, "Feminist Historiography," in *A Companion to Early Modern Women's Writing*, ed. Anita Pacheco [Malden, MA: Blackwell, 2002], 374).

life and euery vertuous lore, / And by descent from Royall lynage came / Of ancient Kings and Queenes" (1.1.5). Kim F. Hall has shown how the linguistic construct of chaste whiteness in poetic descriptions of "fair" or "white" ideals of beauty naturalizes a nascent white supremacist ideology that privileges European ancestry.[12] Here, Una's aestheticized somatic whiteness and noble pedigree mirror her virtuous interiority, whereby the boundaries between white physiognomy, royal blood, and true religion coalesce to produce and patrol exemplary white Protestant womanhood. However, somatic whiteness becomes deceitful simulacra in the absence of an inherently Protestant interiority that points to a godly lineage. In Spenser's Reformed imaginary, epidermal whiteness symbolizes exemplary Protestant womanhood only when it is interlaced with the grace of God, which is granted to members of the elect only. To this, Duessa's whiteness, when she is disguised as "false Fidessa faire," is not enough to countermand her inner falsehood. Furthermore, Duessa's liaison with the Muslim knight darkens her — a point that I will return to later.[13] In the same stanza, the juxtaposition of their "wanton loues" with "the bloud of the vanquisht Paynim bold" (1.7.26) bespeaks the fear of racial mixing, which blackens false Fidessa's whiteness.[14] As Joyce Green MacDonald has observed, somatic whiteness does not "repudiate the idea of racialized norms of femininity, since other kinds of difference — sexual, political, behavioral — will be fully identified as racial matters."[15] Duessa's "borrowed light" hides underneath it "a fowle deformed wight"(1.8.49), as Una proselytizes while she undresses the foreign queen.

12. Hall, *Things of Darkness*, 22.
13. I deliberately choose not to use the label "Saracen" in referring to the Sans Brothers, following Shokoofeh Rajabzadeh's autoethnographic critique of the violence embedded in this term ("The Depoliticized Saracen and Muslim Erasure," *Literature Compass* 16, nos. 9–10 [2019]: https://doi.org/10.1111/lic3.12548).
14. I draw on Royster's "White-Limed Walls," particularly her generative reading of Tamora's whiteness in Shakespeare's *Titus Andronicus*, who is darkened by her sexual relationship with Aaron the Moor.
15. Joyce Green MacDonald, *Women and Race in Early Modern Texts* (Cambridge: Cambridge University Press, 2010), 9–10.

Just as it emblematizes the interdependence of somatic whiteness, true Christian interiority, and noble genealogy, the narrative likewise explores the racializing constructs of falsehood. In the figure of Duessa, racial stigmatization is shaped by sartorial, religious, and sexual modes of differentiation, which pave the way for the poem's ultimate rejection of the foreign woman via the affect of disgust. We first encounter Duessa adrift in Faerie Land, traveling an unfamiliar geographical terrain with the Muslim knight Sans Foy. Unlike Una, whose "wandring in woods and forests" is anchored in Christian clarity, Duessa's mobility is deemed "faire disport and courting dalliaunce" (1.2.9;14). The construction of Duessa's difference starts with a description of excessive materials surrounding her body. She dons "scarlet red, / Pursled with gold and pearle of rich assay" and a "*Persian* mitre" (1.2.13). Even her "wanton palfrey" is adorned in "tinsell trappings" and "golden bells and bosses brave" (1.2.13). In the decadent House of Pride, she basks in "such endless riches, and so sumpteous shew; / Ne *Persia* selfe" (1.4.7). Lorraine Daston and Katherine Park have persuasively argued that wonders, as objects of inquiry, are imbricated with the emotions they evoke.[16] Duessa's movement between her native Persia and Faerie Land, along with her objects of wonder, demonstrate that nobility and lineage signify differently across contexts. Her mobility and opulent surroundings become material signifiers of her spiritual depravity. Despite her noble birth, Duessa is irredeemable because she is an outsider to the true English Church and, by extension, excluded from the divine ordering that grants permission to cross borders. She is the "daughter of an Emperor" (1.2.22), but her traversing of borders, accompanied by material objects and foreign subjects, racializes her in the context of white English Protestantism. As Patricia Akhimie notes, "groupings can never be finite or discrete, since members must continually be evaluated for inclusion or exclusion."[17] The emphasis of Persia as Duessa's place of origin conflates her subjectivity with the pearls associated with the Indian ocean.

16. Lorraine Daston and Katherine Park, *Wonders and the Order of Nature*, 1150–1750 (New York: Zone Books, 1998), 11.
17. Patricia Akhimie, *Shakespeare and the Cultivation of Difference: Race and Conduct in the Early Modern World* (London: Routledge, 2018), 19.

She is the symbolic Persian pearl that evokes wonder, the jewel that white settler colonial ideology strives to hoard. The evocation of strangeness and wonder that accompanies this representation of an Orientalized royal woman moving between borders will morph into feelings of disgust later in the poem. In this formulation, the narrative points to Duessa's overdetermined foreignness, her ostentatious display of wealth, her mobility, and her false beauty. Indeed, Duessa's material hypervisibility, along with the feelings of wonder and desire she rouses, serves as justification for exclusion based on her apostasy, her transgressive sexuality, and her disgusting affect.

The narrative controls erotic desire between racialized bodies by channeling it into feelings of disgust. Duessa represents the dangers of incorporation into the English commonwealth, threatening to corrupt the fantasy of racial purity. In the infamous bathing scene of Book 1, the bleeding, speaking tree Fradubio recounts to Redcrosse his betrayal of Fraelissa for Duessa and the events that led to his metamorphosis into a tree. In the voyeuristic account, Duessa's body produces a warped representational logic that positions the onlooker as, simultaneously, desiring and disgusted. His concupiscence, but more importantly, his need to confirm Duessa's erotic beauty, who "seemde as faire as" Fraelissa, his own "faire lady" (1.2.37), motivated him to watch Duessa bathe, where he "chaunst to see her in her proper hew" (1.2.40). In Fradubio's account of this libidinal spectacle, Duessa's naked, non-white body evokes feelings of disgust. As it turns out, "her proper hew" is not the "fairness" he desired:

> Her neather partes misshapen, monstrous,
> Were hidd in water, that I could not see
> But they seeme more foule and hideous,
> Then womans shape man would believe to bee. (1.2.41)

In drawing attention to Duessa's monstrous reproductive organs, the narrative conjoins the affective energies of desire and disgust with the threat of miscegenation that non-white, non-Christian queens embody. Duessa's "foule" and "hideous" monstrosity justify this moment of violent intimacy, where her reproductive body undergoes a transformation from conduit for progeny into object of odious debasement. But for a brief cinematic moment, in Fradubio's inability to look away from the object of wonder, we witness the scrim separating the erotic thrill from the grotesque repulsion produced by this gendered spectacle of nude bathing. In other words, within the libidinal economy of the poem's racist logic, the embodied allure and threat of a foreign queen become legible through the affective currents of wonder, desire, and disgust that inculcate in the audience appropriate responses to racialized bodies.

By engaging and harnessing the emotional responses of the viewer, and by extension, the reader, the poem creates a new racial language, whereby the embodied otherness of the racialized subject shapes what and how people feel. In his exposé of the cultural meaning of the word "disgust" in the early modern period, Benedict Robinson considers René Descartes's model of aversion as "not the opposite of desire. It is a kind of desire."[18] In Descartes's telling, every aversion constitutes desire, since both affects are rooted in the same passion. However, when the object is considered through time and utility, the relationship to it becomes one of either desire or disgust. Because Fradubio and Redcrosse's desire for Duessa cannot be contained in a generative Protestant marriage, Duessa's body moves in only one direction: from wonder, to desire, to disgust.

Following affect theory's emphasis on the inextricable link between desire and disgust, the relationship between race and desire becomes apparent.[19] Sharon Patricia Holland has shown how erotic desire undergirds processes of racialization: " [the] focus on desire...is important in the process of orientation under colonialism, as desire (longing) marks the place of colonial access"; in this formulation, Holland continues, "the erotic is less like autonomous life and more connected to a matrix of desiring relations that tend to make it difficult to mark where racist ... practice begins and where good desire ends."[20] Spenser racializes the bor-

18. Benedict Robinson, "Disgust c. 1600," *ELH* 81, no. 2 (2014): 554.
19. For example, to Eve Kosofsky Sedgwick and Adam Frank, "only something you thought might delight or satisfy can disgust" ("Shame in the Cybernetic Fold: Reading Silvan Tomkins," in *Shame and Its Sisters: A Silvan Tomkins Reader*, ed. Eve Kosofsky Sedgwick and Adam Frank [Durham, NC: Duke University Press, 1995], 22.
20. Sharon Patricia Holland, *The Erotic Life of Racism* (Durham, NC: Duke University Press, 2012), 50.

der-policing feelings of disgust in his representation of Duessa's allure. When Una finally disrobes Duessa in Canto 8, "fowle Duessa's" (1.8.49) racialized embodiment of disgust comes full circle: her breasts "lyke bladders lacking wind / Hong downe," from which "filthy matter" wells, and "Her wrizled skin as rough, as maple rind." In addition to her vomitive appearance, Duessa reeks of otherness. "And her sowre breath abhominably smeld" (1.8.47), implicating the olfactory in the marking of difference. In mounting this visceral embodiment of her raced otherness, Spenser fundamentally forecloses Duessa's humanity and ultimately legitimizes her expulsion from the land of the redeemed: "She flying fast from heauens hated face, / ... Fled to the wastfull wildernesse apace" (1.8.50). Considering the affective politics of racialization, therefore, gives insight into how the fantasy of white Protestant Englishness impelled the expulsion of diseased, deviant bodies as central to the expansion of hegemonic control.

The poem's animation of disgust coalesces with another powerful racializing discourse of gendered coercion: the vilification of witches. The affective charge of disgust mobilizes an impulse to ward off infection, to "reforme that ragged common-weale" (5.12.26). The unnaturalness of Duessa as a witch contributes to a discourse that welds transgressive sexuality, women's agency, and racialized foreignness to the development of ideologies about gender and race.[21] When we scrutinize witchcraft

21. Spenser's witches include Duessa, Lucifera, Acrasia, Phaedra, Ate, and Munera. Given the scope of this essay, I will only focus on Duessa's witchcraft. The association between heresy and witchcraft has received much critical commentary; as Stuart Clark notes, accusations of witchcraft were "so widespread, so endemic in the discourse of religious difference" (*Thinking with Demons: The Idea of Witchcraft in Early Modern Europe* [Oxford: Oxford University Press, 1997], 532). To feminist critics, the charge of witchcraft was a tool to contain women's agency, regulate their sexualities, and maintain patriarchal control. The relation between early modern witchcraft and patriarchal coercion has been discussed in much detail by feminist critics such as Sylvia Federici, *Caliban and the Witch: Women, the Body, and Primitive Accumulation*, 2nd ed. (Brooklyn, NY: Autonomedia, 2014); Katherine Usher Henderson and Barbara F. McManus, *Half Humankind: Contexts and Texts of the Controversy about Women in England, 1540–1640* (Urbana: University of Illinois Press, 1985); Monica Karpinska, "Early Modern

through the optics of race, particularly when accusations of witchcraft are attached to monstrosity and infection, we can detect how militant Protestants, like Spenser, harness and transform disgust into a method of affective control.[22] In Book 1, representations of Duessa as a witch abound: she is a "false sorceresse" (1.2.34); her golden cup "replete with magick artes" (1.8.14); and her witchcraft rooted in "wicked herbs and ointments," and "secret pyson ... charmes and some enchauntments" (1.2.42; 8.14). Additionally, she is dangerous because the erotic and visual pleasures her magic conjure threaten white futurity.[23] In his witch-hunting handbook, *On the Demon-Mania of Witches* (1580), French political philosopher Jean Bodin considers a witch's defiance of natural law, "one who knowingly tries to accomplish something by diabolical means."[24] More importantly, Bodin's advocacy of witch hunts promoted scrutiny over the gyno-centric areas of pregnancy, birth, and reproduction. To Bodin, witches not only "receive children and offer them to the Devil," they also cause monstrous births, such as one witch who caused "a woman [to give] birth to a toad."[25]

Dramatizations of Witches and Pregnant Women," *Studies in English Literature* 50, no. 2 (2010): 427–44; Julia M. Garrett, "Witchcraft and Sexual Knowledge in Early Modern England," *Journal for Early Modern Cultural Studies* 13, no. 1 (2013): 32–72.

22. For the use of witchcraft in racialized discourse, see Sylvia Wynter's meditation on Sycorax and the demonic in "Beyond Miranda's Meanings: Un/silencing the 'Demonic Ground' of Caliban's 'Woman'" in *Out of the Kumbla: Caribbean Women and Literature*, ed. Carole Boyce Davies and Elaine Savory Fido (Trenton, NJ: Africa World Press, 1992), 355–72. See also Diane Purkiss, "The Witch on the Margins of 'Race': Sycorax and Others," in *The Witch in History: Early Modern and Twentieth-Century Representations* (London: Routledge, 1996), 25075; Karen E. Fields and Barbara J. Fields, *Racecraft: The Soul of Inequality in American Life* (New York: Verso, 2012).
23. My use of the concept of "white futurity" derives from Holland's theorization of the ubiquity of white ontology that rests on anti-Black and racial-colonial violence, arguing that: "the purpose of 'the future' is to wed us to a particular kind of repetition where the reiteration of past practice enlists both heteronormativity and biological belonging on its side to hide racist endeavor in quotidian practice" (*The Erotic Life of Racism*, 34).
24. Jean Bodin, *On the Demon-Mania of Witches*, trans. Randy A. Scott, abr. Jonathan L. Pearl (Toronto: Centre for Reformation and Renaissance Studies, 1995), 45.
25. Bodin, *On the Demon-Mania of Witches*, 138.

Clearly, Bodin's witches, like Duessa, are dangerous because of their proximity to and alignment with reproductive agency, which is itself racialized through connotations of gendered errancy, deviant sexuality, and material excess. Writing in Scotland 1597, the future King of England, James VI of Scotland, warns of the "vnnaturall inuasiones" of witchcraft.[26] The threat of witches lies in their ability to penetrate borders, their gendered agency, and rejections of patriarchal control; to James, "disobedience is as the sinne of Witch-craft."[27]

Likewise, Spenser likens witchcraft to foreign infection, invasion, falsehood, deceit, and waywardness, which are narrativized via the affect of disgust; underneath her "royall robes, and purple pall," Duessa is revealed as "A loathly, wrinckled hag, ill fauoured, old, / Whose secret filth good manners biddeth not be told" (1.8.46). In this sense, then, Duessa can be described as "weyward," which Ayanna Thompson — in reading the racialization of *Macbeth*'s witches, "the secret black and midnight hags" (4.1.48) — defines as "weird, fated, fateful, perverse, intractable, willful, erratic, unlicensed, fugitive, troublesome, and wayward."[28]

Underlining the interconnection between witchcraft, strange queenship, and the biblical allusions attached to the word "hag" reveals much about Spenser's racialization of Duessa. In a poem that is pervaded — one might say obsessed — with genealogies and historical lineages, the semantic affinity between "hag" and the biblical "Hagar" in *Genesis* 16 as social outcasts and racial others generates important meanings.[29] Hagar is the Egyptian slave girl whom Sarah, Abraham's wife, coerced into having sex with her husband in order to preserve the patrilineal line. However, when Sarah bore Isaac, she expelled Hagar into the Sinai desert with her son, Ishmael. Etymologically, the origins of the Hebrew name *Hagar* quite possibly relate to the Hebrew roots *ger*, or *guwr*, which connote "to dwell,

26. James I, King of England, *Daemonologie: In Forme of a Dialogue* (Edinburgh: Robert Walde-grau, 1597), 49.
27. James I, *Daemonologie*, 5.
28. Ayanna Thompson, "What Is a 'Weyward' Macbeth?," in *Weyward Macbeth: Intersections of Race and Performance*, ed. Scott L. Newstok and Ayanna Thompson (New York: Palgrave Macmillan, 2010), 3.
29. I am grateful to James C. Nohrnberg for his help with this point.

abide, reside, emigrate, sojourn," with the prefix *-ha* (the) attached to it.[30] Such etymology, therefore, gives Hagar the literal meaning of "The Immigrant," "The sojourner, the foreigner, or the stranger." In St. Paul's interpretation of Abraham's covenant with Isaac in *Galatians* 4.21–31, Hagar becomes the embodiment of a sexualized and raced body on display, condemned for never arriving, her movement a dalliance, her futurity foreclosed. Indeed, her descendants are not promised salvation, but are associated with the carnality of a fallen, foreign woman. Pauline allegorization of Hagar as a figure of deceit, tainted lineage, and errancy was consolidated by St. Jerome, who read in the word "Saracen" proof that the children of Hagar, called "Agarens," were duplicitous, claiming descent from Sarah.[31]According to Geraldine Heng, "attributing the invention of the name Saracens to the enemy, as a sly act of self-naming by the enemy is … not only a brilliant lie, but one that brilliantly names the enemy as liars in the very act of naming them as enemies."[32] Likewise, Spenser aligns witchcraft with foreign infection, invasion, falsehood, deceit, and waywardness. As *a hag, a Hagar, a harlot*, Duessa's vilified otherness is produced and reproduced time and again. Her non-Christian, non-white lineage, her idolatrous rejection of divine justice, and her defiance of mechanisms of natural law are affronts to the idea of sovereignty and good governance.

Because the body politic and its imagined futures are measured by a queen's coded whiteness, Duessa's indelible markers of religious and racial otherness — her poisonous cup, her sexual relations with Muslim figures, and her deceit — yoked to the feelings of disgust she evokes, cannot sustain the dynastic linearity that the commonwealth of the Godly requires. Quite the opposite, her foreignness threatens fantasies of racial purity, passivity, and constancy. Central to the foreign woman's excision is

30. Paul D. LeBlanc, *Deciphering the Proto-Sinaitic Script: Making Sense of the Wadi El-Hol and Serabit El-Khadim Early Alphabetic Inscriptions*, (Ottawa: Subclass Press, 2016), 239.
31. See Robinson, "'Secret Faith,'" 33.
32. Geraldine Heng, *The Invention of Race in the European Middle Ages* (Cambridge: Cambridge University Press, 2018), 112.

her diminishment in relation to an aggrandized ideal of white Protestant femininity. In the following, I linger on the activation of white feelings, particularly the politics surrounding Una's embodiment of raced sentimentality, to throw into high relief how somatic and affective markers are intimately imbricated in early modern racial formations.

I wish to return to the politics surrounding Una's embodiment of whiteness, particularly the presentation of her raced sentimentality, to reveal how somatic and affective markers are intimately imbricated. When we first encounter Una, we learn that she "Inly mournd," and "seemed in heart some hidden care she had" (1.1.4). Una is mourning the aborted project of the true English church, but it is important to highlight how Una feels white, or evokes positive emotions, and how her sentimentality transmits to the sensing bodies of readers. Joseph Campana notes "Una's conversion into a figure of sentimental beauty whose appeal and triumph are underwritten by a displaced violence directed at demonized figures of feminine materiality, such as Duessa."[33] This triumph of Una's sentimentality over Duessa's racialized materiality is conducive to what Lauren Berlant, in theorizing the political work of the sentimental genre, calls "the pleasure of being morally elevated by consumption."[34] In Una's case, Spenser's readers access the pleasures of sympathizing with her sentimentality, which arrives racially coded. Indeed, Clare Hemmings looks at the ways affect "manifests precisely not as difference, but as a central mechanism of social reproduction." In this context, Una's sentimentality, or "affective intensity," to use Hemmings's term, "strengthen[s] rather than challenge[s] a dominant social order."[35] In the poem, when Una is associated with positive affects such as pity in "piteous words" and "piteous plaints" (1.3.33; 44); a "royall virgin" who "wailes and weeps" (1.2.7); and "sore grieved in her gentle brest" (1.2.8), her embodiment and materiality embed her in the

33. Joseph Campana, *The Pain of Reformation: Spenser, Vulnerability, and the Ethics of Masculinity* (New York: Fordham University Press, 2012), 49.

34. Lauren Berlant, *The Female Complaint: The Unfinished Business of Sentimentality in American Culture* (Durham, NC: Duke University Press, 2008), 54.

35. Clare Hemmings, "Invoking Affect: Cultural Theory and the Ontological Turn," *Cultural Studies* 19, no. 5 (2005): 551.

machinations of white biopower. What is strengthened is an emotional code necessary to uphold the demarcation between virtuous reproductive bodies, on the one hand, and raced and oversexed ones, on the other. White supremacy's project of racial differentiation is in full production.

In the figure of the disgusting foreign queen, Spenser produces feelings to identify a collective threat that needs to be purged. This activation of feelings to draw racial boundaries is a precursor to what Kyla Schuller calls "the biopolitics of feeling" in the nineteenth-century United States, when state-sponsored programs used affect as a "broad regulatory technology."[36] In the nascent ecology of settler colonialism, the organization of feelings contributes to the dehumanization of non-white women. Contrarily, the valorization of sentimental white womanhood becomes an equally powerful mode of domination in the colonies. In sharp contrast to Una's white affect, Duessa's insensate body is base, volatile, and impenetrable. Notice, for example, how Spenser prompts his readers to dismiss Duessa's suffering in the Legend of Holiness. First, the poem ridicules her "crocodile tears" as she mourns the death of her Muslim lover, Sansfoy. Spenser doubles down on his construction of racial identities. Not only is Duessa incapable of feeling grief, since hers is a "false griefe hyding … harmefull guile," but also the very object of her grief, her slain Muslim lover, is not worthy of pity. Spenser redirects his readers' compassion to the "mournefull plight" of the weary wanderer, a "foolish man" for sympathizing with Duessa's "cares" (1.5.18).[37] To be moved by Duessa's grief or to feel pity for the dead Muslim knight is to transgress a racialized boundary that is reserved for white bodies only. It is a construction that undergirds the early formations of the racialized subject as incapable of both

36. Kyla Schuller, *The Biopolitics of Feeling: Race, Sex, and Science in the Nineteenth Century* (Durham, NC: Duke University Press, 2018), 9.

37. Joseph Campana notes that it is an ethical fallacy to deny the truthfulness of Duessa's emotions ("Crocodile Tears: Affective Fallacies Old and New," in *Affect Theory and Early Modern Texts: Politics, Ecologies, and Form*, ed. Amanda Bailey and Mario DiGangi [New York: Palgrave Macmillan, 2017], 129–52).

absorbing affect and generating it — at once unimpressible and unworthy of Protestant pity.[38]

In adjudicating whose bodies are amenable to experiencing morally superior affects, Spenser contributes to a nascent white supremacist discourse that considers non-white bodies impervious to pain and suffering. Indeed, the creation of disgust in readers foregrounds the kind of dehumanizing ideological work that justifies the expulsion of non-white people, and later on, their enslavement as means of production only. If Spenser's central concern in *The Faerie Queene* is "making virtue active in the world," as Kimberly Anne Coles argues, how does this vision encompass the vast expansion of dominion? How does this project reckon with irredeemable subjects who have diseased souls and depraved complexions?[39] These questions become particularly urgent at the end of Elizabeth's reign, when the propagation of the Tudor progeny had unquestionably failed and the prospect of racial mixing — possibly with England's mortal enemy, Roman Catholic Spain — lurked on the horizon. This crisis makes the specter of racial and religious contamination a clear and present danger. I turn here to the dynastic politics of this temporal juncture, which brought the ideological ramifications of foreign queenship to the fore.

As early as the 1580s, secret negotiations between Spain and James VI of Scotland, Elizabeth's presumed successor, were already underway to map the future of dynasticism in Europe.[40] Far from raising the mantel of Protestant providentialism, the Scottish King worked every channel to

38. In Book 5, Spenser conflates Catholicism with Islam, using the same affective charge of pride in his depiction of the "proud Souldan" (5.8.30). Souldan is read as an allegorical stand-in for Philip II of Spain; as Michael O'Connell has argued, "[t]he Souldan's high war chariot aptly portrays the turreted Spanish galleons of the Invincible Armada" ("*The Faerie Queene*, Book V," in *The Spenser Encyclopedia*, ed. A. C. Hamilton (Toronto: Toronto University Press, 1990), 282.

39. Kimberly Anne Coles, "Gender in the 1590 *Faerie Queene*," in *Edmund Spenser in Context*, ed. Andrew Escobedo (Cambridge: Cambridge University Press, 2016), 357.

40. Peter Lake and Michael Questier, *All Hail to the Archpriest: Confessional Conflict, Toleration, and the Politics of Publicity in Post-Reformation England* (Oxford: Oxford University Press, 2019), 12.

ensure his accession to the English throne. He suggested Spain was interested in a match between the future Prince of Wales and the Spanish infanta, or a daughter of the Prince of Savoy, King Philip's niece, as part of a larger agenda of peace.[41] In the resounding words of Andrew Hadfield, "Spenser died thinking that his worst fears were about to be realized and that the result of years of bad female rule would be the triumph of a pincer movement – or even an alliance – between the Stuarts and the Spanish to outflank and threaten the rump of England."[42] Indeed, on the heels of his accession to the English throne, King James I – the self-appointed *rex pacificus* – sought a peace that would include a dynastic marriage with England's mortal enemy, Roman Catholic Spain, as well as Catholic tolerance for English recusants.[43] The homogeneity of the realm is endangered when the racialized are granted passage into the enclosed garden, the gated community, the walled nation-state.

If intimacy and purity forged the ideal of white Protestant Englishness, then interracial marriage was a threat to the commonwealth. *The Faerie Queene*'s investment in rooting out infection to serve divine purposes

41. For James's peace negotiations with Spain in the 1590s, see Alexandra Gajda, "Debating War and Peace in Late Elizabethan England," *The Historical Journal* 52, no. 4 (2009): 852. For a discussion of an Anglo-Spanish alliance prior to James's accession to the English throne, see Paul Allen, *Philip III and the* Pax Hispanica, 1598–1621: *The Failure of Grand Strategy* (New Haven, CT: Yale University Press, 2000), esp. 99–114; Robert Cross, "To Counterbalance the World: England, Spain, and Peace in the Early 17th Century" (PhD diss., Princeton University, 2012), esp. 57–58, 64, 243, 513.
42. Andrew Hadfield, "War Poetry and Counsel in Early Modern Ireland," in *Elizabeth I and Ireland*, ed. Brendan Kane and Valerie McGowan-Doyle (Cambridge: Cambridge University Press, 2017), 260.
43. See Kenneth Fincham and Peter Lake, who point out that James's "belief in Christian unity, based upon a very limited number of crucial Catholic doctrines," could allow him to incorporate a "range of religious opinions in the heart of the church" ("The Ecclesiastical Policies of James I and Charles I," in The Early Stuart Church, 1603–1642, ed. Kenneth Fincham [Stanford, CA: Stanford University Press, 1993], 31). For James I's rhetorical use of the *via media*, see W. B. Patterson, *King James VI and I and the Reunion of Christendom* (Cambridge: Cambridge University Press, 1997). On "loyal Catholics," see Michael Questier, "Catholic Loyalism in Early Stuart England," *English Historical Review* 123, no. 504 (2008): 1132–65.

and determine God’s favor dovetails with its lessons on how to *feel* as a community under threat. In this grand narrative of English Protestant providentialism, the process of racialization is interrelated with affective energies. As a result, the poem’s affective construction of sentimental, chaste, white womanhood in opposition to Orientalized, Blackened, foreign queenship indexes anxieties about procreating bloodlines amidst a succession crisis. Spenser’s fantasy of a white Protestant realm not only shapes the moral and religious timbre of the virtuous commonwealth, but more effectively, stokes feelings of desire and disgust that function to exclude non-white, non-Christian queens from its ideal imaginings.

3. New World Encounters and the Racial Limits of Friendship in Early Quaker Life Writing

MEGHAN E. HALL

In May 1676, English Quakers Alice and Thomas Curwen boarded a shipping vessel bound for Barbados. The Curwens were itinerant missionaries: for two years, they had journeyed between New England and the mid-Atlantic colonies, evangelizing the Quaker faith and lending support to newly-formed Quaker communities. Alice had steered the couple's travels thus far; by contrast, it was Thomas who proposed going to the Caribbean, insisting that God had called them to "travail," or serve, there. And while the Caribbean Islands were a common stopover for Quaker missionaries on their way to or from England, Alice hesitated.[1] In the brief narrative Curwen wrote in 1679, *A Relation of the Labour, Travail and Suffering of that Faithful Servant of the Lord Alice Curwen*, she recalls feeling afraid: "A great Fear fell upon me, considering my own Weakness, and the Highness

1. For the most part, Quakers relied on commercial shipping vessels for traveling. English vessels regularly traced a triangular route between London, the New England Colonies, and the Caribbean Islands, so missionaries commonly traveled by way of the Islands when making journeys to and from New England. Beginning in the 1650s, a small Quaker planter class had begun to form on islands such as Barbados, Antigua, Jamaica, and Bermuda, and Nevis. For discussions of Caribbean Quaker communities, see Larry Dale Gragg, *The Quaker Community on Barbados: Challenging the Culture of the Planter Class* (Columbia: University of Missouri Press, 2009), 22–57; Jordan Landes, *London Quakers in the Trans-Atlantic World: The Creation of an Early Modern Community* (New York: Palgrave Macmillan, 2015), 147–65; Hilary Hinds, *George Fox and Early Quaker Culture* (Manchester: Manchester University Press, 2013), 121–45; Kristen Block, "Cultivating Inner and Outer Plantations: Property, Industry, and Slavery in Early Quaker Migration to the New World," *Early American Studies* 8, no. 3 (2010): 515–48.

of all sorts of people there, and fearing lest they should even trample upon my little Testimony, and lest I should suffer Loss."[2]

If we take her at her word, Curwen feared the anti-Quaker hostility she anticipated from the Anglican colonists of Barbados. And certainly, this hostility was very real. From the religion's beginnings in 1650 to the end of the century, Quakers were welcomed in few places around the world, resented for their outspokenness against Anglican and Catholic clergies and feared by authorities for the religion's popularity with England's poor. In England and many of its colonies, Quakers were frequently jailed, beaten, publicly humiliated, stripped of their possessions, exiled, and in some cases, executed.[3] Some colonies even passed legislation banning Quakers completely. In Barbados, the small Quaker planter class was more or less tolerated by the Anglican authorities, but anti-Quaker prejudice had escalated in recent years. This was due in large part to fears that Quaker missionary activity would disrupt the slave economy on which Barbados was built. A fundamental tenet of the Quaker religion was the spiritual equality of all people, regardless of their ethnicity or prior religious affiliation. Though the Quakers did not generally advocate for emancipation – many of the Quaker planters enslaved people themselves – they did include enslaved Black and Indigenous people in their worship, which the Anglicans feared would empower the rapidly expanding slave

2. Anne Martindell, *A Relation of the Labour, Travail and Suffering of that Faithful Servant of the Lord Alice Curwen* (n.p.: London, 1680; Early English Books Online, accessed 10 May 2019), 6. Upon her death in 1679, Curwen entrusted the care of her narrative to Anne Martindell, a close friend who was present at her deathbed. In 1680, Martindell appended a collection of letters and memorial testimonies from Curwen's family and arranged the narrative's publication.
3. There is a sizeable body of Quaker literature from this period that documents the persecution suffered by the religion's followers. For contemporary historical overviews, see Craig W. Horle, *The Quakers and the English Legal System, 1660–1688* (Philadelphia: University of Pennsylvania Press, 1988), 101–50; Amanda Herbert, "Companions in Preaching and Suffering: Itinerant Female Quakers in the Seventeenth- and Eighteenth-Century British American World," *Early American Studies* 9, no. 1 (2011): 73–113; Adrian Davies, *The Quakers in English Society, 1655–1725* (Oxford: Oxford University Press, 2000), 161–90.

class to rebel. After an uprising plot was discovered in 1674, the planters blamed the Quakers, and in 1675, they were legally banned from including enslaved people in their worship.[4]

It was true, then, that relative to previous years, the Quakers were facing intensified hostility in Barbados. Nonetheless, Curwen's admission of fear in this passage contrasts with her self-presentation in earlier sections of the narrative. Up to this point, Curwen appears to have been fearless in the face of persecution, bolstered by her conviction that to suffer for the sake of her faith was an inevitable and righteous part of being a Quaker. In Boston, she had brazenly flouted local laws and had subjected herself to the rude hands of Puritan authorities in order to give her public testimony. In Flushing, she had delivered a sharp retort to a constable threatening to arrest her, and though she suffered violence and imprisonment in response, she returned to the same place to worship publicly again. She had been dragged, flogged, jailed, and driven into the wilderness. And, of course, Quakers had already been executed for trespassing on the Boston Colony — news of the Boston Martyrs is what spurred Curwen to travel in the first place — so she must have been aware that her missionary activity could get her killed. If Curwen met all these previous threats with resolve, what was it about Barbados that elicited fear?

We could speculate about what changed Curwen's state of mind. Perhaps it was her fatigue at this point in a four-year journey, or the fact that the Caribbean was Thomas's idea. However, this essay is less interested in the root of Curwen's personal feelings about Barbados and more interested in the function served by Curwen's admission of fear towards it. By admitting fear of Barbados and "all sorts of people there," Curwen transforms herself from the stoically suffering agent of God in the New World that we see in earlier parts of the narrative to a timid and unassuming believer whose "little testimony" can be threatened. The word "trample" contributes to this transformation by conjuring an image of chaotic and unruly crowds stepping on those unlucky enough to fall underfoot,

4. For a discussion of the uprising and anti-Quaker legislation in Barbados, see Hilary Hinds, "An Absent Presence: Quaker Narratives of Journeys to America and Barbados, 1671–81," *Quaker Studies* 10, no. 1 (2006): 18–26.

an image that refers obliquely to how densely populated and diverse the island was. Barbados was at this time the largest producer of sugar in the region and a major hub for the transatlantic slave trade. Aside from Quakers, the island was made up of a wealthy Anglican planter class; indentured laborers from the vagrant populations of England and Ireland; Sephardic Jews who worked for the slave trade in the Dutch West Indies; and enslaved Black and Indigenous peoples. The island was far more heterogenous than anything Curwen had experienced in the New England colonies or even in London, and her phrase "all sorts of people" references the diversity of religions, cultures, and ethnicities present on the island. Additionally, the growing population of enslaved Black and Indigenous peoples may lie behind Curwen's fear of diversity. By 1680, the enslaved population would outnumber the population of free white people two to one, a proportion that made Anglican planters and others nervous. Though Barbados was certainly governed by the English planters, the island appeared to be nearing a tipping point at which the enslaved population could take control of the island and its resources.

Curwen thus subtly marks out Barbados as fundamentally distinct from the other New World spaces she visited thus far. By expressing a vague fear of the place and its (all sorts) of people, she also constructs emotional distance between her expected readers — fellow Quakers — and the people of Barbados, foreclosing on some of the intimacy her readers might expect to feel with the people of the island, particularly with those who were enslaved. In doing so, she circumvents the problem that Barbados' slave economy posed to her own convictions; namely, that the enslavement and cruel treatment of Black and Indigenous peoples conflicted with the fundamental Quaker belief in the spiritual equality of all mankind.

Although fear appears infrequently in Curwen's narrative, it coincides almost exclusively with her encounters with non-Europeans: both the enslaved peoples in Barbados and the Indigenous tribes living around New England. This essay explores fear not only as an affect within a particular historical time and place, but also as a technology of race-making. By transforming herself into a fearful subject, Curwen directs her readers to feel a similar sense of fear toward the non-Europeans. At the same time, Curwen neglects to acknowledge or even raise the possibility of the Black and Indigenous peoples feeling fear themselves, even though they experienced far greater horrors than Curwen and were undoubtedly often afraid. Therefore, fear in Curwen's narrative remains a particularly white, particularly Quaker trait, marking out which peoples have the full humanity to be included in the Quaker promise of salvation.

In admitting fear of Barbados, Curwen participates in what Sara Ahmed has theorized as an affective economy. For Ahmed, emotions do not originate, reside, and eventually extinguish with an individual (as we often assume), but rather "involve a process of movement or association, *whereby feelings take us across different levels of signification, not all of which can be admitted in the present.*"[5] Rippling out from the individual and acting upon others, affects move laterally, sticking to different "signs, figures, and objects," evoking past associations and projecting future outcomes.[6] Fear, in particular, works to tether individuals together through their "past histories of association" by designating a fearsome object outside of the group.[7] Thus, Curwen uses fear as a technology of gathering whiteness together at moments when the presence of non-Europeans threatens to unsettle her convictions, despite being extremely critical of non-Quaker Europeans in other sections of the narrative.

Curwen "sticks" Barbados's diversity and population density to her fear through subtle allusions and metaphor, evoking long-standing European views of the Caribbean Islands as a wild region where both English immigrants and others often lived in danger and quasi-lawlessness. In doing so, she gathers her Quaker readers together through their shared experiences of whiteness in a European society that viewed others as less-than-human, even as she claimed to view all of humanity as spiritually equal.

This could not have been a casual slip for Curwen. Like many poor women in this period who sought personal distinction through religious zeal, Curwen was devoted to expanding the Quaker religion and sustaining the bonds of Quaker Friendship. This Friendship was characterized by intense emotional connections and a (sometimes extreme) sense of inti-

5. Sara Ahmed, *The Cultural Politics of Emotion* (London: Routledge, 2004), 44, original emphasis.
6. Ahmed, *The Cultural Politics of Emotion*, 45.
7. Ahmed, *The Cultural Politics of Emotion*, 63; 66.

macy between Quakers, who understood their love for each other and their love for God to be one and the same. As Rachel Warburton has shown, the correspondence between Quakers was filled with a spiritually erotic language of devotion that emphasized the physical proximity (though, importantly, not the sexual union) of the two parties.[8]

For example, in a letter addressed to the Curwens from Salem Quaker Mary Milles, Milles co-opts the opening lines of a wedding ceremony to address her fellow Quakers: "My dearly Beloved in the Lord, Read me here and feel me here, even in that which Tongue cannot express, nor Lips declare; for truly in [God's love] are you dear and near unto me."[9] Milles's address reads like a love letter and, in many ways, it is: Invoking their shared relationship to God, her words aim to activate in the Curwens the same affection, intimacy, and obligation she feels toward them. The way her address blurs the lines between reading and touching, the letter and her body, collapses the space between herself and her addressees. The Curwens are meant to feel the presence of Milles's body near them as they read. Though it is tempting to speculate that a deeper relationship – even just a close friendship, in the traditional sense – existed between Milles and the Curwens, there is no indication that they ever even met, as the Curwens did not visit Salem on their journey. Indeed, it was not uncommon for Quakers to write oaths of love to fellow believers they had never met.

The Curwens wrote similar letters to their fellow Quakers. Friendship sustained the Curwens on their travels, both in the literal sense of providing friendly persons to lend shelter, provision, and guidance along their way, and in the spiritual sense. In many cases, they were trusting strangers with their lives, yet they did not consider any Quaker to be a stranger. Community, in the Quaker religion, was forged and sustained through the mutual love and obligation offered between any who believed.

8. Rachel Warburton, "'The Lord Hath Joined Us Together, and Wo Be to Them That Should Part Us': Katharine Evans and Sarah Cheevers as Traveling Friends," *Texas Studies in Literature and Language* 47, no. 4 (2005): 402-424.

9. Martindell, *A Relation of the Labour, Travail and Suffering of that Faithful Servant of the Lord Alice Curwen*, 41.

This is important because the gathering that Curwen's fear accomplishes is not the gathering of Quaker Friendship, which did not, in theory, have a definite outgroup – according to Quaker doctrine, all people were born with saving light within themselves and could elect to join the religion. No one was higher than another in the eyes of God, and while the Quakers were critical of persons outside of the religion, they were always potential Quakers. Curwen was particularly committed to convincing new members. In his memorial testimony, Thomas Curwen recalls that his wife's conversation "was as becometh the Gospel; for her Children *and many more* were Convinced by her Wise Walking before them."[10] Curwen's expression of fear, then, stands out as an anomaly in this commitment. As we will see, fear designates for Curwen's reader who is excluded from the bonds of Quaker Friendship.

While in Barbados, Curwen wrote a now well-known letter to Martha Tavernor, a Quaker plantation owner who had barred those she enslaved from attending Quaker worship. In the letter, Curwen chastises Tavernor for believing herself higher than her Black "servants," the term Quakers insisted on calling them:

> I Cannot pass by, but in Love write to thee, for in Love we came to visit thee, and to invite thee and thy Family to the Meeting; but thou for thy part art like him that was invited to work in the Vineyard, and went not: And as for thy Servants, whom thou callst thy *Slaves*, I tell thee plainly, thou hast no right to reign over their Conscience in Matters of Worship of the Living God; for thou thy self confessedst, that *they had Souls to save as well as we*: Therefore, for time to come let them have Liberty, lest thou be called to give an Account to God for them, as well as for thy self: So in thy old Age chuse rather, as a good Man did, that both thou and thy whole Family may serve the Lord; for I am perswaded, that if they whom thou call'st thy Slaves, be Upright-hearted to God, the Lord God Almighty will set them Free in a way that thou knowest not;

10. Martindell, *A Relation of the Labour, Travail and Suffering of that Faithful Servant of the Lord Alice Curwen*, 9 emphasis added.

> for there is none set Free but in Christ Jesus, for all other Freedom will prove but a Bondage.[11]

At first glance, Curwen's letter appears to advocate for abolition, with its frequent references to liberty and her insistence that the enslaved "have souls to save as well as we." Moira Ferguson has powerfully argued as much. In addition to reading Curwen's call for freedom as a call for the emancipation from bondage, Ferguson interprets the word "servant" as a symbolic rejection of the legitimacy of slavery.[12] Brycchan Carey builds on Ferguson's argument, adding that when Curwen invites Ferguson's family, she includes the enslaved, insisting on their humanity in a place where they were commodified.[13]

But Curwen's letter is not as straightforward as her biting tone makes it seem. Recent scholarship highlights the letter's equivocations. Most notably, Hilary Hinds argues that for Curwen, "freedom" and "liberty" refer to a narrow definition of spiritual freedom through Christ.[14] Curwen's call for Tavernor to "let them have liberty" refers not to their release from bondage, but rather their release from their ignorance of the Quaker religion. The letter's final lines, in which she states quite plainly that real freedom is achieved through knowledge of Christ, reroute the language of freedom through the Quaker model of salvation. Curwen thus sidesteps the problem slavery poses to her beliefs: The enslaved "have souls to save as well as we," yet are still subjected to inhumane treatment at the hands of English planters and Curwen's fellow Quakers. The letter, therefore, obscures the material violence suffered by the enslaved in the temporal world by reframing the issue as a spiritual one.

11. Martindell, *A Relation of the Labour, Travail and Suffering of that Faithful Servant of the Lord Alice Curwen*, 18 original emphasis.
12. Moira Ferguson, *Subject to Others: British Women Writers and Colonial Slavery, 1670–1834* (London: Routledge, 2014), 60.
13. Brycchan Carey, *From Peace to Freedom: Quaker Rhetoric and the Birth of American Anti-Slavery, 1658-1761* (New Haven, Conn.: Yale University Press, 2012), 66–69.
14. Hilary Hinds, "An Absent Presence: Quaker Narratives of Journeys to America and Barbados, 1671–81." *Quaker Studies* 10, no. 1 (2006): 19–23.

This letter exposes the limits of Curwen's commitment to Quaker Friendship: Black and Indigenous peoples may certainly join in Quaker worship, but they will not be fully embraced by the community they worship alongside. At least two hypocritical sentiments underlie these limits. One is Curwen's quiet acknowledgment that while slavery conflicted with fundamental Quaker beliefs, it was nonetheless a profitable institution through which her fellow Quakers in the Caribbean were gaining power and influence. Wealthier Quakers, like Tavernor, owned or invested in the sugar plantations that were bringing massive wealth to Barbados, while other Quakers worked within the slave trade itself as brokers. Particularly in the Caribbean, Quakers were at best complicit and at worst active participants in the continuation of the slave trade. In her letter, Curwen quietly acquiesces to this reality by not challenging the institution of enslavement fully.

Fear also underlies Curwen's limits, signifying a hypocritical stance in Quaker encounters in the New World. If we return to the fear that traveling to Barbados prompted in Curwen and to her veiled references to the island's diversity, we can surmise that Curwen may prefer English control of the island. If all Barbados plantation owners were to free the enslaved, the Black and Indigenous population would significantly outnumber their former enslavers, shifting control of the island from the enslavers to the formerly enslaved. Here, Curwen likely shares in the widespread Anglican anxiety percolating in Barbados that the enslaved would "rise and cut their master's throats."[15]

Even if Curwen did not anticipate violent retribution from freed Black and Indigenous peoples, she certainly favored the English – and preferably the Quakers – maintaining control of Barbados. From its beginnings, the Quaker religion sought global expansion. Founder George Fox was famously shown a vision of God's people gathering across the world. Quaker writings from this period teem with images of "God's Empire"

15. William Edmundson, *A Journal of the Life, Travels, Sufferings, and Labour of Love in the Work of the Ministry, of … William Edmundson, Who Departed This Life, the Thirty First of the Sixth Month*, 1712 (London: 1712; Early English Books Online, accessed 12 June 2019), 66.

sweeping across the seas and enveloping the earth.[16] Thus, the Quaker community's discourses on freeing the enslaved were meant to construe such "redemption" as part of God's plan of expansion. Many Quaker writings from this period frame enslavement as a means of recruiting more Quaker members. George Fox's 1657 epistle, "To Friends Beyond the Sea, that Have Blacks and Indian Slaves," urged white Quakers to see to it that "the gospel is preached to every creature under heaven, which is the power that giveth liberty and freedom."[17] By redefining "liberty" and "freedom" for the enslaved as that which comes with salvation, Fox both sidesteps the question of freedom from actual bondage and implicitly promises a kind of spiritual freedom if the enslaved submit to a Quaker education. His 1679 epistle, "To Friends in America, Concerning Their Negroes and Indians," exhorts white Quakers to "preach the gospel to [slaves], and other servants, if you be true Christians ... Christ commands it to his disciples, 'Go and teach all nations, baptizing them into the name of the Father, Son, and Holy Ghost.'"[18] The enslaved here are redefined as

16. The fact that the movement was invested in the global dominance of their religion is easily overlooked due to the Quakers' pacifism and refusal to employ violent or overtly coercive means of "convincing" members. The word "convince" approximates the term "convert," with an important distinction. The Quakers believed that all people held a divine light within them, though not all were ready to recognize it. To be "convinced" was not to be persuaded toward Quakerism, but rather for the inner light to be activated by hearing the words of a current Quaker. Though their refusal to force or coerce people into the fold meant that their vision of religious expansion was far less violent than that of other English colonists (who also conquered in the name of Christianity), the nature of convincement informed a more insidious sense in the Quakers' right to occupy foreign spaces, as other populations were understood as future Quakers who were simply awaiting their arrival.
17. George Fox, "An Exhortation to Friends Beyond the Sea (1666)," in *A Collection of Many Select and Christian Epistles, Letters and Testimonies Written on Sundry Occasions, by that Ancient, Eminent, Faithful Friend and Minister of Christ Jesus*, vol. 2 (London: 1698; Early English Books Online, accessed 10 May 2019), 17.
18. George Fox, "To Friends in America, Concerning Their Negroes and Indians," in *A Collection of Many Select and Christian Epistles, Letters and Testimonies Written on Sundry Occasions, by that Ancient, Eminent, Faithful Friend and Minister of Christ Jesus*, vol. 2 (London: 1698; Early English Books Online, accessed 10 May 2019), 426.

both a kind of servant and as the members of a foreign "nation," a redefinition that obfuscates the structures of violence that not only forced enslaved Africans into labor, but also subjected them to the Quaker religion.

Fox goes on in this epistle to frame the education of the enslaved as an "open[ing of] the Promises of God to the ignorant," implicitly redeeming slavery as the vehicle for salvation for those who would otherwise remain unsaved.[19] While the inclusion of the enslaved in Quaker Meetings, and therefore the willingness to see them as Friends, would form the foundation of later abolitionist movements, it also predicated Quaker critiques of slavery and its practices on a presumption that the enslaved would join their numbers. Though the enslaved were not expected to become itinerant preachers themselves, their convincement contributed to the Quakers' numbers and influence in the Caribbean.

Curwen was also devoted to the Quakers' expansion; it was one of the driving forces of her and her husband's journey to the Americas. Thus, her fears of the English losing control of the island are related not solely to the possibility of violence, but also to the Quakers losing their foothold. Her investment in the spatial expansion of the Quakers in the Caribbean butts up against the egalitarian impetus of the Quaker worldview, leading Curwen to sidestep questions of the enslaved population's freedom in order to maintain her already precarious position of power. Put another way, Curwen had a vision of a thriving Quaker community on Barbados. Granting the enslaved their freedom — and therefore power over themselves and the spaces they inhabited — threatened that vision.

Fear appears again in Curwen's depictions of the Indigenous tribes of North America. Though she refers to them as Indians, she likely encountered the Sakonnet, Patuxet, Nemasket, Neponset, Wessagunset, Nonatum, and Penacook tribes in her travels between Rhode Island and present-day New Hampshire. The Indigenous populations of New England occupy a remarkably small portion of Curwen's narrative. She mentions them only twice, in fact, and in both cases, the people themselves are conspicuously absent. Instead, Curwen reads landscapes they have allegedly

19. Fox, "To Friends in America, Concerning Their Negroes and Indians," 427.

destroyed as evidence of their violence. As the Curwens made their way from the Rhode Island port to Boston, they encountered "the Woods and Places where the devouring *Indians* had made great Desolation in many places."[20] "Desolation" characterizes Indigenous lands and peoples in two conflicting ways. The term simultaneously refers to the devastation of a landscape — "laying waste to a land, destroying its crops and buildings" — and — derived from the French *desolé*, "to be left alone" — to the depopulation of an area.[21] Thus, Curwen's use of "desolation" concurrently conjures the land's violent and wasteful inhabitants and emphasizes a lack of inhabitants. This echoes a familiar script of early colonialism, one that framed the American landscape as "open" and available for settlement by the English.

With the term "devour," Curwen rhetorically divests the Indigenous populations of their humanity, imposing animalistic qualities on them: literally meaning "to swallow up," the term connotes the indiscriminate consumption of an animal predator and echoes popular representations of American Indigenous peoples as animalistic and cannibalistic.[22] By reducing them to the status of animals, she marks them as beyond the pale of

20. Martindell, *A Relation of the Labour, Travail and Suffering of that Faithful Servant of the Lord Alice Curwen*, 6, original emphasis.
21. OED *Online*, s.v., "desolation," n. 1, accessed 3 June 2019, www.oed.com/view/Entry/50924. It is worth noting that while we cannot know for sure what Curwen is describing when she uses the term "desolation" (as in, what she is seeing), the images of barren wastelands that the term conjures may in fact refer to burned land. It was common in Indigenous agricultural communities of the Northeast to practice a form of semi-nomadic crop rotation. Communities would build living and working structures around the planting of their crops and, after a few years, would move on to nearby lands to allow the soil to replenish its nutrients. In some practices, the crop residues might be set on fire in a controlled burn to quicken the decomposition process, leaving a literal scorched earth. This is not to say that Curwen was simply misreading the landscape, if it was in fact what she saw, but that her investment in the lands of the New World — as a place for her and other Quakers to occupy and move through — was threatened by a competing, and much older, use of the land. See William E. Doolittle. "Permanent vs. Shifting Cultivation in the Eastern Woodlands of North American Prior to European Contact." *Agriculture and Human Values* 21, no. 2 (2004): 181–189.
22. OED *Online*, s.v., "desolation," n. 1.

her community, beyond the pale of the possibility of community. Unlike her disparaging portrayals of New England Anglicans, whom she also considers violent but whom she maintains are capable of being saved, the Indigenous peoples here have no human presence, no apparent soul, and therefore, no potential for salvation. She wields her own fear to foreclose on the possibility of her readers empathizing with the Indigenous populations.

Curwen mentions the Indigenous populations once more. She recalls that as they traveled to Dover, "We came to a Friend's house beyond the River, where there were about two hundred people, some Friends, some others, who were come thither for Safety, and had fortified the House very strongly for fear of these Bloody *Indians*, which had killed two of our Friends within three miles of that place."[23] It is difficult to know precisely what Curwen means by "fortification." The term can simply mean "to strengthen," and may refer to the settlement steeling themselves against expected attacks. The term also refers to bearing arms.[24] In a related sense, fortification was an architectural term in colonial New England, referring to a style of house designed after English forts of the period. The "Fortified House" was built of thick, rough-cut timber, and featured "embrasures," small, angled holes from which to shoot firearms. Fortified Houses were becoming the preferred architectural style in Dover, New Hampshire, around the time of King Philip's War (1675–1678), as raids by the Abenaki and Narragansett tribes on the colonial settlement increased dramatically in response to English aggression.[25] Therefore, it is not much of a stretch to assume that the settlers' "fortification" of the house involved preparing the structure for battle. Curwen's antipathy toward the "Indians" comes into sharper focus here. In this case, the

23. Martindell, *A Relation of the Labour, Travail and Suffering of that Faithful Servant of the Lord Alice Curwen*, 8, original emphasis.
24. OED *Online*, s.v., "fortify," v. 1 and 3.
25. The popularity of fortified or "garrison" houses in the New Hampshire colonies in the second half of the seventeenth century is evidenced by their sheer numbers. For descriptions of surviving houses and their features, see The New Hampshire Society of The Colonial Dames of America, *The Colonial Garrisons of New Hampshire* (Exeter, N.H.: News-Letter Press, 1937).

attacks have led the Quakers to consider defending themselves, potentially with violence. Despite enduring anti-Quaker hostility in the colonies, this is the first instance of Curwen witnessing Quakers returning the hostility. This sits at odds with their willingness to embrace suffering as martyrs. As I have discussed, the calm submission to violence perpetrated against them, including execution in some cases, was a hallmark of early Quaker life. To bear arms, even in self-defense, would sit uncomfortably with a devout Quaker. And while Curwen herself is not necessarily participating in the fortification, her silence makes her complicit.

Additionally, we can read the act of building structures as a kind of violence, one committed by building houses meant to exclude the land's original inhabitants. Because the Quakers were often banished from English settlements, their own building took place on the outskirts. Although this heightened their precarity – unable to rely on the defenses of Anglican settlers, the Quakers had to decide whether or not to defend themselves – it also expanded the English presence in the New World by colonizing wilderness they considered to be open.

As in Barbados, Curwen shared in a Quaker vision for the space of the New England wilderness, an admittedly peaceful vision. But what this vision fails to account for is the fact that taking up space is itself an act of violence and violation. At best, the Quakers were encroaching on the living space of the Indigenous populations abroad, and at worst, they were participating in the violently expansionist program of the budding English Empire. While one might argue that Curwen simply does not recognize her occupation of space as a form of violence against Indigenous populations, the rhetorical strategies that she uses to disavow their humanity suggest otherwise. Curwen quietly sides with England's colonial project by reversing the directionality of the violence. By rhetorically divesting them of humanity and the potential for salvation in her narrative, it is the Indians who are encroaching on Christian territories. Turning away from the universalist vision of a world united by Friendship, Curwen implicitly insists on the innate difference of the Indigenous people.

Curwen's writing on the New World is particularly valuable to contemporary scholars of early modern race because it exposes how alternative communities – in this case, a persecuted religious minority – came to define themselves against racial others, even when doing so conflicted with their own values. It also exposes the role affect plays in foreclosing on the intimacy Curwen's Quaker readers might expect to feel with Black and Indigenous peoples in the Americas. In Curwen's scant admissions of fear, we see an intentional gathering of people through their shared experience of whiteness at moments when her usual inclusivity fails to serve her visions of Quaker expansion. Here, the limits of Quaker Friendship lie along the axes of territorial power and race.

4. Early Modern Affect Theory, Racialized Aversion, and the Strange Case of *Foetor Judaicus*

DREW DANIEL

What Does Affect Mean?

Upon mentioning to a colleague that I was contributing an essay to a volume on affect in early modernity, she didn't mince words: "I'm sick of talking about affect. I mean, what does that word even mean anymore? Do you know what I mean?" This dispute along methodological battle lines is hardly surprising, given that modish objects of scholarly interest inevitably draw skeptical fire as excitement turns to doubt. One scholar's keyword is another's sacred cow, and a precarious job market mobilizes us to speed up the metabolism by which we surf and then denounce trends.[1] That said, the phrasing of my colleague's question braids thinking and feeling together. The hostility of the assault on the utility of the word affect ("what does that word even mean?") is modulated by the status-checking bid for empathy implicit in the closing gesture ("do you know what I mean?"), which we might parse as "do you feel the way that I do? Please don't be offended. Please be on my side and in sync with me." Venturing towards the psychoanalytic logic of the symptom, one could then note the revealing overdetermination of the word "mean," which pops up three times but does double duty: it is at once the issue under dispute (affect does not mean anything, affect is an empty buzzword) and a signifier of emotion in play (in lashing out aggressively at her colleague's field of study the speaker is, herself, being "mean" and then noticing and dial-

1. The highwater mark of skeptical critique of affect's intellectual currency is surely Ruth Leys, "How Did Fear Become a Scientific Object and What Kind of Object Is It?" *Representations* 110, no. 1 (2010): 66–104. Though she too is my colleague, I hasten to add that she is assuredly not the unnamed source of the anecdote with which this essay begins.

ing back that exact performance). Such an analysis would lead in turn, to a new question: If "affects," in the plural, surge across and are transmitted by the same statement that disavows "affect," in the singular, as a poorly defined and therefore worthless object of study, does that vindicate the utility of the word? Or, does it exemplify the slipperiness of application that prompts such objections in the first place? What does that word "affect" even mean, anyway?

So far, so defensive: such a response is hardly neutral where affect is concerned, nor does it address the core objection: "affect" has no meaning *because* it has, or has had, too many meanings. Promiscuously various in its disciplinary reach across theology and philosophy and medicine and psychology and neuroscience, worryingly polysemous in its plural definitions that stretch from classical Greece to contemporary laboratories, the elastic disciplinary reach and long historical range of this keyword appeal to some and repel others. To risk a cruel parody of new historicist critical ambitions, at this late point in the game, "affect" names that which is held in common across a cumulative trans-historical conversation about emotional embodiment between a hodgepodge of dead people (including ancient Stoics, Thomas Rogers, René Descartes, Baruch Spinoza, Sigmund Freud, Gilles Deleuze, Silvan Tomkins, Eve Kosofsky Sedgwick, Teresa Brennan, and Lauren Berlant) and a hodgepodge of living people (including Antonio Damasio, Jane Bennett, Heather Love, Ann Cvetcovitch, Rei Terada, Eugenie Brinkema, Sianne Ngai, and Brian Massumi).[2] The frame of what counts as "affect theory" or "affect studies" could be widened to

2. Because I am discussing the wider uptake of "affect theory" as a movement in the humanities across many contemporary fields, I strategically omit the numerous scholars in early modern studies — including those editors and many of the other contributors to this volume — whose work on the passions and emotions has and continues to inform my own thinking: a list that includes but is not limited to Gail Kern Paster, Bruce Smith, Susan James, Mary Floyd-Wilson, Victoria Kahn, Douglas Trevor, Janet Adelman, Amanda Bailey, Mario DiGangi, and Michael Schoenfeldt constellates just part of how the field of early modern studies has worked through these topoi, with its own complex methodological disputes and points of contact. I regard their work as disciplinarily distinct from what has been generally recognized as "affect theory" because of its historically specific frame.

swallow entire fields and periods, or shrunk to a tiny list of central canonical authors, texts, and tributary notions.[3]

Acknowledging the elasticity of a term that is asked to link somatic reflexes and complex ideological formations, here is my working definition of, if not "what affect means," then what I think I mean by, affect. Affects are movements, arcs of force that ramp up or down in intensity within material bodies as those bodies change their states, sometimes putting those bodies into motion, sometimes bringing them to rest. Accumulating as potential energy and then discharging as kinetic acts of emotional expression, they unfold dynamically and processually. Affects flow across one body and, as they are encountered and taken up by other bodies, delivering their force beyond the frame of the body in which they originate, they communicate outward in a manner that is material, transpersonal, and observable, yet frequently open to interpretation and dispute. Affects are variable, pervasive, and creative. They are grounded in particular bodies, but take on the legibility of social signs. They travel across bodies and bond them into new assemblages in the process.[4]

Such a broad formulation of course prompts objections, the need for refinement, specificity, more methodology, the proffering of credentials, the carping of the critical, and the shrugging of the unconvinced. Are we really talking about bodies or just the parts of bodies called minds? Are we talking about actual liquid flows, solid motions, gaseous diffusions, or electrical discharges? Or is all this flowing and moving and diffusing

3. For more on the current state of intersections between these theories and early modern studies specifically, see Amanda Bailey and Mario DiGangi, eds., *Affect Theory and Early Modern Texts: Politics, Ecologies, and Form* (New York: Palgrave Macmillan, 2017).
4. My definition more or less resembles commonly held positions across recent affect theory, but I demur from taxonomizing the affects or enumerating their primitives (as in Spinoza or Tomkins or, to an extent, Sedgwick). I do not refer to "affect" in the singular but "affects" as a plural array. I regard this plural array as causally prior to the various forms of emotional display through which said affects become expressive and thereby legible to others. In sympathy with Brennan and Terada and Berlant, I am hoping to de-subjectivize the interpretive scene in which affects unfold. In sympathy with Brinkema, I am interested in formal description. In sympathy with Katrin Pahl, I am interested in changes of state.

and discharging a matter of metaphors that draw upon the thingly force of their vehicles on behalf of emotional tenors? Are rage, pleasure, fear, joy, and shame a matter of conscious experience or postures of muscular expression? What does it mean to observe an affect, and what would be its archive of evidence? Is it a matter of tracking changes in conductivity, measured on the surface of the skin or in terms of heart rate, like a lie detector? Would this archive of evidence include amounts of blood rushing to a blushing face or an erect nipple? Or is this archive of evidence less material and more ambient? Is it like the collectively shared feeling of tension in the air before an anti-police-brutality protest or a couple's imminent public argument? Is it like the corkscrew to the heart that one recognizes as grief; or the neurons that happen to fire in brains, which produce that as conscious experience? These are questions about practices, competence, and disciplines, but they are also basic questions about human beings as such.

These questions are arguably anticipated in a familiar song from *The Merchant of Venice* that condenses them into a speculation about the nature of affect:

> Tell me where is fancy bred,
> Or in the heart or in the head?
> How begot, how nourishèd?
> Reply, reply. (3.2.63–66)[5]

There is a character-specific agenda here, but the song's question lingers even for those who are not being cued by its end-rhymes to pick the lead casket. That question can be boiled down to a childlike paraphrase: where do our desires and aversions come from? Answering the doubled urgency of the imperative to "reply, reply," one can imagine a (very) rough sketch of the intellectual history of affect theory's archives as a cascade of possible responses:

5. William Shakespeare, "The Merchant of Venice," in *The Complete Works of Shakespeare*, 7th ed., ed. David Bevington (Boston: Pearson, 2014), 202.

1. From our souls.
2. From our humors.
3. From our affects and passions.
4. From the mental faculties of fancy and imagination.
5. From the unconscious and the drives.
6. From chemical and neuronal events in our brains.

Different thinkers in the history of what is now gathered together under the rubric of "affect theory" would select different options from this list, some making multiple selections, others angrily insisting upon the equivalence of some of these options at different ontological levels of description. Bodies are in history, and as species evolve, the natures and capacities of those bodies, and the brains and brainstates and minds and emotional expressions that go with them, have changed and will continue to undergo change. Correspondingly, the disciplines through which we produce truths about bodies and desires undergo change. But do our affects *themselves* change over time, or do we simply alter the cultural names and disciplinary homes from which we encounter and taxonomize their legible expressions as emotions? Part of doing work upon affect is recognizing that we are arresting a flow in the moment of its historical expression. The case is never closed.

What's Race Got to Do With It?

In comparison with "affect," "race" as a scholarly keyword also indexes an elastic interface between bodies and social forms, to which is added the ethical ballast of an inescapably substantial archive of lived experiences of harm and injury that follow from its ongoing theorization and relentless application. With reference to its circulation across diverse disciplines and contexts and historical periods, Justin E. H. Smith has described race as "an extremely tenacious illusion," and not something that early modern scholars should reify in the present as if we already now know what race "really" is.[6] Geraldine Heng notes that "in principle, race theory ... understands, of course, that race *has* no singular or stable referent,"[7] yet many within the humanities tend to regard modernity as the de facto location of "racial time," as if "race" only begins with the dawning of scientific racism, despite the proliferation of evidence that race thinking pervades medieval texts, documents, laws, and practices. Contesting this historiographic mistake, Heng has argued persuasively that "*race is a structural relationship for the articulation and management of human differences, rather than a substantive content.*"[8] As a fine-grained meshwork of responses and cues that subtend the everyday and show up as tacit feelings of belonging and disconnection, affects play a significant role in the ongoing work of articulation and management through which race is constituted — precisely because affects are labile enough to accommodate and fill out the open cultural spaces provided by race's cruel combination of incoherence and omnipresence.

To see the everyday meshwork of race and affect in action, consider another moment in *The Merchant of Venice*, when the Prince of Morocco spots a potential snag in the midst of courtship:

> Mislike me not for my complexion
> The shadowed livery of the burnished sun
> To whom I am a neighbor and near bred. (2.1.1–3)

Race matters here, and it matters because it shows up as a cluster of affects: pride, fear, aversion. As Kim F. Hall points out, "The Prince, 'a tawny Moor', in making himself a Petrarchan suitor, shows an awareness of the cultural values surrounding skin color and also of the grounds for

6. Justin E. H. Smith, "Toward a Historical Ontology of Race," in *Nature, Human Nature, and Human Difference: Race in Early Modern Philosophy* (Princeton, NJ: Princeton University Press), 69.

7. Geraldine Heng, "The Invention of Race in the European Middle Ages, I: Race Studies, Modernity, and the Middle Ages," *Literature Compass* 8, no. 5 (2011): 319.

8. Heng, "The Invention of Race in the European Middle Ages, I," 319 original emphasis.

erotic competition."[9] Portia is quick – a little too quick – to parry the Prince's direct gesture towards the possibility that she "mislikes" him; she responds with the coolly witty double entendre that he is as attractive to her as any other of her potential suitors seen so far. Portia punts into a cruel sort of demi-politeness that anticipates the "colorblind" proceduralisms and rhetorical camouflages of the present. But as we learn from her parting aside to the audience, "Let all of his complexion choose me so" (2.7.78), Morocco's concern is in fact well-founded, and all too apt. Premodern critical race studies has documented the richly various, but also inescapable and pervasive, intellectual genealogies by which race was mobilized within early modernity, and accordingly has taught our field – or those within our field willing to learn from it – much regarding how to understand the valence of "complexion" in scenes such as these.[10]

But, to ask a question in resonant sympathy with this edited collection, what is the relationship of "misliking" to "complexion"? That is, how might affects express, enact, and translate race into feelings, actions, and outcomes? Affects can help us think about the structures of feeling that surround race, the surges of attachment and detachment that script the experience of being racialized as an intersubjective encounter. It feels a certain way to encounter one's own being as it undergoes racialization by others, and that very recognition implies a prior nexus of expectations and associations that cluster around the presentation of embodiment. Insofar as early modern texts show us raced bodies becoming objects of desire or aversion, they provide a significant archive through which to examine race as an affective forcefield.

The Smell of the Other

While the cultural primacy of the visual means that seeing constitutes the most intuitively apparent sensory pathway through which bodies are

9. Kim F. Hall, *Things of Darkness: Economies of Race and Gender in Early Modern England* (Ithaca, NY: Cornell University Press, 1995), 94.
10. See Patricia Akhimie, *Shakespeare and the Cultivation of Difference: Race and Conduct in the Early Modern World* (London: Routledge, 2018).

constituted as racially identifiable, the remit of this essay will consider a particularly painful example of the role that olfactory experiences of disgust performed for early modern people. One could call this a kind of race-smelling that was primed by, and served to reinforce, race-thinking. Smells are not affects, but they are the occasion for an affective response of pleasure or displeasure; as such, the cultural work of translation implicit in turning a smell into a speech act can capture affect in its sparking moment of articulation. Specifically, I am interested in how textual evocations of bodily odors, insofar as they are cut free from the material support of any corroborating bodily experience, solicited secondhand sympathetic disgust in readers that worked to consolidate, and perhaps also eventually to dissolve, racialized assemblages of belonging and exclusion.[11] As medical historian Jonathan Reinarz argues, "the cultural embeddedness of racial scents underscores the absoluteness of social boundaries," a dynamic exemplified in the persistent pattern through which non-Western cultures in racist discourse are "denigrated as malodorous."[12] While I also draw upon discussion of the "smelly other" by social anthropologists and sensory historians, my interest in this topic derives its impetus from the scholarly work of Carol Mejia LaPerle, who reads Caliban's allegedly "fishy" odor and the expressions of racialized aversion it prompts in the Italian characters in *The Tempest* as an example of "the affective ecology of bodies."[13] Pushing off from LaPerle's provocative reading as one example of a broader possibility that premodern critical race studies might consider the function of smell in the making of race, I analyze a key example of premodern racialized affect: the *foetor judaicus*,

11. For an account of olfactory symbolism and the problem of the "smelly others" that uses the El Carmel neighborhood in Barcelona as a site for thinking the politics of smell, see Diana Mata-Codesal, "El olor del cuerpo migrante en la cidudad desodorizada: simbolismo olfativo en los procesos de clasificacion social," AIRB: *Revista de Antropologia Iberoamericana* 13, no. 1 (2018): 23–43.
12. Jonathan Reinarz, "Odorous Others: Race and Smell," in *Past Scents: Historical Perspectives on Smell*, (Urbana: University of Illinois Press, 2014), 86.
13. Carol Mejia LaPerle, "Race, Affect and the Olfactory," *The Sundial*, 16 August 2019, https://medium.com/the-sundial-acmrs/race-affect-and-the-olfactory-f69659deab04.

the bizarre but persistent anti-Semitic fantasy that Jewish bodies generate a "distinctive and unpleasant" aroma.[14] Sensory historians have traced this allegation back to its classical sources in Ammianus Marcellinus's reference to "foetentes Iudeos" and Martial's objection to the smell of "the breath of the fasting Sabbatarian Jews." These founding phrases were routinely cited by later medieval and early modern writers as supporting evidence for this supposed defect.[15]

Reduplicated by reverence for classical authority and reinforced by anti-Semitic prejudice and the love of natural-philosophical curiosa, the allegation of *foetor judaicus* circulates promiscuously across early modern texts.[16] In *Jews in the Early Modern English Imagination*, Eva Johanna Holmberg has collected a number of exemplary cases in Thomas Nashe's "The Unfortunate Traveler," Christopher Marlowe's "The Jew of Malta," Thomas Dekker's "The Whore of Babylon," and others.[17] A particularly grotesque example of *foetor judaicus* appears in Gervase Markham's translation of one of Ariosto's *Satyres* (1608) on the material ingredients used to make cosmetics. Markham imagines that men kissing their mistresses do so in ignorance of the foul brew required:

14. Joshua Trachtenberg, *The Devil and the Jews: The Medieval Conception of the Jew and its Relation to Modern Anti-Semitism* (Philadelphia: The Jewish Publication Society, 1983), 47.
15. Reinarz, "Odorous Others," 95.
16. Scholars of religious thought tend to distinguish "anti-Judaism" as a theological and doctrinal discourse of refutation from "anti-Semitism" as a rhetoric of slander and targeting; sometimes this distinction is drawn on historiographic grounds, with "anti-Semitism" being regarded as a later phenomenon. I regard the *foetor judaicus* as anti-Semitic, and take its classical origin and tenacious transhistorical survival to complicate the claim that anti-Semitism is a relatively late phenomenon. See Robert Chazan, *Anti-Judaism to Anti-Semitism: Ancient and Medieval Constructions of Jewish History* (Cambridge: Cambridge University Press, 2006).
17. Eva Johanna Holmberg, "Framing Jewish Bodies and Souls," in *Jews in the Early Modern English Imagination: A Scattered Nation* (London: Ashgate, 2011), 105–51. I am indebted to Holmberg's scholarship for my examples, but diverge in my methodological goals, insofar as smell is simply part of a catalogue of anti-Semitic fantasies examined in her book, and Holmberg is not chiefly interested in the affective dimension of racialization as such.

He knowes not, did he know it he would spewe
That paintings made with spettle of a Iewe,
(For they best sell) nor that loathsome smell,
Though mixt with muske and amber nere so well,
Can they with all their cunning take away
The sleame and snot so rank in it doth stay.
Little thinks he that with the filthy doung
Of their small circumcised infants young,
The fat of hideous serpents, spaune of snakes,
Which slaues from out their poisonous bodies takes.[18]

As Holmberg indicates, Markham's phantasmagoria collapses Jewish religious practices of circumcision with standing anti-Semitic slurs depicting Jews as poisoners.[19] The serpent imagery naturally suggests poison, but, to go beyond Holmberg's analysis, it perhaps also draws upon the serpentine stories coiled around Moses in the Hebrew Bible: the transformation of Aaron's rod into a serpent in Exodus 7:10; the fiery serpents sent against the nation of Israel by God in the Book of Numbers 21:4–9; the "brazen serpent" subsequently worshipped before its destruction in 2 Kings 18:4. But far from a scriptural exegesis, Markham's poem hits below the belt, associating the bodies of Jews with both a scatological cornucopia of substances (spit, mucus, and feces) and a surreptitious agenda of concealment beneath apparent luxury commodities. Jews are imagined as both disgusting and insidious, capable of scattering and spreading their material markers and hidden traces across even the most intimate surfaces.

I have dilated upon this unsavory example because I think its notable qualities of virulence and vicariousness are related. In order to generate and hopefully relay its powerful affective charge of disgust, Markham attempts a synaesthetic sleight of hand: whether we read the poem as words upon a page or hear it as language within our ears, in either case we are encouraged to sensorially experience its juicy, noisome inventory

18. Ariosto, Ariosto's *Satyres* (1608), qtd. in Holmberg, "Framing Jewish Bodies and Souls," 132–33.

19. Holmberg, "Framing Jewish Bodies and Souls," 133.

of words and images in olfactory and haptic terms. Whether we actually vomit or not, we are encouraged by the text to imaginatively inhabit an affective reflex of disgust that is sourced in a virtual encounter with an imagined smell and its imagined sources; crucially, the text holds out to the reader the capacity to become forearmed through reading so that a new olfactory priming — essentially, *knowing what to smell for* — might produce some future confirmation of a deceitfully encrypted truth about both women's apparent beauty and malevolent Jewish practices. Misogyny against women for resorting to "painting" sits cheek by jowl with hatred of and disgust at the Jews who are imagined to supply such poisonous wares.

The association of Jews with serpents that Markham's text reinscribes rests upon a persistent link in anti-Semitic discourse between Jews and the ultimate serpent, Satan. As many scholars have suggested, this cluster of Christian associations overwrites the classical sources for the concept of *foetor judaicus* with a kind of super-cessionist force. In *The Devil and the Jews*, rabbi and independent scholar Joshua Trachtenberg argued that by the medieval period the meaning of the *foetor judaicus* had become fundamentally theological:

> the notion of the *foetor judaicus*, so prevalent in the Middle Ages ... carried a deeper meaning to the medieval Christian ... its meaning is clearly indicated when we read that the Jew emits a foul odor as punishment for his crime against Jesus ... according to common Christian belief during the Middle Ages good spirits emit a marked fragrance, while evil spirits, and in particular, of course, Satan, are distinguished by an offensive stench. Myrrh gushes forth like fountains from the grave of martyrs, we are told, and when the coffin of the martyred St. Stephen was opened his body filled the air with fragrance .... *The foetor judaicus, then, is another distinctive sign of the "demonic" Jew.*[20]

Trachtenberg's reading gets further support when we consider that the *foetor judaicus* was regarded, at least by some, as miraculously fungible

20. Trachtenberg, *The Devil and the Jews*, 47–48.

in cases of conversion. Relaying the fanciful climate of hearsay in which such doctrines circulated, Reinarz notes that "if a Jew converted to Christianity, it was said, the Jewish stench transformed immediately into a fragrance sweeter than ambrosia."[21]

What sort of early modern people believed in the *foetor judaicus*, and how widely accepted were such claims? Endorsement was surely subject to wide variation, as sheer individual caprices of prejudice no doubt inflected how it circulated and who chose to believe it. The shaky basis for such fanciful "beliefs" is apparent when, with reference to travel writings of the period, Holmberg notes that "the Jewish body seems to have been produced to fit the needs and narratives following from the writers' various agendas; the truthfulness of these stories — of Jewish male menstruation, hemorrhoids, and smells — was often hazy, and was not spoken of in terms of medical or empirical concepts."[22] That is, there is rarely a kind of firsthand affirmation of a material basis for the *foetor judaicus*; it arrives into discourse as an *idée recue* from elsewhere, a somatic innuendo that is sufficient to invoke as a prior allegation for its faint twinge of sour perfume to resurface. *Foetor judaicus* wafts across the intellectual landscape as a diffusely racialized attitude, a matter of ambience, common knowledge. The idea is not a "dead metaphor" so much as it is a culturally recirculated "dead affect," a trace of someone else's alleged or imagined sensory encounter that occasions a vivid recharge, or a skeptical ramping down, each time it gets repeated.

Holmberg confirms Trachtenberg's earlier reading of the fundamentally religious symbolic importance of the *foetor judaicus*, but situates that reading in a consideration of the broader connotations of odors in the period:

> Odours and bad smells were suspicious to early modern people for several reasons. Bad odours were often connected with putrefaction, disease and poverty. Miasmic vapours could be carried on the poison air and make people fall victim to various diseases; the

21. Reinarz, "Odorous Others," 95.
22. Holmberg, "Framing Jewish Bodies and Souls," 128.

> most dangerous of these was the plague, which attacked London several times during the sixteenth and seventeenth century. Early modern Englishmen identified two distinct causes for the Jewish smell: one divinely ordained and the other couched in terms of natural philosophy.[23]

Perhaps the generality implicit in Holmberg's troika of "putrefaction, disease and poverty" tells us something important about the overspecificity of the *foetor judaicus* as a compensatory formation. Affixing the allegation of a particular and knowable aroma onto the Jew as scapegoat constitutes a means of disavowing uncomfortable scenarios in which Gentiles come to be odorous corpses, sick people, or paupers themselves. Marking the Jew as the bearer of the onus of stench, Christians pass a smell test of their own devising by default.

Having traversed Holmberg's archive of *foetor judaicus*, I here step beyond it, to ask: Are affects voluntary, like beliefs, or involuntary, like reflexive responses? The conceptual elasticity of what "affect" names has consequences for how we think the circulation of *foetor judaicus* beyond its status as a curious and discredited delusion. If "affect" names both somatic responses that feel immediate, such as "disgust" and "startle" and more properly "emotional" scripts that require complex attitudes and rationales and epistemological situations ("pride" and "shame" require a significant circumstantial backdrop of beliefs to happen), then the olfactory jolt of recoiling from a bad smell would seem to be on the material, somatic, pre-voluntary end of the spectrum. Yet in the case of *foetor judaicus*, we are not dealing with an imminent sense of disgust at an actual smell, but *an imagined right to be disgusted* that rests upon a necessarily prior belief that Jews just do have a particular, identifiable and noxious odor. Thus, *foetor judaicus* reworks disgust itself, leveraging the pre-voluntary affective script on behalf of a heavily stage-managed ideology.

The affective phenomenology of the *foetor judaicus* might seem like an odd, even recalcitrant, object of analysis. The *foetor judaicus* is a prejudicial slur without any material basis that circulated primarily at the level

23. Holmberg, "Framing Jewish Bodies and Souls," 131.

of folk discourse, even as it was recirculated in the tributary discourses of theology, medicine, and literature. If, as Holly Dugan has pointed out, "smell bridges acute sensory perception and brute bodily materiality," then the *foetor judaicus* amounts to a collective hearsay, an accusation in circulation that would precede any immanent material moment of encounter.[24] It is not so much a description of actual felt disgust as the implication that a virtual feeling of disgust at a virtual odor, were it to happen, would be justified.

It thus reveals the intersubjective system of race formation that the purely imagined or ascribed affect of disgust accomplishes. In imagining their own virtual capacity to smell the *foetor judaicus*, the Christians' own identity shores itself up, and the fact of Jewish difference is reinforced and preserved, without any actual contact required. Above all, the *foetor judaicus* is imagined as already self-evident, as a given. In the process, the observer-dependent relationality of "offensiveness" is massaged away; "offensiveness" is projected outwards onto the imagined stench of a "smelly other," whose mere existence is now rescripted as provocative, extravagant, and, above all, identifiable.[25] As Janet Adelman puts it, this scripting speaks to a fundamental problem in the representation of Jewishness:

> Jews ... are generally depicted as physically unmistakable, with red or black curly hair, large noses, dark skin, and the infamous *foetor judaicus*, the bad smell that identified them as Jews. But apparently Jews could not be counted on to be reliably different: although allegedly physically unmistakable, Jews throughout Europe were nonetheless required to wear particular styles of

24. Holly Dugan, "Strong, Invisible Perfumes," in *The Ephemeral History of Perfume: Scent and Sense in Early Modern England*, (Baltimore, MD: Johns Hopkins University Press, 2011), 2.
25. Mata-Codesal, "El olor del cuerpo migrante en la cidudad desodorizada: simbolismo olfativo en los procesos de clasificacion social."

> clothing or badges that graphically enforced their physical unmistakability — as though they were not quite different *enough.*[26]

This overdetermination of the Jewish body as simultaneously recognizable and at risk of becoming surreptitious reveals the Gentile need to make difference manifest, to produce race at the level of sensory input. In its very weakness and infra-thin evanescence, the *foetor judaicus* was culturally useful. Unlike, say, the fantasy that Jewish men have horns, the imagination of an olfactory experience requires the least possible perceptual support, falling beneath the threshold of immediately apparent evidence. Smells travel light.

Against the credulous backdrop of its broad cultural circulation, Sir Thomas Browne's debunking of *foetor judaicus* in *Pseudodoxia Epidemica* marks a decisive shift. Browne's text is compelling, both for the terms with which it recapitulates and then contests received opinions on the subject, and for its primarily empirical orientation.[27] In Chapter X of Book IV, titled "Of the Jews," Browne maintains a genial attitude of cheery impartiality, even as the inclusion of this item within the overall catalogue of "vulgar errors" that make up the *Pseudodoxia Epidemica* implicitly suggests skepticism: "THAT the Jews stink naturally, that is, that in their race and nation there is an evil savour, is a received opinion we know not how to admit; although concede many questionable points, and dispute not the verity of sundry opinions which are of affinity hereto."[28] Browne's coy authorial mode is epitomized in his casual manner, protesting too much that he will "dispute not" the verity of opinions that he cannot resist quoting but which he also clearly intends to undermine. What goes unremarked is the metonymy whereby a chapter titled "Of the Jews" is *only* about *foetor judaicus*, as if the question of this slanderous allegation was, unto itself, sufficient to exhaust the topic of Jews as such. Numerous other books

26. Janet Adelman, *Blood Relations: Christian and Jew in* The Merchant of Venice (Chicago: University of Chicago Press, 2008), 79 original emphasis.
27. Sir Thomas Browne, *Pseudo-doxia Epidemica, or, Enquiries into very many received tenets and commonly presumed truths* (London: Printed by T.H. for E. Dod, 1646).
28. Browne, *Pseudo-doxia Epidemica*, Book IV, Chapter X, 166.

of the *Pseudodoxia* are taken up with discussion of events in the Hebrew Bible, so Browne can hardly have believed this, and yet at the level of the book's own encyclopedic structure, it curiously mirrors Chapter X of Book VI, "Of the blackness of Negroes," by creating a numerically paired set of chapters devoted to the somatic constitution of racialized bodies.

At the level of tone, Browne seems open to belief in the *foetor judaicus* if the facts will support it, and yet also altogether happy to point out that, judging from his consideration of the evidence, they do not. Here he is not the "bad physician" made familiar by Stanley Fish's polemic, reaching for rhetorical effects at the expense of the truth; rather, Browne seems keen to boost his bona fides as a natural philosopher. The passage from textual allegations to "Experience" transmits an implicit shift from the pleasurable relay of literary arcana to the claims of empirical evidence, which is notably given the last word: "Lastly, Experience will convict it; for this offensive odor is no way discoverable in their Synagogues where many are, and by reason of their number could not be concealed: nor is the same discernible in commerce or conversation with such as are cleanly in Apparel, and decent in their Houses."[29] The very fact that Browne should write these sentences in the first edition, published in 1646, three years before Johanna and Ebenezer Cartwright would author the first formal petition for the readmission of Jews to England, is both of a piece with shifting attitudes afoot in "admissionist" circles, and yet still startling in its willingness to reconsider centuries of demonizing prejudice.[30]

At the level of prose style, Browne's casual implication of firsthand familiarity with the aroma of Synagogues could index his travels across Montpellier, Leiden, and especially, given its prominent Jewish community, Padua; but it also registers the free indirect discursive mode by which the textual authorities and secondhand information from various other authors that Browne collated here become transubstantiated into

29. Browne, *Pseudo-doxia Epidemica*, Book IV, Chapter X, 168.

30. See Todd M. Edelman, *The Jews of Britain, 1656 to 2000* (Berkeley: University of California Press, 2002).

the authoritative voice of (textual, vicarious) "experience."[31] Individual Jews may or may not be "cleanly" or "decent," but that is only ever an individual matter and not a collective trait, and that is that. Summing up, Browne, at last, comes to rest in a qualified rejection of the premise that has occupied the entirety of the chapter's meanderings across supporting and skeptical trajectories, deflating the *foetor judaicus* with a flourish of farewell:

> Thus therefore, although we concede that many opinions are true which hold some conformity unto this, yet in assenting hereto, many difficulties must arise: it being a dangerous point to annex a constant property unto any Nation, and much more this unto the *Jew*; since this quality is not verifiable by observation; since the grounds are feeble that should establish it; and lastly: since if all were true, yet are the reasons alleadged for it, of no sufficiency to maintain it.[32]

It is tempting to see in Browne's cheerful myth-busting an anticipatory dawn of liberalism, and to find in Browne's skepticism about anti-Semitic disgust a proleptic indication of the Readmission to come under Oliver Cromwell in the following decade. We would do well to remember that many of the relatively philosemitic and tolerationist attitudes of the period have themselves been glossed by Alexandra Walsham as, in a piquant phrase, examples of "charitable hatred," retractable largesse offered from within disapproval "to the adherents of an inherently false religion."[33] In contrast to the sheer virulence of Markham's slanderous insinuations about Jewish "doung" and "spewe," the magnanimity of Browne's genial manner can make him seem like an avatar of tolerance and truth.

31. Reid Barbour, "Padua, 1632–1633," in *Sir Thomas Browne: A Life* (Oxford: Oxford University Press, 2013), 145–83.
32. Browne, *Pseudo-doxia Epidemica*, Book IV, Chapter X, 169–70.
33. Alexandra Walsham, *Charitable Hatred: Tolerance and Intolerance in England, 1500–1700* (Manchester: Manchester University Press, 2006), 4.

But as we know, the abeyance of theological frames and the coming age of the sciences of man would witness a further articulation of racism rather than its decisive abolition, bringing about what Denise Ferreira da Silva terms "the production of the analytics of raciality,"[34] analytics that stem from a foundational reorientation of human projects around the Promethean tool of scientific reason. Pushing back against supernatural folk doctrines about inherently cursed bodies but casually open to being convinced that Jews really do smell after all on the empirical grounds of cultural and culinary difference, Browne's position models both the fond hope that empirical evidence will demolish our attachment to "race," and the curious elasticity of racialized aversion in its affective form along the long march towards secular modernity. As such, Browne's mingling of stances offers us a revealing moment of transition in what Ronnie Po-Chia Hsia has termed "the Christian ethnography of Jews."[35] Browne's text anticipates later sublations of the somatic into the cultural, both in its redemptive philosemitic mode – rescuing the Jews from credulous fantasies of bodily difference – and in the culturalist preservation of difference all the same: the Jew stays "separate," isolable, knowable in the wake of this corrective, an object of knowledge to be taxonomized alongside the "Negroes" and rabbits and comets of natural philosophy.

Browne's closing rhetorical maneuvers, in which he grants that the allegation of the *foetor* could simply be a matter of Jewish dietary practices rather than inherent somatic difference, meshes uncomfortably with Trachtenberg's description of the actual outcome of the *foetor judaicus* as it passed out of the supernatural realm and, as it were, went secular and mainstream. Trachtenberg states that the *foetor judaicus* "is still prominent in the folk literature in a 'refined' version, namely, that the Jews are guilty *en masse* of the egregious sin of 'garlic eating.' This is 'modern'

34. Denise Ferreira da Silva, *Toward A Global Idea of Race* (Minneapolis: University of Minnesota Press, 2007), 99.

35. Ronnie Po-chia Hsia, "Religion and Race: Protestant and Catholic Discourses on Jewish Conversions in the Sixteenth and Seventeenth Centuries," in *The Origins of Racism in the West*, ed. Miriam Eliav-Feldon, Benjamin Isaac, and Joseph Ziegler (Cambridge: Cambridge University Press, 2009), 268.

antisemitism, as distinguished from the medieval variety."[36] Writing in the immediate aftermath of the Shoah, Trachtenberg's words powerfully demonstrate the capacity of stereotypes and fantasies to outlive the religious prejudices and bygone cultural contexts that birthed them, and to linger long after widespread belief in their ontological support systems has shriveled.

I began with a usefully difficult encounter in which the value and meaning of "affect" was called into a question: "What does that word even mean, anyway?" It is a question worth asking, and worth trying to answer. It has been the intuition of this essay that we can best know "what affect means" by tracing the particular histories of what particular affects have made possible, and at whose expense. I have argued that affects are variable, pervasive, and creative, and that they are grounded in particular bodies, and that they take on the legibility of social signs. The strange case of *foetor judaicus* shows us that this creative power and this legibility yield bitter harvests; across a spectrum from violent discourses of somatic difference to tacitly segregationist forms of culturalist tolerance, affect can become a medium through which racialized forms of knowledge find their seeming confirmation in the everyday givenness of sensory experience. Contributing to the "*articulation and management of human difference*,"[37] the first progenitors of the myth of *foetor judaicus* sought to fix peoples in persistent relations of antagonism founded upon an invisible and seemingly incorrigible difference, a difference they summoned through the evocation of a powerfully involuntary affect: disgust. The power of passing sensations of disgust and aversion to render race portable across time and territory shows us at least one form that the race-making force of affect has taken. I hope that it models why critical attention to affects might inform our capacity to recognize, in LaPerle's words, "how race feels."[38] For those hailed by the strange case of *foetor judaicus*, it feels like a painful flinch of misrecognition at a smell that never existed.

36. Trachtenberg, *The Devil and the Jews*, 49.
37. Heng, "The Invention of Race in the European Middle Ages, I," 319 original emphasis.
38. LaPerle, "Race, Affect and the Olfactory."

Section II

Racialized Affects of Sex and Gender

5. Conversion Interrupted: Shame and the Demarcation of Jewish Women's Difference in *The Merchant of Venice*

SARA COODIN

Recent scholarship on the history of race has made clear that Jews have long been central to the logic of racial supremacy and were targets of distinctly racialized persecution in Europe as early as the thirteenth century.[1] "Jewish looks" and "looking Jewish" have not always been at the forefront of the discriminatory logic designating Jewish difference, but it is impossible to deny the long-standing intransigence of convictions that Jews are essentially and ineradicably "other."[2] In Jews and Judaism's complex and ongoing imbrication within ideas about race, racializing structures, and racism, an unstable relationship to visible forms of racial difference, including whiteness and Blackness, emerges.[3] Thus, this chapter takes a

1. On this point, see Geraldine Heng, *The Invention of Race in the European Middle Ages* (Cambridge: Cambridge University Press, 2018), Chapter 2. Heng discusses English Jews as the first racialized minority in Europe and England as the first racial state. For a different perspective, see M. Lindsay Kaplan, *Figuring Racism in Medieval Christianity* (Oxford: Oxford University Press, 2018), who examines Jews' status within medieval Christian theology and argues that Jews came to be marked with an inherited inferiority relative to Christians during this period. Robert C. Stacey, "The Conversion of Jews to Christianity in Thirteenth-Century England," *Speculum* 67, no. 2 (1992): 263–83, argues that Jewishness in medieval Europe was understood to be irreducible, even for converts who had become Christian. The operative idea was that even when Jews converted to Christianity, they were thought to still remain Jews.
2. See Susan A. Glenn, "'Funny, You Don't Look Jewish': Visual Stereotypes and the Making of Modern Jewish Identity," in *Boundaries of Jewish Identity*, ed. Susan A. Glenn and Naomi B. Sokoloff (Seattle: University of Washington Press, 2010), 64–90.
3. In this essay, I capitalise "Blackness" and "Black" where it applies primarily to racial identity or category. This spelling is in accordance with recent arguments that emphasize the "elements of shared history and identity" of Black culture (https://www.nytimes.com/2020/07/05/insider/capitalized-black.html). However, I

step back from the physiological as a primary source of Jewish difference and turns instead to the more diffused structures of feeling implicated in marking and perpetuating Jewish difference — especially the difference of Jewish women.

In contrast to Jewish men, Jewish women are often figured as less racially distinct and more assimilable, a feature reflected in the English literary canon through their imagined amenability to Christian marriage and conversion.[4] *The Merchant of Venice*'s Jessica provides a formative and influential example of the narrative of Jewish female responsiveness to normative Christianity and its potential to "whiten" Jewish converts. As an eligible, unmarried woman, Jessica is described using the period's typical language of fairness. Her skin is figured as "ivory" to her father's "jet" and her blood described as "rhenish" — light — in contrast to her father's, which is likened to the darker "red wine" (3.1.35–36).[5] And yet, despite her association with whiteness, Jessica's entry into Christian marriage remains conclusively ambivalent. Rather than being defined through conversion, Jessica is instead characterized through her repeated professions of religious self-loathing and shame. These affects forestall what are ultimately left unstaged: her transformative conversion and marriage.

also want to call attention to the ways in which early modern writing frequently deploys the language of color — blackness and whiteness — to designate hue as well as racial category in ways that can prove extraordinarily difficult to prise apart. In cases where both racial concept and pigment are possibilities, I have chosen to leave the terms "black" and "blackness" uncapitalized as a way of emphasising the ways in which the two meanings, material pigment and racial designation, were beginning to shift into conceptual alignment. Leaving those instances un-capitalised allows readers to parse the conflation of the two senses, and consider the ways in which natural properties like pigment have historically shifted to become terms for artificial, culturally constructed racial categories. This essay's consideration of where Jews fit into the categorical designations "Black" and "white" in many ways epitomises that very process, since Jewish identity has shifted across time and geography many times.

4. This argument is made persuasively in M. Lindsay Kaplan, "Jessica's Mother: Medieval Constructions of Jewish Race and Gender in *The Merchant of Venice*," *Shakespeare Quarterly* 58, no. 1 (2007): 1–30.
5. All references to the play are from William Shakespeare, *The Merchant of Venice*, 3rd Series, ed. John Drakakis (London: The Arden Shakespeare/Bloomsbury, 2010).

Rather than focusing on discourses of bodily difference – complexion or blood – as key anchors of Jewish racial difference, I investigate Jessica's deployment of religious self-loathing and shame as racially formative. Affect remains under-studied in its capacity to map social and political spaces and subjects along racial lines, despite the passions' current centrality as a scholarly topic. This chapter considers self-loathing and shame as vitally important and distinctly political forms of currency in *The Merchant of Venice*, intimately bound up with race and the processes that attend the racial othering of Jewish women.

In its modern iteration, shame has overwhelmingly been understood as a private, inward condition rather than a public or political force. Jewish self-loathing in the nineteenth and twentieth centuries was particularly prone to psychologizing interpretations that designated it as a pathology of the mind. Fin de siècle Jewish "self-hatred" was considered a psychopathology of assimilated European Jewish intellectuals, evidenced through public figures such as journalist Karl Kraus and philosopher Otto Weininger, both of whom spoke out forcefully against the mannerisms of the "uncouth" *Ostjuden* (Eastern European Jews) from whom they sought to distinguish themselves.[6] In a twentieth-century American context, the term "inferiority complex" used before the Second World War became known by the 1940s and 1950s as "Jewish self-hatred," a concept "as attractive as ... the Oedipal complex"[7] had been in the 1920s and 1930s in its capacity to illuminate the Jewish psyche.[8] "Jewish self-hatred" entered into the cultural lexicon as part of a "broader psychological moment in American social science, public policy, and public culture."[9] Heavily influenced by the work of refugee scholars arriving from Nazi Germany, the postwar years brought an intensive focus on the affective experiences

6. Susan A. Glenn, "The Vogue of Jewish Self-Hatred in Post-World War II America," *Jewish Social Studies* 12, no. 3 (2006): 96.
7. Glenn, "The Vogue of Jewish Self-Hatred in Post-World War II America," 98.
8. "Jewish self-hatred" was meant to describe the psychological self-loathing born of internalized antisemitic persecution and Holocaust trauma. This trauma was thought to result in an attempted erasure of all signs of Jewish origin in order to assimilate seamlessly into white Anglo-Saxon Protestant American culture.
9. Glenn, "The Vogue of Jewish Self-Hatred in Post-World War II America," 100.

of persecuted minorities, particularly Ashkenazi or "European" Jews. Although the various iterations of modern Jewish self-loathing were also known to encompass a range of topical sociopolitical issues — prewar German Zionism, post-Holocaust trauma, Jewish assimilation in America — the framework for understanding the phenomenon itself remained insistently rooted in a psychologized view of the Jewish subject as a self-divided person, almost always depicted as male and presumed to be pale-skinned and Ashkenazi.

Whereas shame's modern meaning has come to denote an inward condition — a self fundamentally in conflict with itself that maps external strife onto an interiorized terrain — by contrast, early modern accounts of shame emphasize a public, exteriorized constitution. Early modern shame was generated in an interpersonal social milieu, the product of being seen and perceived by others. Reflecting on how "men make no doubt of doing that in secret, which for shame they would not do openly," Timothy Bright's 1613 treatise on melancholy declares that shame depends on public scrutiny, without which there is no corresponding inner sense. Therefore, according to Bright, "[t]hough a man be greved & sorie therefore, yet before it be known to others is he not ashamed."[10] An interiorized feeling of shame follows only after the public recognition of a misdeed.

Early modern shame's distinctly public contours, as a form of experience inscribed outwardly and communicated in a social environment, would appear to confirm the recent scholarly claim that Renaissance emotions themselves were profoundly sociable, transactional entities.[11] Similar notions have also underwritten poststructuralist and new historicist scholarship theorizing the social constructs of interiority.[12] Much of that work has succeeded in challenging the post-Enlightenment concept of selfhood as a contained and inwardly generated thing. And yet, though such theories succeeded at challenging modern assumptions about self-

10. Timothy Bright, *A Treatise of Melancholy* (London, 1613), 203–204.

11. Steven Mullaney, *The Reformation of Emotions in the Age of Shakespeare* (Chicago: University of Chicago Press, 2015), esp. 22.

12. On this point, see See Francis Barker, *The Tremulous Private Body: Essays on Subjection* (Ann Arbor: University of Michigan Press, 1995).

hood and estranging the early modern from the modern, they also often remain intensively psychological in their focus. Several have rebuilt the Renaissance psyche by first emptying out its modern contents, and then pouring back into it a series of worldly elements, from geohumoralism to Elizabethan structures of authority, without attending significantly to race.[13] Early modern shame has been extensively theorized as a form of inherently social communication and a site of socializing discipline enforced on women's bodies; however, those same discussions have also elided race from the picture of the social environments in which affective signals were apt to circulate.[14]

Emotion's sociability, and shame's in particular, points insistently towards the racial hierarchies in which shame is enmeshed — hierarchies that shame often helped to constitute. Rather than functioning as the marker of incomprehensibly premodern inwardness, or a form of discipline for bodies without discernible racial identities, or bodies characterized by an unmarked implicit whiteness, the affective experience of shame actually represents a remarkably legible form of race-making technology in the Renaissance and beyond, one that presides over the process of racial othering. Within Western moral-philosophical and sci-

13. See Mary Floyd-Wilson, "English Mettle," in *Reading the Early Modern Passions: Essays in the Cultural History of Emotion*, ed. Gail Kern Paster, Katherine Rowe, and Mary Floyd-Wilson (Philadelphia: University of Pennsylvania Press, 2004), 130–46; "Temperature, Temperance, and Racial Difference in Ben Jonson's *The Masque of Blackness*," *English Literary Renaissance* 28, no. 2 (1998): 183–209; Gail Kern Paster, *The Body Embarrassed: Drama and the Disciplines of Shame in Early Modern England* (Ithaca, NY: Cornell University Press, 1993).
14. One of the most detailed recent discussions of the phenomenology of early modern shame and women's bodies is in Jennifer Panek, "*The Nice Valour*'s Anatomy of Shame," *English Literary Renaissance* 48, no. 3 (2018): 339–67. Panek's work, like her previous study of shame and pleasure in *The Changeling* ("Shame and Pleasure in *The Changeling*," *Renaissance Drama* 42, no. 2 [2014]: 191–215), adopts a historicized approach focused on the particular representations of early modern women's shame; however, her approach does not take up questions of race. Paster's *The Body Embarrassed* represents the most influential historicized study of early modern shame, but also does not address race substantively, despite its careful attention to early modern embodiment and women's embodiment in particular.

entific traditions, shame has functioned as a powerful tool for demarcating boundaries between types, groups, and categories of living things. As far back as Aristotle, shame and its most visible token, blushing, have been used to mark distinctions between male and female; between humans and other animals; between persons imagined capable of moral emotions as opposed to those excluded from a full range of capacities and therefore deemed less sensible, less civilized, even less-than-fully human.[15]

Shame's racializing capacity during the Renaissance was bound up in complex ways with the discourse of complexion. As a prerequisite for certain forms of Christian virtue, the blushing cheek presupposes a skin tone light enough to redden with shame. Renaissance Spanish literature proverbializes the equation of light complexions with the capacity for virtue in expressions such as, "how can he be trusted who knows not how to blush," a formulation that emphasizes pale skin's inherent moral superiority over dark. Miguel de Cervantes reformulates this same commonplace slightly in *Don Quixote* as, "better a blush on your face than a blot in your heart."[16] English Jesuit Thomas Wright offers a similar conclusion in his description of the relative merits of European and especially English complexions over other nationalities: "The very blushing also of our people showeth a better ground whereupon Virtue may build that certain brazen faces, who never change themselves although they commit, yea, and be deprehended in enormous crimes."[17] Light skin becomes the prerequisite for virtues that, for women, are spelled out in English Renaissance moral codes centered on female modesty, silence, and sexual chastity or virginity, whose token is the blush. For men, temperance is

15. Charles Darwin cites blushing as a "most peculiar and the most human of expressions," and he admits that though monkeys visibly redden when they become impassioned, "it would require an overwhelming amount of evidence to make us believe that any animal could blush" (*The Expression of Emotions in Man and Animals* [Chicago: University of Chicago Press, 1965], 309).
16. "do no hay verguenza en cara que mancilla en corazon" (Miguel de Cervantes, *Don Quixote*, ed./trans. John Rutherford (New York: Penguin Classics, 2002, part 2, chapter 44).
17. Thomas Wright, *The Passions of the Mind in General*, ed. William Webster Newbold (New York: Garland, 1986), 82.

often read as the key sign of the capacity to self-moderate, something of which dark-skinned populations are routinely imagined incapable in the period, just as they are excluded from the capacity to blush.

Despite the widespread association between complexional lightness and the capacity for shame and its associated virtues in Renaissance writings, these same texts often go on to discuss the ways shame also positions the body as fundamentally ambivalent rather than eminently readable. Even in the face of such supposedly clear signs as skin tone, shame has the capacity to destabilize the moral hierarchies that European Christian writers use to make sense of ethno-racial and religious difference. For travel writers, meditations on shame often shift into occasions for self-reflexive assessment in which the critical gaze is refocused back onto the European observer, who begins to critique the mores and morals of his fellow Europeans. Unguarded displays of nudity in New World Indigenous populations often prompt these kinds of episodes, in which the inherent moral superiority of normative Christian values is called into question. In the 1550s, Jean de Léry concludes in his written reflections on the Tupinumba of Brazil that the native tribespeople not only fail to conceal their bodies, but also are not ashamed of going about as naked as the day they were born.[18] Though unmistakably moralizing in its intent, de Léry's account of the Tupinumba's nudity also identifies a prelapsarian innocence in the tribespeople's unclothed bodies, which then prompts him to reflect critically on the habits of European women. He concludes that French aristocratic women's proclivity for jewelry, superfluities, and sartorial excess[19] generates a far more lascivious tableau than the Tupinumba's unclothed simplicity.[20] De Léry's reflection where he

18. "non seulement sans cachers aucunes parties de leurs corps, mais aussi sans en avoir nulle honte ni vergogne, demeurent & vont coustumierement aussi nuds au'ils sortent du ventre de leur mere" (Jean de Léry, *Histoire d'un voyage fait en la terre du Bresil*, [La Rochelle: Antoine Chuppin, 1578], 110).

19. "baubances, superfluitez, & exces en habits" (de Léry, *Histoire d'un voyage fait en la terre du Bresil*, 131).

20. Léry, *Histoire d'un voyage fait en la terre du Bresil*, 131. For a discussion of European expedition writing in the Renaissance and beyond, see Brian Cummings, "Animal Passions and Human Sciences: Shame, Blushing and Nakedness in Early Modern Europe

encounters the Brazilian "other" threatens to dissolve the moral imperative of his voyage and the theological mission that underwrites it, which is patterned on a conclusive conversion of the "savage" to Christianity. This same reflexive turn is also present in Michel de Montaigne's meditation on the Tupinumba's simplicity in "On Cannibals." The unclothed tribesperson's lack of shame generates a turn towards self-scrutiny, one that moves into cultural self-critique as well as the self-dissolving skepticism that characterizes many of Montaigne's more extended reflections throughout the *Essais*.

Within Renaissance European travel writing, the naked body of the tribesperson promises to afford unguarded visual access to something vital that is kept closely hidden in a European context. The apparent absence of shame amongst Indigenous populations in faraway lands represents an occasion for the Christian observer to look more closely. Instead of disclosing its hidden secrets, however, the shame-less body of the "other" can only occasion a series of inconclusive attempts at meaning-making. The Christian narrative of prelapsarian innocence is introduced in de Léry's account as a possible explanation for what he observes; however, de Léry cannot reconcile that account with his Christianizing mission, which views the tribespeople as unredeemed and primitive. The unclothed, shame-less body of the tribesperson resists facile moral explanations or easy location within a familiar hierarchy. Instead, discussions of shame and its absence turn the observer's own gaze back on itself. In its capacity to destabilize, shame occasions a collapse of the interpretive enterprise and thereby occasions a kind of hermeneutic crisis, a phenomenon that Sujata Iyengar has argued constitutes shame's signal feature in Renaissance writing.[21]

Shame's capacity to incite hermeneutic instability is not only a feature of European observers' encounters with the bodies of exotic "others," but

and the New World," in *At the Borders of the Human: Beasts, Bodies, and Natural Philosophy in the Early Modern Period*, ed. Erica Fudge, Ruth Gilbert, and Susan Wiseman (New York: Palgrave Macmillan, 1999), 26–50.

21. Sujata Iyengar, *Shades of Difference: Mythologies of Skin Color in Early Modern England* (Philadelphia: University of Pennsylvania Press, 2005), 108.

it is also endemic to familiar, local, and pale-skinned European Renaissance bodies. Women's shame was particularly prone to signal multidirectionally. Markers such as the blush functioned as sites where moral truths were thought to be communicated; however, blushes had the capacity to indicate either guilt or innocence, wantonness or chastity. As a site of extraordinary significance for measuring the moral worth of individuals, women's shameful blushes were simultaneously opaque in what they actually signaled. Thought to reflect the body's transmission of blood to the face, Renaissance English accounts of the physiological processes underwriting blushing were awash with contradictions. Wright's explanation cites the rush of "the purest blood" to the face as "a defence and succour the which effect, commonly, is judged to proceed from a good and virtuous nature, because no man but allow it, that it is good to be ashamed of a fault."[22] Blushing signals virtue, a subject's purest and innermost awareness of a fault's inherent viciousness, and is therefore a sign of innocence. And yet Wright also asserts, contradictorily, that individuals blush "because nature being afraid, lest in the face the fault should be discovered."[23] Wright's comments appear to assert that blushing is both a sign of innocence and its opposite: an attempt to conceal a fault's discovery, and therefore a sign of guilt.

In *The Merchant of Venice*, Jessica rehearses some of the key elements and contradictions that attend Renaissance discussions of shame, including the complexional whiteness that is imagined as a prerequisite to blushing and its corresponding Christian virtues. However, her blush also occasions some of the signature destabilizations that are equally endemic to Renaissance accounts of blushing, in ways that bear on her racial mobility. At the moment of her absconsion, Jessica calls attention to the "lightness" of her transgression and pronounces, "What, must I hold a candle to my shames? They in themselves, good sooth, are too too light. Why, tis an office of discovery, love, and I should be obscured" (2.6.42–45). Jessica's juxtaposition of fairness, awareness of sin, and desire for the

22. Thomas Wright, *The Passions of the Minde in Generall*, (London: Valentine Simmes, 1604), 30.
23. Wright, *The Passions of the Minde in Generall*, 30.

cover of night as she engages in transgressive activities communicates that she is cognizant of her current "sins," which include theft, betrayal of her father, and elopement with a Christian man. Her shame therefore indicates her subjection to, and awareness of, a shared moral framework that regards such things as wrong, even as she playfully casts them as "light" or un-serious. The term "light" also references a complexional paleness that facilitates her participation in a shared Christian moral framework — one that, according to the conquistador's logic, is framed according to skin tone and necessarily precludes dark complexions.

Through her turns of phrase, Jessica appears to situate herself as rightfully belonging to the world of Christian Venice, a milieu centered on the vilification of dark complexions that radiates through the play from Belmont outwards, and frames Shylock's Jewishness as both theologically depraved and dark. Jessica's characterization of shame through the language of color communicates a desire for belonging within a social community in which membership is prefaced on skin pale enough to register a blush. Here, Jessica aspires to be, and presents herself as, sufficiently light-skinned to enter that world.

Jessica's mention of shame not once but twice as she absconds in Act 2, Scene 6 implies that she is capable of blushing even prior to conversion. But were Renaissance Jewish women imagined to be capable of blushing? Could conversion effect such a shift, even if a Jewish woman's natural color was imagined to reflect darker tones? As she prepares to depart from her father's home, Jessica calls out to Lorenzo in a speech that draws attention to her as a blushing subject while asking him to avert his eyes:

> I am glad 'tis night you do not look on me,
> For I am much ashamed of my exchange.
> But love is blind, and lovers cannot see
> The pretty follies that themselves commit,
> For if they could, Cupid himself would blush
> To see me thus transformed to a boy. (2.6.35–40)

Jessica's insistence on the moment of her absconsion as an "exchange" draws attention to several illicit elements that underwrite the scene, including her donning of male clothing to disguise her departure; the transgressive looting of her father's coffers; the transfer of those funds to Lorenzo in lieu of a legitimate dowry; and the underlying fact of Lorenzo's "marrying down" by eloping with a Jewish woman, however beautiful and richly endowed. All of these circumstances are rightful causes for blushing since they violate a host of protocols governing marriage and fidelity.

However, Jessica's body – the very thing to which she calls attention in this episode, even as she implores her viewing audience to look away – is also a profoundly destabilizing entity. Her somewhat embarrassed joke about looking like a boy resonates meta-theatrically with the presence of the boy actor behind the young woman who dons the male disguise. The scene's layers of theatrical artifice also extend to the actor's other illusions, including the application of marks of shame through cosmetic rouge and white face paint, which formed part of the assemblage of cosmetic preparations sold to women in Renaissance England.[24] Even as she urges her onlookers to look away, Jessica calls attention to the signifying blush while simultaneously revealing its contingency as a construct produced, or at least producible, through the skilled illusions of makeup and actorly impersonation. In this scene, Jessica's "lightness," her pale skin and all of the social and racial mobility bound up with it, are de-stabilized through her call to look-but-not-look at her blushing face.

As Kimberly Poitevin has argued, early modern cosmetics could "disrupt the intersecting categories of race, nation, and religion" that were thought to mark – and render legible – a person's complexion in Renaissance England.[25] This capacity, and the application of cosmetics, was predominantly associated with women in Renaissance England, unlike cosmetics' use abroad, which travel writings ascribed to both men and women alike.[26] By recalling the blush and the spectral presence of the actor who plays Jessica's role – a role characterized by the fluidity of disguise – Jessica

24. See Kimberly Poitevin, "Inventing Whiteness: Cosmetics, Race, and Women in Early Modern England," *Journal for Early Modern Cultural Studies* 11, no. 1 (2011): 59–89. For a comprehensive analysis of the period's cultural preoccupation with cosmetics, see Farah Karim-Cooper, *Cosmetics in Shakespearean and Renaissance Drama* (Edinburgh: Edinburgh University Press, 2006).
25. Poitevin, "Inventing Whiteness," 81.
26. Poitevin, "Inventing Whiteness," 66.

destabilizes the connection between Jewish women and racial whiteness. In this moment of transition that forecasts her imminent conversion from Jew to Christian, the unsettling of clear racial belonging suffuses Jessica's Jewish body with uncertainty and contingency. Within the parameters of the play, the Jewish woman's body is revealed to be underwritten by a series of unstable signifiers. While it remains subject to transformation through the process of whitening-through-conversion described in some medieval texts, it can also be "painted" through the artful application of cosmetics. Jessica invites her lover, along with the play's audience, to examine the "pretty follies" that actively unsettle her image as a chaste maiden, reminding them that what proves her modesty is ultimately a boy actor dressed as a young woman and the specter of makeup in the blush. Even the contingent phrasing surrounding the blush itself ("for *if* they could, Cupid himself *would* blush) and the blush's obscure subvisibility in this scene — never directly perceived, and yet repeatedly recalled — further unmoors the scene's anchoring in clearly visible racial, moral, and physiognomic categories. Does the Jewish would-be convert blush, or doesn't she? Jessica's reply only invites further obfuscation and scrutiny. Like the stories of European travel writers, Jessica's account of blushing calls attention to the body while simultaneously revealing its opacity as a source of determinate meaning.

Jessica's absconsion scene de-stabilizes the firm anchoring of Jewish racial difference via skin color. Historically, Jews have had a range of skin tones and physical attributes ascribed to them in a European context, shifts also reflected in ideas about their perceived religious, racial, and ethno-national identities in relation to normative Christianity. In medieval European medical texts, Jews were ascribed a humoral melancholy, and their complexions associated with melancholy's attendant color: black. Melancholy's association with mud (*luteus*) and lead (*lividus*) also invoked a range of other colors associated with Jewish complexions, present in graphic depictions of Jews that included white, tawny shades of brown or red, blue, blue-black, gray, and grayish-black hues.[27] One fourteenth-cen-

27. M. Lindsay Kaplan, "The Jewish Body in Black and White in Medieval and Early Modern England," *Philological Quarterly* 92, no. 1 (2013): 42–44.

tury text comments on Jews as melancholic and pale due to blood loss tied to hereditary punishment for the crucifixion.[28] The exegetical commentary of Ambrose of Milan aligns Jews with Ethiopians, black because the sun no longer shines on them, but redeemable to whiteness upon their conversion.[29] Medieval psalter depictions of Jesus's Jewish tormenters cast them with distorted features, including large noses, grimacing mouths, black or brown skin, bulging foreheads, red hair; however, these features exist alongside others typically used to depict Christians, such as blonde hair, white skin, and unremarkable facial features.[30]

By the seventeenth century, European writers expressed conflicting opinions about Jewish appearance and skin color, with some ascribing blackness to Jewish complexions, and others, such as François-Maximillian Misson in his 1691 *New Voyage to Italy*, declaring all European Jews white, with the exception of the Portuguese.[31] In some English texts, assertions of Jewish physical difference are belied by initial confusion over whether an unknown interlocutor might be Jewish, only to be followed by assertions that the author in fact registered a distinctly Jewish appearance from the start. To that end, Sebastian Munster's 1655 *The Messiah of the Christians and the Jews* recounts a story wherein a Christian interlocutor discovers a man to be Jewish only after attempting to converse with him in Hebrew. He then attempts to overwrite his initial uncertainty by declaring that he had seen visible tokens of the man's Jewish complexion from the start: "I knew you to be a Jew: for you Jews have a peculiar color of face, ... for you are black and uncomely."[32]

28. Kaplan, "The Jewish Body in Black and White in Medieval and Early Modern England," 44.
29. Kaplan, "The Jewish Body in Black and White in Medieval and Early Modern England," 46.
30. Kaplan, "The Jewish Body in Black and White in Medieval and Early Modern England," 49–52.
31. François-Maximillian Mission, *New Voyage to Italy*, qtd. in Kaplan, "The Jewish Body in Black and White in Medieval and Early Modern England," 55.
32. Sebastian Munster, *The Messiah of the Christians and the Jews* (1655), qtd. in Kaplan, "The Jewish Body in Black and White in Medieval and Early Modern England," 55.

Whereas Jewish men were identified by a range of physiological characteristics, some of them indistinguishable from those of Christians, Jewish women's visible difference was rendered more obscure and intangible during the early modern period. M. Lindsay Kaplan has argued that medieval English Christianity viewed Jewish women as both racially undifferentiated and amenable to racial transformation through conversion. In combination with newly circulated and popularized Aristotelian ideas about gender and reproduction, women were identified as more physiologically malleable than men, and therefore unable to transmit their own racial identity to their offspring. Jewish women's bodies were thereby imagined to be far less racially distinctive and formative than the bodies of Jewish men.[33]

Rather than serving as a locus of indisputable proof and racial belonging, Jessica's body in *The Merchant of Venice* instead calls attention to multiple levels of ambiguity. Furthermore, the ambivalence of Jessica's racial Jewishness as she absconds in Act 2, Scene 6 is bound up with shame's broader ambivalence in the Renaissance. Rather than the body speaking for itself, blushing as a sign of shame requires us to think through the ways the body communicates the social judgments levied upon it. The body's ability to register shame is neither endowed with absolute nor clear significance; instead, it remains subject to ongoing revaluation depending on context and on who is positioned to interpret it. Unlike visible forms of difference figured in the complexional darkness of Launcelot's Moorish lover, Jewish difference is provisionally amenable to whitening and Christian conversion, which is particularly useful in the context of the play's concern with transactionality.

The play's exploration of transactionality imagines the possibilities for a subversion of Portia's — and Belmont's — Christian purity through the influx of strangers who vie for the chance to marry and procreate with her. *The Merchant of Venice* also follows this trail in the opposite direction, testing out ways racialized "others," like Jessica, seek to become whitened and Christianized. In moving financial assets from her father's coffers to Lorenzo's waiting hands, Jessica helps to facilitate the play's revaluation

33. Kaplan, "Jessica's Mother."

of wealth as something that can come to reflect a particular concept of virtue when it is removed from the "wrong" hands and placed into the "right" ones. Like the proverbial convert to Christianity, money is subject to "whitening" and can be revalued, depending on who possesses it. By ensuring that the money ends up in the coffers of the play's Christian men, *The Merchant of Venice* enacts a kind of wish fulfillment, illustrating the ideal flow of capital within a white supremacist Christian universe. Money, jewels, households, and their contents, including children, as well as sacred texts and divine providential blessings, are all redirected. They are taken from the hands of the Jewish moneylender and redirected into the hands of Belmont's Portia, before finally coming to rest in the coffers of its Christian Venetian men.[34] The play's comic resolution manifests what Kim F. Hall describes as "the redistribution of wealth from women and other strangers to Venice's Christian males," ensuring that "the uneven balance of wealth in the economy is righted along racial and gender lines."[35] Hall also remarks on the play's inability to assimilate its exogamous dark-complexioned "others," even those who, like the offspring of Launcelot and his unnamed Moorish lover, form part of Venice's forecasted ethno-racial future. Hall concludes by dwelling on the product of Launcelot's sexual liaison with the Moor, the mixed child whose "blackness may not be 'converted' or absorbed within the endogamous, exclusionary values of Belmont,"[36] and who is ultimately excluded from the play's concluding figuration of Venetian marriage, fertility, and procreation.

Jessica's performance of blushing as shame makes possible a social mobility deployed precisely by Jewish women's complexional indeterminacy, which Jessica depicts as a product of her white-presenting, blushing face. Unlike the Moroccos and Moorish lovers of the play, Jews are not the

34. For an extended discussion of how the play stages a complex negotiation between Christian and Jew over the ownership of sacred texts, see Sara Coodin, Is *Shylock Jewish? Citing Scripture and the Moral Agency of Shakespeare's Jews* (Edinburgh: Edinburgh University Press, 2017), Chapter 2.
35. Kim F. Hall, "Guess Who's Coming to Dinner? Colonization and Miscegenation in The Merchant of Venice," *Renaissance Drama* 23 (1992): 99–100.
36. Hall, "Guess Who's Coming to Dinner?" 105.

exogamous strangers from without, but strangers within, as Janet Adelman's work has illustrated convincingly.[37] Theologically, this positioning was reflected through Protestant Christianity's concern over the implicit threat that Jews, and converts in particular, posed to Christian theological supremacy. Since Jews constituted the original "chosen nation" favored by divine blessings and providential advantage, it required considerable theological explanation to discount their claim to greater primacy than Protestant Christians.

And yet despite Jews' resemblance and dangerously close proximity to Christians, Jewish difference, and Jessica's in particular, is continually reasserted throughout the play. She is a stranger at Belmont according to Portia's description. The antisemitic taunts rehearsed by Launcelot and recirculated by Lorenzo and others occasionally settle on invisible sites of ineradicable difference — such as the inner recesses of her blood or paternal lineage — as the source of her inherited inferiority. In the absence of visible, empirical forms of difference, however, Jewish difference relies increasingly on forensic modes of differentiation and racialization that have significant performative dimensions. The legacy of those attempts is well represented in the history of spectacular public shamings of Jewish rabbinical authorities that took place in staged theological disputations between Christians and Jews intended to reenact Christian supersessionism in medieval Europe.

♦♦♦

Shame in an early modern European context constituted a powerful technology for marking and situating Jewish bodies imagined to be amenable to whitening, as Jessica's clearly is. Particularly for bodies that were read as racially indeterminate and hence mobile, affective modes of discipline like shaming ensured that any potential for mobility and success remained strictly limited. The processes that attend blushing are both inherently theatrical in their optics and deeply forensic in subject-

37. Janet Adelman, *Blood Relations: Christian and Jew in* The Merchant of Venice (Chicago: University of Chicago Press, 2008).

ing vulnerably positioned individuals to interrogation. Women's bodies were particularly apt to be identified this way and positioned as objects of intensive moral scrutiny.[38] Part of the underlying logic of that kind of marking involved their identification as sufficiently pale and blank enough to bear the imprint of normative Christian dominance, able to be inscribed with male meaning, and circulated within an economy where marks of shame signal not only moral, but also ethno-racial and religious availability, even malleability.[39]

Shame manages to firmly fix its subjects within the crosshairs of an authoritative, evaluative gaze, in ways that also reflect powerful patriarchal dominance. When Lorenzo engages in an extended discourse with Jessica on the civilizing powers of music in Act 5, Scene 1, he insists that there is a hidden structure to the universe that underscores all things, visible in the night's sky when the "floor of heaven / Is thick inlaid with pattens of bright gold" (58–59). Despite the heavenly music's inaudibility to those with preoccupied and "attentive spirits" like Jessica's, Lorenzo insists that its harmonies will eventually pacify the "wild and wanton" strains of Jessica's rebellious nature (71). Lorenzo's lesson is intended to apply not only to Jessica uniquely, but also to the entire ethno-religious group for which she stands, rendered in the speech's pluralized animal imagery featuring not just a single wild horse, but an entire "herd, / Or race, of youthful and unhandled colts" (72). In theological terms, Lorenzo forecasts the conversion of the Jews and their submission to a universalizing Christianity whose harmonies remain inaudible to Jewish ears so long as Jews remain unredeemed by conversion. Unconverted Jews remain stuck in the "muddy vesture of decay" (64–65) of intransigence and literal-mindedness that forms the core of a set of antisemitic Christ-

38. On this point, see Derek Dunne, "Blushing on Cue: The Forensics of the Blush in Early Modern Drama," *Shakespeare Bulletin* 34, no. 2 (2016): 233–52.

39. Kim F. Hall, *Things of Darkness: Economies of Race and Gender in Early Modern England* (Ithaca, NY: Cornell University Press, 1995), 87, has argued that an emerging complexional whiteness in Renaissance England marked women's availability to be commodified within a patriarchal social order. Shame's potential to determine a body's worth also represents a powerful way women's bodies could be inscribed with racial meaning and value in a Renaissance context.

ian theological tropes that resonate throughout the play. Lorenzo's insistence that his young colt's "savage eyes" can be "turned to a modest gaze" (78) manages to emphasize not only Jewish theological submission, but also the gendered domestications that attend Christian marriage, which Jessica repeatedly conflates with her longed-for conversion. The natural energies and vigor that characterize the herd of young colts will become subjugated by the inaudible but diffuse tempos that structure the world that Jessica longs to enter, on whose threshold she stands perched in this scene as the couple awaits entry to Portia's home in Belmont. Those tempos promise to keep Jessica firmly fixed in her designated place, even where her contrarian opposition – "I am never merry when I hear sweet music" (69) – suggests that its sounds may remain forever inaccessible to her, its rhythms perpetually elusive.

Unlike the proselytizing Christianity that promises to erase all difference as it enfolds exogamous "others" into its universal truths, Jessica's spirit is here positioned as still virile and not particularly amenable to Lorenzo's instructive lesson. The rhythms of domestication are juxtaposed against bucking images of potent rebellion, which are only ever temporarily mollified into submission within the terms of Lorenzo's lesson. His speech forecasts a young Jewish woman and her Christian husband within a union replete with ongoing tension and unresolved distinctions between the two lovers. At the outset, Lorenzo lays out the gleaming allure of celestial imagery to draw Jessica into a more compliant acceptance of her assigned place. But his speech soon evolves into an object-lesson in the soothing capacities of diffuse but universal harmonies that promise to pacify even the quickest of spirits. His speech then shifts again, switching out the carrot of gilded and beautiful skies for the stick of enforced discipline and threats of reprisal. Lorenzo concludes with a warning:

> The man that hath no music in himself,
> Nor is not moved with concord of sweet sounds,
> Is fit for treasons, stratagems, and spoils;
> The motions of his spirit are dull as night
> And his affections dark as Erebus.
> Let no such man be trusted. Mark the music. (83–88)

Lorenzo articulates a promise that reads as indistinguishable from a threat: the rhythms that govern his world are not only aspirational markers, but also forms of discipline to be marked. Through affective processes like shame, the bodies of Jewish female "others" are positioned submissively, able to be marked by normative Christian imperatives. But Lorenzo's speech suggests that they also resist being completely overwritten, even as they remain perpetually out-of-tune with the overarching beat of the Christian world they inhabit. Because of the ongoing problem of their perpetual dissonance, they risk sliding into alignment with the villainized "dark affections" and complexions that the play relegates beyond the pale of social acceptability and membership. In having to be told to "mark the music" that she cannot fully hear, Jessica is positioned for ongoing surveillance that is also a form of subjugation.

The logic of early modern Jewish racialization centers not on stable physiological differences observed in Jewish bodies, but rather on forms of affective currency that subject those bodies, and particularly women, to forensic modes of scrutiny. Affective experiences like shame have proven remarkably successful at generating and policing the boundaries of ethno-racial belonging, even in the absence of clearly identifiable signs of Jewish difference. The sense that Jews do not quite fit in because they are unable to fully grasp the subtle contours of things like English irony, as former Labour Party leader Jeremy Corbin insisted in 2003,[40] turns Jewish difference into something that is simultaneously harder to identify than visible physical marks like dark skin; and much harder to pin down because of its diffuseness and elusive contours. The perceived invisibility of Jewish difference, at least of the kind assigned to certain white-presenting, Ashkenazi Jews, also helps account for shifting perceptions about Jews' relationship to racial whiteness over time, and to the tendency for Jews' position relative to normative racial categories to shift quickly and sharply, as has been the case within just the last century. In moving away

40. This episode is drawn from one of Jeremy Corbyn's remarks that was recorded on video. There are multiple news outlets that aired them, including https://www.theguardian.com/politics/2018/aug/24/corbyn-english-irony-video-reignites-antisemitism-row-labour

from the body as a primary locus for Jewish difference, it becomes clearer that Jews as a group are particularly prone to such revisions, which often results in unique forms of isolation, as it does for Jessica, even where it promises to afford opportunities for mobility that are denied to those with more visible forms of racial otherness.

6. Navigating a Kiss in the Racialized Geopolitical Landscape of Thomas Heywood's *The Fair Maid of the West*

KIRSTEN N. MENDOZA

> Gold and Jewels she had great quantity, with a house richly furnished after the Indian fashion. For this consideration, I perswaded myself to marry her; and with several arguments alleaged, I gained so much conquest over myself that I could kiss her without disgorging myself: and by accustoming my self to her company, methought I began to take some delight in it.
>
> – Richard Head, *The English Rogue* (1665)[1]

As a central element of early modern popular culture, English commercial theater is a productive locus for analyzing the shifting contours and frictions of erotic meaning-making in a global early modernity. When characters onstage respond to a caress with praise or reprimand, or when they voice their attraction, disgust, excitement, pride, or shame, they give early modern playgoers a way to make sense of their emotional reactions and to navigate their affective registers. As Sara Ahmed cogently explains, what attracts and repels us shapes how we orientate ourselves.[2] Emotions encourage us to respond, to move toward or away, to cohere or to reject. The *Oxford English Dictionary* defines orientate, the intransitive verb, as "to turn or face towards a specified direction."[3] However, orientation is not limited to the physical positioning of the body; it also applies to the

1. Richard Head, *The English Rogue: described in the life of Meriton Latroon, a witty extravagant, being a compleat history of the most eminent cheats of both sexes* (London: Printed for Henry Marsh, 1665), 460.
2. Sara Ahmed, *Queer Phenomenology: Orientations, Objects, Others* (Durham, NC: Duke University Press, 2006).
3. OED *Online*, s.v., "orientate," v. 1.

process of opening oneself toward particular aspirations, values, and ideologies while shifting away from others. The decisions we make, the goals we set for ourselves, and the actions we perform all derive from an accretion of previous orientations. "The history of bodies," Ahmed writes, "can be rewritten as the history of the reachable," and "what is reachable is determined precisely by orientations that we have already taken."[4] If history results from the accretion of orientations — of turnings toward, away, askew, and back again — then even the most seemingly insignificant or fleeting of affective responses contribute in some way to what will be. Attention to the history of race-making, therefore, is incomplete without a study of the role emotions have played in helping to differentiate and essentialize human beings. These modes of differentiation, I argue, enable the accumulation of power and privilege for some while rendering others threatening, base, and necessarily vulnerable. While affect in the singular is malleable and protean, affect en masse shapes human connections and, thereby, the racist history that continues throughout our present. This chapter focuses on early modern theater's participation in the accumulation of orientations toward an English identification with desirable whiteness.

Through the iconic character of Bess Bridges, Thomas Heywood's *The Fair Maid of the West* Part I (ca. 1597–1603) twins an English nationalism with the representation of white femininity.[5] And, it is precisely in the site of Bess kissing and being kissed that the play manifests the power of emotions to demarcate dimensions of race. Transgressive and proper, diplomatic and sexual, the playful and dangerous ambiguity of a kiss lends itself as the perfect vehicle to explore the excitement and anxieties attached to England's desire for commerce in an increasingly global marketplace. A caress requires both power and vulnerability since one must be within reach to gain access to the body of another. While the play, unsurprisingly, highlights Bess's fair complexion to symbolize the moral superiority of the English as well as the threat of racial contamination, I argue that it also

4. Ahmed, *Queer Phenomenology*, 55.

5. All quotations are from Thomas Heywood, *The Fair Maid of the West*, Parts I and II, ed. Robert K. Turner, Jr. (Lincoln: University of Nebraska Press, 1967).

charges whiteness with affective value that was central to Bess's success as an entrepreneur. In other words, Heywood's play provides a particularly incisive example of how the accretion of emotional responses – from the overtly dramatic to the trivial and innocuous – orientates audiences toward whiteness as the prerogative of the English and as a coveted tool for mercantile, colonial, and cultural domination.

From humble beginnings as a tanner's daughter and tavern maid, the savvy Bess Bridges rises as an entrepreneur and becomes a cross-dressing privateer, traversing hostile seas from English ports to the Azores and eventually to the Moroccan coast. Through her circulation abroad, fair Bess accrues global prestige and is eventually hailed by her fellow Englishmen, her Spanish captives, and even the King of Fez as a paragon of beauty and virtue. As she gains more followers and international fame, Bess also amasses gold for herself and for her countrymen. Therefore, the play entwines the construction of Bess's whiteness as an emblem of constancy and beauty with her lucrative circulation in a global economy.

Bess's reputation among Englishmen depends on her geographic placement. While in England, her virtue is rendered suspect because of her attractiveness and occupation as a tapstress, which makes her body accessible and in circulation among men. Discourses of propriety are employed to assess and police her chastity. Before audiences first see Bess onstage, they learn about her from several male characters, who either assert their opinion that she is honest or insist on the seeming incompatibility of chastity with a tavern worker who is both desirable and vocal about her desires. When her beloved Spencer enters the Plymouth tavern and calls for her, he learns that she is above "with three or four gentlemen" (1.2.32). Although her occupation makes inevitable the company of several men at once, the indefinite number of male patrons she serves titillates audiences with the thought of what may be occurring offstage. Later, Spencer attempts to convey his trust in Bess's virtue to the disbeliever Goodlack with this account:

> I have proved her
> Unto the utmost test, examin'd her
> Even to a modest force, but all in vain.
> She'll laugh, confer, keep company, discourse,

And something more, kiss; but beyond that compass
She no way can be drawn. (1.2.58–62)

When Spencer seduces Bess, he tests her virtue by judging her forms of reciprocity. Despite applying the Ovidian precept "force is pleasing to girls," Spenser reports that Bess remained virtuous and could not be moved to engage with any other sexual act beyond that of a kiss.[6] As subject and agent, Bess's sexual will is highlighted in Spencer's account. He details the various forms of verbal and physical relations — all inflected with sexual meanings — into which Bess willingly entered. Early modern perceptions of women's laughter often mirrored that of unruly speech. As Joy Wiltenburg underscores, "the word "giggle," referring to foolish laughter, already had gendered associations in the sixteenth century."[7] Risibility in women was frowned upon by social commentators who viewed the propensity to laugh as a sign of frivolity, lack of self-control, vulgarity, and even sexual laxity. Laughter, as Gail Kern Paster has written, was understood by the early moderns to make the body potentially out of one's voluntary control, leading to an experience of bodily shame.[8] In a 1683 manual on the art of polite conversation, the writer warns: "to laugh as women do sometimes, with their hands on both sides, and with a lascivious agitation of their whole body, is the height of indecency and immodesty."[9] Despite these invectives, which "give a rather solemn impression of human relationships," Bernard Capp urges scholars today to "remember that people … [found] time for laughter and fun."[10] Thus, Spencer's descriptions of Bess portray a maid who straddles innocence and wanton-

6. Cynthia E. Garrett, "Sexual Consent and the Art of Love in the Early Modern English Lyric," *Studies in English Literature, 1500–1900* 44, no. 1 (2004): 37–58, highlights the conflation of seduction and rape in the Renaissance lyric.
7. Joy Wiltenburg, "Soundings of Laughter in Early Modern England: Women, Men, and Everyday Uses of Humor," *Early Modern Women* 10, no. 2 (2016): 26.
8. Gail Kern Paster, *The Body Embarrassed: Drama and the Disciplines of Shame in Early Modern England* (Ithaca, NY: Cornell University Press, 1993), 123.
9. Qtd. in Bernard Capp, *When Gossips Meet: Women, Family, and Neighbourhood in Early Modern England* (Oxford: Oxford University Press, 2003), 4.
10. Capp, *When Gossips Meet*, 140.

ness, inviting audiences to imagine her conversation as agreeable and also too light, indicative of sexual indecency.

In this trial of Bess's virtue, distinctions between courtship and seduction collapse. Spencer ostensibly views Bess as marriageable because she is accommodating, but not so accommodating as to be classified as a whore. However, like her engagements with Spencer listed above that code as both good-natured affability and immodesty, Spencer's repeated assertions of his faith in Bess's honesty, in fact, work to undermine his claims. The conclusive test Spencer administers unsettles the very outcome it proves, troubling the distinction between chaste will and savvy performance. As Laura Gowing writes, "[t]he attempt to distinguish between whore and wife, between 'kindness' and whorishness, as so often, becomes impossible."[11] Bess's kiss, in particular, at once serves as the hinge exemplifying her virtue and the precise act that undoes it. When Bess kisses, does she receive them in return? Are they mutually enacted? Furthermore, do her lips touch Spencer's cheek, his mouth, or another part of his body? As these questions reveal, in the imagination of playgoers, the innocent meaning of a kiss — a form of affection, a touch of the lips — could just as easily flirt with the pornographic. Ultimately, the inevitable restrictions of such misogynistic tests that attempt to diagnose women's inner virtue through their outward signs can only prove that Bess is chaste with Spencer — that she withholds from performing other acts with *him*. When Bess caresses an Englishman, her sexual act engenders discomfort since it simultaneously codes as virtuous *and* incriminating.[12]

The playful ambiguity of a kiss, then, always bears some risk due to the manifold interpretations of and responses to the performance of a caress. Audiences not only hear about the kiss Bess bestows on her beloved, but

11. Laura Gowing, *Common Bodies: Women, Touch and Power in Seventeenth-Century England* (New Haven, CT: Yale University Press, 2003), 104.
12. For more on how Bess's economic independence and financial savviness confuse Englishmen in Foy, requiring Bess to reeducate these men, see Jennifer Higginbotham, *Girlhood of Shakespeare's Sisters: Gender, Transgression, Adolescence* (Edinburgh: Edinburgh University Press, 2013), 20–61.

they also witness these acts in Part I, albeit not with Spencer himself. When Goodlack returns to Foy, he bears the news of Spencer's death and final requests. Should Goodlack find Bess free of scandal, she will receive five hundred pounds per year as dictated in Spencer's will. But, should she be of ill repute, branded "amongst the loose and lewd" (2.2.95), Goodlack must take away Spencer's picture from the "whore" and for his faithfulness will receive Spencer's legacy in her stead. With the incentive to unmake Bess to make himself, Goodlack slanders the heroine and threatens to take away Spencer's portrait. Speaking to the image, Bess cries: "Oh thou, the perfect semblance of my love / And all that's left of him, take one sweet kiss / As my last farewell" (3.4.43–45). Playgoers get a taste of the "[t]wenty thousand kisses" (3.4.4) Bess claims to have given to the idol of her affection. Through Goodlack, who is converted to one of her followers, the play seems to treat this scene with pathos.

As a woman grieving her lover's recent death, the audience may be inclined to view her touching kiss as a demonstration of earnest devotion to the memory of the man she has lost. At the same time, however, her kiss — with its religious worship of an image — may also raise ambivalent responses due to the idolatrous Catholic undertones of the scene.[13] Prior to Bess's overseas circulation, the play uses discourses of propriety to load a kiss with meaning by troubling the protagonist's reputation as a chaste maid. While in England, it is Bess who elicits an assortment of emotions, including sexual arousal, distrust, and even the ire and disgust of Spencer when he imagines her potential promiscuity. Although Bess eventually converts all those who doubt her virtue into believers, she is nonetheless forced to prove her chastity and defend the boundaries of her body. The narrated and staged kisses set in her domestic homeland incite the sexualization of Bess, open her to the ridicule and denigration of men, and turn her agency into a potential threat to her male counterparts.

13. Elizabeth Williamson, *The Materiality of Religion in Early Modern English Drama* (Burlington, VT: Ashgate, 2009), 134, argues that the kissing of portraits — even when portraits were not of religious icons — would have been perceived by English Protestants as a gesture steeped in Catholic Idolatry.

This vexed ambiguity of a kiss continues throughout the play, but the parameters by which emotions are policed alter as the potential threat is displaced from Bess to Mullisheg, King of Fez. Audiences are made to wait until Bess travels to Northern Africa before they see her kiss a man and enjoy a reunion with her beloved Spencer. The man she kisses twice onstage, however, is not her fellow Englishman but the newly established King of Fez and of Morocco. After having arisen victorious from a lengthy war, Mullisheg announces the three pillars that will guide his reign: the safety of his kingdom; the enrichment of the public treasury; and pleasure. In fact, his first order forces Christian merchants who had previously enjoyed freedom of trade to surrender their "ship and goods" since they had "conceal[ed] / The least part of our custom due to us" (4.3.17–19). While these forfeitures may initially seem like just penalties for Christian swindlers, Mullisheg explains that this additional revenue will be put toward his depleted treasury. Thus, as the king regains the wealth that had been lost in the establishment of his reign on the backs of entrepreneurial Christians, just retribution codes as savvy opportunism.

The play sexualizes Mullisheg through the character's carnal language that mirrors an insatiable appetite already whetted for Christian goods. Mullisheg boasts that he has "tasted" the profits of laws that target Christian merchants (4.3.24), and, when he instructs Alcade to bring him a variety of concubines, the first he names are the "fairest Christian damsels" (4.3.29). Stereotypical of racist English early modern discourses of Moors, Turks, and Africans, commercial and sexual predation conflate in the play's introduction of the King of Fez, who is depicted as driven by overwhelming desire and innate lasciviousness.[14] For Mullisheg, the attainment of pleasure serves as the mark of a king (4.3.27-8). This introduction to the King of Fez orientates audiences to view him as a conniving com-

14. See, for example, Ania Loomba, *Gender, Race, Renaissance Drama* (Manchester: Manchester University Press, 1989); Nabil Matar, *Turks, Moors, and Englishmen in the Age of Discovery* (New York: Columbia University Press, 1999); Virginia Mason Vaughan, *Performing Blackness on English Stages, 1500–1800* (Cambridge: Cambridge University Press, 2005); Arthur L. Little Jr., *Shakespeare Jungle Fever: National-Imperial Re-Visions of Race, Rape, and Sacrifice* (Stanford, CA: Stanford University Press, 2000).

mercial competitor and sexual threat to Christian Europeans. Ahmed theorizes orientation as the movement toward that to which one aspires because one understands "identity as the mark of attainment."[15] This points, then, not simply to the development of a commercial rivalry but, more importantly, to a perpetual and racialized state of war since it is only through subduing the constructed other that Mullisheg and Christian merchants are able to attain the identities they desire.[16]

In the previous acts of the play, we witness how misogyny sexualizes Bess and initially leads English characters to doubt her self-identification as a chaste and constant woman. However, this dynamic crucially changes along with the geopolitical setting of the play. In the Azores and later Morocco, duplicity does not receive censure, but rather praise. Duplicity is coded as the savviness necessary of entrepreneurs. Furthermore, as Jane Hwang Degenhardt insightfully reveals, Bess's targeted plunder of Spanish ships and subsequent demonstration of compassion toward her captives are presented in the play as cosmic retributions against the Spanish whose greed for gold led to the slaughter of Amerindians in the Americas.[17] The representation of Bess's unassailable virginity and her staged acts of mercy perform affective labor that "purifies the pursuit of gold by merging its material accumulation with an economy of moral

15. Ahmed, *Queer Phenomenology*, 56.

16. Although Europeans were not the only Christians in the sixteenth century early modern world, nor was Europe comprised solely of Christians, Alcade's justification of the seizure of goods from "Christians that reap profit by *our* land" (4.3.25 emphasis added) forges religion as the primary distinction between their territories in Northern Africa and foreign, presumably Christian European, agents. Furthermore, while the play mentions the duplicity of Christian merchants who have cheated Mullisheg of customs that were owed, what this scene reveals is a competitive commercial market in which both the King of Fez and the merchants aspire to "make" themselves through mutual exploitation. See Richard Wilson, "Visible Bullets: Tamburlaine the Great and Ivan the Terrible," *English Literary History* 62, no. 1 (1995): 57.

17. For more on Bess's affective labor that aligns the successful enlargement of English wealth with intrinsic goodness and moral value, see Jane Hwang Degenhardt, "Gold Digger or Golden Girl?: Purifying the Pursuit of Gold in Heywood's *Fair Maid of the West, Part I*," in *Historical Affects and the Early Modern Theater*, ed. Ronda Arab, Michelle M. Dowd, and Adam Zucker (London: Routledge, 2015), 152–65.

value."[18] I wish to emphasize that the symbolism attached to Bess's fair complexion magnifies the perceived moral divide between the constructions of the valiant, honorable English and the cruel Spanish, from which the Black Legend derives. But, the affective function of white womanhood in Heywood's play does not end with infusing a sense of national pride in English audiences to obscure the dissolute activities that necessarily attend mercantile and colonial pursuits. It also primes playgoers to consider what English whiteness can mean to imperial rivals, as well as to potential commercial allies.

As the play transfigures piracy into an act of merit, it also presents Bess's exploitation of a Muslim Moroccan ruler as the moral prerogative of a fair Christian woman. As Kim F. Hall has argued, the iconography surrounding Bess's namesake — Queen Elizabeth I — constructed the image of an inviolable English superiority tied to whiteness.[19] To an English audience, then, when the King of Fez seeks the fairest of Christian women, the play reveals whiteness to be a rare and exoticized commodity and, in so doing, extols the attribute of whiteness with which the English identified themselves. Although beautiful women come in all types, Mullisheg's emphasis on his desire for the fairest of Christian women prepares audiences to view Bess's flirtation with the King of Fez as shrewd rather than indecent — her manipulation is righteous, rather than obscene. As portrayed in the movement of a kiss, Mullisheg's desire for a fair English lass renders him vulnerable. After all, he consensually and wholeheartedly capitulates to Bess's will. Thus, the play explicitly shows the benefits of yoking an English identity to whiteness in a racialized world that hierarchizes complexion based on the ideological superiority of fair beauty. Bess is an export that Mullisheg seeks to acquire, and he submits to the English of his own volition. It is in this way that whiteness is wielded as a construct that justifies domination and serves as an ideological tool for success in commercial, colonial, and imperial pursuits.

18. Degenhardt, "Gold Digger or Golden Girl?," 152.

19. Kim F. Hall, "'These Bastard Signs of Fair': Literary Whiteness in Shakespeare's Sonnets," in *Post-Colonial Shakespeares*, ed. Ania Loomba and Martin Orkin (London: Routledge, 1998), 64–83.

Bess's virginal white body yields an affective power, enabling an English commoner to dominate a reigning monarch. When Bess states that it is no "shame for Bess to kiss a king" (5.1.66), she strategically highlights Mullisheg's regal status and effaces the king's racial and religious otherness by omitting his name as well as that of his kingdom. Significantly, Bess's volition is couched in terms of propriety through which she reinscribes the significance of Mullisheg's request by reverting to the acceptable and innocent English custom. Bess's defense of propriety also highlights her agency. While Mullisheg is made to ask for her favor, the fair English woman is the one who acts. Furthermore, she defines for Mullisheg, the Moroccan court, her fellow Englishmen, and for early modern audiences, her terms of representation.

The play cultivates the superiority of fair beauty through Mullisheg's perception of Bess as his means to access godliness. When the King of Fez inquiries about the customs in England, it is Goodlack who first prompts Mullisheg and Bess to kiss as a form of salutation:

> *Goodlack*: Our first greeting
> Begins still on the lips.
> *Mullisheg*: Fair creature, shall I be immortaliz'd
> With that high favor?
> *Bess*: 'Tis no Immodest thing
> You ask, nor shame for Bess to kiss a king. (5.1.61–66)

Significantly, it is Mullisheg, a king, who proclaims that he is deified through receiving a kiss from a commoner and not the reverse. While there are different kinds of kisses — ranging from the platonic and familial to the romantic and erotic — it is evident that this first caress between Mullisheg and Bess occupies several registers at once. In this exchange, Mullisheg asks for Bess's consent to the act that he perceives as more than a diplomatic or mundane greeting and, thereby, heightens the potential eroticism of the kiss. This register is confirmed when Mullisheg proclaims that the "kiss hath all [his] vitals ecstasied" (5.1.67).[20] While the scene positions audiences to view whiteness as transcendent, Mullisheg's experience of bodily ecstasy grounds him in the corporeal and carnal, thus reifying the perception of Black desire as corruptive and tied to the flesh.

The cultivation of an ideology that hinges upon the dual transcendence and desirability of an English whiteness attempts to assuage the anxieties attached to intercourse with strangers, while simultaneously proffering whiteness as a tool that can be strategically deployed for the commercial interests of the commonwealth. Despite Goodlack's introduction that presents the kiss as an inconsequential greeting, he is well aware of Mullisheg's sexual interest in Bess. When Bess unveils herself before the king, one of Mullisheg's first responses is to give Goodlack gold for bringing the English virgin to his court. After observing Mullisheg's love for Bess, Roughman opportunistically states with a hint of resignation: "Well, let her / Do as she list, I'll make use of his bounty" (5.1.69–70), a statement with which Goodlack heartily agrees. Jean E. Howard persuasively argues that Bess's initiatives with Mullisheg "invites being read as the sexual wanton Spencer and others earlier expected her to be."[21] The willingness of the Englishmen to condone Bess's flirtatious commerce with Mullisheg resonates with global early modern politics — specifically, Elizabeth I's diplomatic exchanges with Morocco. Elizabeth sent the London merchant Edmund Hogan and agent John de Cardenas to promote commercial and economic ties in Morocco designed to help the English reach their aspi-

20. Daniel Vitkus, *Turning Turk: English Theater and the Multicultural Mediterranean, 1570–1630* (New York: Palgrave Macmillan, 2003), 107–63, describes how the kisses shared between Bess and Mullisheg embody the fears, worries, and tensions surrounding the possibility of too much cross-cultural exchange leading to a Christian "turning-Turk."

21. Jean E. Howard, "An English Lass Amid the Moors: Gender, Race, Sexuality, and National Identity in Heywood's *The Fair Maid of the West*," in *Women, "Race," and Writing in the Early Modern Period*, ed. Margo Hendricks and Patricia Parker (London: Routledge, 1994), 116. Howard further suggests that the anxieties arising from Bess's transgressive sexuality as a desirable and actively desiring woman is displaced onto the hypersexualized Moors, who are safely rendered effeminate and inferior to the English.

rations for international eminence.[22] Affective responses to scenes of miscegenation, like the unease expressed when Bess's countrymen observe her intercourse with Mullisheg, parallel English anxieties concerning the accumulation of wealth through — as Hall succinctly puts it — global "commercial interaction [that] inevitably foster[s] social and sexual contact."[23] Bess, like Elizabeth I, must engage in commerce and alliances with foreign powers, despite the dangers associated with cultural and sexual exchange, to pave the way for future English prosperity.

The kisses shared between Bess and Mullisheg are immediately policed and navigated in an attempt to define their meaning categorically as either diplomatic or sexualized, proper or improper, even though the boundaries of such classifications often blur. After all, the intention, effect, and reception of a caress do not always align perfectly. As with Bess's defense of the favor she bestows on the king, Roughman also underscores the Englishwoman's agency at Mullisheg's expense. I emphasize again that Mullisheg willingly submits to Bess's pleasure when he promises to load her boat with gold once she has tired of their "sunburnt clime" (5.2.36). His self-debasing description explains the existence of dark complexions as scars caused by sun exposure — deviations from unblemished, originary whiteness. Furthermore, like Roughman, Mullisheg highlights his subjection to the vagaries of Bess's pleasure. Anxieties surrounding Bess's sexual will, dominating the first acts of the play set in England, continue when her countrymen find themselves in Northern Africa. However, their disapproval and concerns regarding her sexual agency and the threat of miscegenation are bracketed by the material gains that the English stand to benefit from Bess's pleasure.

The seemingly minor negativity couched in Roughman's wary approval of Bess's intercourse with Mullisheg accumulates when placed in conver-

22. Jesús López-Peláez Casellas, "'What Good Newes from Barbary?': Nascent Capitalism, North-Africans and the Construction of English Identity in Thomas Heywood's Drama," *Atlantis* 29, no. 1 (2007):123–40; Gary K. Waite, "Reimagining Religious Identity: The Moor in Dutch and English Pamphlets, 1550-1620," *Renaissance Quarterly* 66, no. 4 (2013): 1264–6.

23. Kim F. Hall, "Guess Who's Coming to Dinner? Colonization and Miscegenation in *The Merchant of Venice*," *Renaissance Drama* 23 (1992): 88.

sation with more spiteful affective responses to one of her kisses. The king asks for a kiss from Bess to pardon a Christian preacher, which she quickly performs, stating: "Thus I pay't" (5.2.79). From a modest salutation, the kiss becomes currency for exchange. Rather than justify the act, Bess immediately engages in the transaction. While her noble cause – to save the life of a fellow Christian – likely removes the need for a defense of propriety, the payment does raise feelings of disgust from at least one observer. This second caress elicits the vulgar disapproval of her servant Clem, who complains: "Must your black face be smooching my mistress's white lips / with a Moorian? I would you had kiss'd her a – " (5.2.80–81).[24] Unlike the first kiss, which underscores Bess as an agent, Clem focuses on the Black visage that caresses Bess's fair mouth. Clem's response differs from his mistress's assertion that she paid the fee, which implies that Bess is the agent who acts rather than the object that receives. Clem's xenophobic remarks, in comparison, redundantly stress Mullisheg's racial difference and turns the king into the agent who pollutes and threatens white femininity. More fitting, Clem begins to state, would have been the king stooping to place his lips on Bess's derriere.

Rather than react to a king who condescends to a commoner, Clem's disgust unsurprisingly ignores the class differences between Mullisheg and Bess. Instead, he relies on racial, religious, and gender stereotypes, casting the fair Christian woman with the status of one in need of protection against dark non-Christian men. Although Part I shows Roughman being far more brazen in his attempts to assault Bess, Englishmen are provided with the opportunity to reform their ways, to be forgiven, and, most importantly, not to be classified as people with predatory sexuality. Dennis Austin Britton and Sujata Iyengar have each shown that the early moderns often interpreted an embodied darkness as indicative of the internal and, ultimately, unalterable state of a person's soul.[25] Imagining Bess, who

24. Turner glosses "Moorian" as "a play on 'murrain'; *with a murrain* = plague on it!" (*The Fair Maid of the West*, 87). This racial slur uses phonetic repetition to "stick" the association of Moors with disease, contagion, and death.

25. Dennis Austin Britton, *Becoming Christian: Race, Reformation, and Early Modern English Romance* (New York: Fordham University Press, 2014); Sujata Iyengar, *Shades of Dif-*

stands for England, to be defiled by granting a kiss to Mullisheg, a North African king, is a form of biopolitical racism because it normalizes the perception that certain populations are deserving of protected status and of forgiveness, while others are conceived as irredeemable threats to the state. In Part II, when Mullisheg reneges on his promise to respect Bess's will to be the wife of a Christian Englishman, the play reifies the belief in what Leerom Medovoi describes as an "*interior* raciality."[26] Mullisheg's perceived internal immutability from his original state of lust cultivates the understanding of Christian Europeans being perpetually at "war" with Muslim North Africans, even when bonds of commerce unite them.

I suggest that Clem's affect – disgust – may have served as a mouthpiece for some playgoers' responses to the sight of a fair woman's lips on an actor in blackface playing a North African man. And, while Heywood's play does provide space for such blatant and racist disapproval, it invalidates – to some extent – Clem's outburst. Unlike the other Englishmen who realize that the meanings of sexual acts and the anxieties they induce shift (for the benefit of the English) in another geopolitical landscape, Clem does not seem to understand the new codes that prevail in the erotic exchanges between Bess and Mullisheg. His lack of fluency extends to a general inability to grasp the interactions between the English and the Moroccans, which leads Clem to ask for the "honor" designed for Spencer, a request that results in the subsequent unintended loss of his "best jewels" (5.2.127).

Clem's folly, which brings about his castration, demonstrates a deficient understanding of how persons and things circulate in a global setting. Indeed, Clem and the Englishmen he serves share discomfort when witnessing a cross-racial kiss; but, while Clem may be too simple to understand the ways geopolitical specificities alter the meanings attached to

ference: Mythologies of Skin Color in Early Modern England (Philadelphia: University of Pennsylvania Press, 2005).

26. Leerom Medovoi, "Dogma-Line Racism: Islamophobia and the Second Axis of Race," *Social Text* 30, no. 2 (2012): 66 original emphasis. Medovoi argues that "religion gradually came to model the calculation of ideological dispositions, the *interior* raciality of populations" (66 original emphasis).

Bess's interactions, the more powerful and worldly of Englishmen compartmentalize their reservations through politic tact in service of their commercial interests.[27] The castration of xenophobic Clem serves as both punishment and proof of his inability to negotiate the different kinds of honor and propriety that result from Anglo-Moroccan alliances and the circulation of Englishmen and women abroad.[28] However, it is important to underscore that Clem's negative reaction magnifies the slight disfavor uttered previously by Roughman. When these staged affective responses accumulate, what "sticks" — to use Ahmed's term — is discomfort in response to erotic exchanges between a white woman and a Black man.[29] It is precisely through these nuanced, individual, and seemingly ephemeral affective responses that the play validates xenophobic feelings in the process of cultivating racism. The mundane and quotidian, like expressions of slight displeasure, move audiences to perceive Bess's caress as necessary but not ideal, a negative that is further accentuated by Clem's racist outburst. The play, therefore, performs the work of cultivating everyday feelings that, as Sharon Patricia Holland explains, "circumscribe [desire's] possible attachments" and "articulates and keeps the

27. None of Clem's fellow Englishmen nor his mistress (who earlier in the play protected him from abuse) intervene to prevent his castration. The nationalist ethos of Heywood's play that consolidates through racial discourses splinters along the lines of gender and class, marked by the irrevocable lack that also codes as both racial otherness and religious apostasy.
28. Joshua Mabie, "The Problem of the Prodigal in *The Fair Maid of the West*, *A Christian Turned Turk*, and *The Renegado*," *Renascence* 64, no. 4 (2012): 299–319, interrogates the anxieties surrounding apostasy in Part II of Heywood's two-part play, stating that Clem's castration "remains throughout the play not only fodder for bawdy jokes but also a source of general awkwardness" (303). Clem's inability to judge honor and propriety in the Moroccan court leads to ostracization from his countrymen made absolute through an irreversible mark.
29. Sara Ahmed, "Affective Economies," *Social Text* 22, no. 2 (2004): 117–39, theorizes how emotions become attached to particular signs through circulation. The movement between signs throughout history enables a collective coherence in which certain affects "stick" and become the attributes of others.

flawed logic of race in its place."[30] Thus, although *The Fair Maid of the West* ostensibly invalidates Clem's outburst (since the most xenophobic reaction comes from a foolish lower-class individual who eventually suffers castration), Heywood's popular drama nonetheless affirms racist reaction as an uncouth, visceral, and — therefore — innately English response.

The racist demarcations constructed through the feelings of characters are affirmed at the conclusion of the play when Bess is proclaimed by all her followers, Spencer, and even Mullisheg, as a beauteous maid whose constancy is deserving not of concubinage to a powerful monarch, but of the ultimate prize of marriage with her fellow Englishman.[31] The union of Bess and Spencer conforms to nationalist and religious bias while reconciling the exogamic "niceties" she shares with Mullisheg. By the end of Part I, Bess succeeds at converting all men to her followers, including (momentarily) Mullisheg, whose esteem for Bess is then extended to Spencer as well. Spencer uses this leverage to request a favor concerning an English merchant who had surrendered his "ship for goods uncustom'd" (5.2.143). Before Spencer even finishes his suit, Mullisheg magnanimously grants Spencer the opportunity to do what he wishes with the forfeitures, which implies that those goods will be returned to Spencer's countryman. In other words, Spencer gets Bess as well as the ability to decide the fate of his fellow Englishman's goods; Mullisheg does not even care to demand the bare minimum — the customs rightly due to the treasury of Morocco. Although Mullisheg began his reign with

30. Sharon Patricia Holland, *The Erotic Life of Racism* (Durham, NC: Duke University Press, 2012), 43, 6. Holland contends that our erotic lives cannot be uncoupled from racism and the racist practices that limit erotic desire.

31. Access to marriage and to the rights attached to that union serve as signs of racial difference. The ideals of white femininity coincide with the legitimating and protected status of lawful wife. See Lynda E. Boose, "'The Getting of a Lawful Race': Racial Discourse in Early Modern England and the Unrepresentable Black Woman," in *Women, "Race," and Writing in the Early Modern Period*, ed. Margo Hendricks and Patricia Parker (London: Routledge, 1994), 35–54. In the Antebellum South, the denial of marriage rights to the enslaved increased a white slaveholder's control of the reproductive bodies of Black women. See Dorothy E. Roberts, *Killing the Black Body: Race, Reproduction, and the Meaning of Liberty* (New York: Vintage, 1997).

a proclamation that he will endeavor to increase his treasury through Christian swindlers and will acquire sexual pleasure from the bodies of fair Christian women, by the conclusion of the first part of the play, he willingly relinquishes both.

Critics have pointed to Mullisheg's benevolence as evidence exemplifying Bess's virtuous power that can dominate even the most stereotypically lust-driven character types in English drama, a conversion that proves ephemeral in the King of Fez who reverts to the racist trope of the lascivious Moor at the start of Part II.[32] I emphasize that Bess's influence over Mullisheg goes beyond momentarily stifling the king's purported inordinate appetite for wealth and sexual gratification. The conclusion of Part I that has Mullisheg renege on the customs owed by the English merchant portrays the North African king completely enthralled by the affective power of white femininity. This state of volitional submission leads Mullisheg to capitulate fully to the commercial desires of the English, who reap the benefits of trade without paying taxes.[33] By aligning Bess's handling of Mullisheg with favorable outcomes for the English, *The Fair Maid of the West* makes legible the centrality of white womanhood in a racialized proto-capitalist landscape to enable exploitation without violence and consensual submission without coercion.

To highlight further Bess's superiority, the play has Mullisheg proclaim the Englishwoman to be "a girl worth gold" (5.2.153).[34] Gold, a precious metal that symbolized royalty and divinity in the early modern period, was deeply enmeshed in the commercial significance of Africa to fif-

32. See Anthony Gerard Barthelemy, *Black Face, Maligned Race: The Representation of Blacks in English Drama from Shakespeare to Southerne* (Baton Rouge: Louisiana State University Press, 1987), 165.
33. Heywood participates in orientating audiences toward what Jane Hwang Degenhardt describes as a fantasy of "effortless commerce" and "the ability to attain a foreign commodity while bypassing the means of production and contingencies of exchange" ("The Reformation, Inter-Imperial World History, and Marlowe's *Doctor Faustus*," PMLA 130, no. 2 [2015]: 402–403).
34. Degenhardt insightfully reveals that Bess's unassailable virginity represented an intrinsic value of gold, which addressed English concerns about "the loss of English bullion through London trade" ("Gold Digger or Golden Girl?," 158).

teenth- and sixteenth-century Europeans. Rather than go through well-established North African Muslim merchants, Europeans sought means to establish their own direct trade with regions of high gold production located south of the Sahara.[35] However, gold was not the only African commodity to which the English desired direct access. Bess names her ship *The Negro*, which in turn gives rise to several interpretations. The Englishmen fear that it bodes ill for their ventures while Mullisheg muses that perhaps it is a sign that she will "bosom with a Moor" (5.1.9). However, Bess professes that there is yet another meaning, a conceit, for the name she gives to the ship. While black represents a state of mourning, which expresses her own feelings of loss when she mistakenly learns of Spencer's death, Anthony Gerard Barthelemy rightly points out that just as her "ship is wholly owned and dominated by her and her men, so too must Mullisheg be dominated and controlled."[36] Thus, Bess's command that her ship be "pitch'd all o'er: no spot of white, / No color to be seen, no sail but black" (4.2.78–79) conforms to expectations of feminine constancy while also preparing playgoers to view her interactions with Mullisheg as her handling of him in a way that will allow a young English commoner to manipulate and control an African king.

The desirability of whiteness enables Bess to engage in a process of exploitation rather than commerce with Mullisheg who promises that "[her] *Negro* shall be ballast home with gold" (5.2.37). In this way, the play orientates audiences towards the superiority of whiteness and the ways it could be deployed to the advantage of the English in the traffic of wealth, goods, and bodies. Before Bess and her crew arrive in Northern Africa, they defeat the Spanish in a naval battle near the "fort ... call'd Fayal" (4.4.7) that previously "English Raleigh won and spoil'd" (4.4.31). These details suggest that their location is the Fort of Santa Cruz on the island of Faial in the archipelago of the Azores that was attacked and pillaged by Sir Walter Raleigh and his men, an act of plunder widely celebrated in England. Atlantic islands such as Faial were integral to the start of the transatlantic slave trade since they made southern exploration of Africa viable

35. See David Arnold, *The Age of Discovery, 1400–1600* (London: Routledge, 2002), 35.
36. Barthelemy, *Black Face, Maligned Race*, 165.

and provided the Portuguese with more direct routes for contact with African societies.[37] As Hall reminds, although Elizabeth officially espoused aggression toward the African trade, she surreptitiously sought means through her privateers like John Hawkins to undermine the Spanish and Portuguese monopoly, and it was "under Elizabeth that England gained a foothold in the Atlantic Trade."[38] The image of a fair woman at the helm surrounded by her fellow Englishmen in complete command of black objects – the ship, sail, and flags – symbolically parallels the growing desire for more involvement of the English in the trade of enslaved African people.

Through the imagery of a dominant fair Bess sailing south on her black ship, Heywood uses the representation of the white female body as a conduit to charge audiences with a sense of pride and excitement that turns the profit of privateering into a moral prerogative. These emotions, I contend, move playgoers to support more than just trade in gold. *The Fair Maid of the West* puts the idea of justified plunder within conceptual reach of the English and orientates audiences to aspire towards commercial eminence, which includes involvement in the kidnapping and rapine of Black men, women, and children. Through staging a kiss, Heywood reveals the role of affect in cultivating and habituating the logics of race-making, such as the fears of miscegenation and the transglobal longing for whiteness. Actions that may ignite censure, distrust, and disgust within Christian England become the anxiety-inducing but necessary work of the courageous, the resourceful, and the virtuous. In a global context and when applied to people who have been vilified, objectified, and subjugated, these actions mobilize the ideological dominance of whiteness. As a fair Englishwoman and privateer, Bess can kiss and be kissed. She can *be* promiscuously in the world without losing value but only through her

37. See Herbert S. Klein, *The Atlantic Slave Trade* (Cambridge: Cambridge University Press, 2010).
38. Kim F. Hall, *Things of Darkness: Economies of Race and Gender in Early Modern England* (Ithaca, NY: Cornell University Press, 1995), 20. See also Kenneth R. Andrews, *Elizabeth Privateering: English Privateering During the Spanish War, 1585–1603* (Cambridge: Cambridge University Press, 1964).

alignment with nationalist and economic ambitions upheld by the affective construction of a specifically white, Christian, and English superiority.[39]

39. I am grateful to *Carol Mejia LaPerle* for her attentive and generous feedback on this project and for her support of my work. Thanks also to Dennis Austin Britton for his guidance on an early draft of this piece.

7. Branded with Baseness: Bastardy and Race in *King Lear*

MARIO DIGANGI

In William Shakespeare's *King Lear*, bastardy functions as a nexus for the racializing mechanisms of lineage, sexuality, and gender. The racial implications of bastardy come to the fore through the experiences of Edgar and Edmond, each of whom soliloquizes about what it feels like to be dispossessed. As Benjamin Minor and Ayanna Thompson have shown, Edgar, a legitimately born first son and heir who is renounced by his father, consciously adopts blackface to exile himself from legitimate society as a rogue or gypsy. Signifying his alienation from kin, court, and nation, Edgar's disguise as Poor Tom functions as a "marker of radical racial difference."[1] Although Minor and Thompson acknowledge Edgar's illegitimate younger brother Edmond as "the obvious 'other' in *King Lear*," the racial implications of his bastard status have yet to be explored.[2]

1. Benjamin Minor and Ayanna Thompson, "'Edgar I Nothing Am': Blackface in *King Lear*," in *Staged Transgression in Shakespeare's England*, ed. Rory Loughnane and Edel Semple (New York: Palgrave McMillan, 2013), 153.
2. Minor and Thompson, "'Edgar I Nothing Am,'" 153. Studies of race in *King Lear* have mostly been confined to adaptation studies. See Frederick Luis Aldama, "Race, Cognition, and Emotion: Shakespeare on Film," *College Literature* 33, no. 1 (2006): 197–213; Sylvaine Bataille and Anaïs Pauchet, "Between Political Drama and Soap Opera: Appropriations of *King Lear* in US Television Series Boss and *Empire*," in *Shakespeare on Screen: King Lear*, ed. Victoria Bladen, Sarah Hatchuel, and Nathalie Vienne-Guerrin (Cambridge: Cambridge University Press, 2019), 202–18; Pierre Kapitaniak, "Negotiating Authorship, Genre and Race in *King of Texas* (2002)," in *Shakespeare on Screen: King Lear*, ed. Victoria Bladen, Sarah Hatchuel, and Nathalie Vienne-Guerrin (Cambridge: Cambridge University Press, 2019), 111–24; Baron Kelly, "Ira Aldridge: Prophet of Protest," in *Ira Aldridge, 1807–1867: The Great Shakespearean Tragedian on the Bicentennial Anniversary of His Birth*, ed. Krystyna Kujawińska Courtney and Maria Lukowska (New York: Peter Lang, 2009), 33–39. See also Martin R. Orkin, "Cruelty, *King Lear*, and the South African Land Act, 1913," *Shakespeare Survey* 40 (1988): 135–43. Urvashi

Because it is always already about social illegitimacy, sexual sin, and bodily impurity, bastardy puts into relief the intersecting racializing mechanisms of lineage, sexuality, and gender.[3] Advocating the need for a "materialist theory of politics or agency," Diana Coole and Samantha Frost attest to "the role played by the body as a visceral protagonist within political encounters."[4] Edmond's soliloquy, bristling with strong feelings that might be variously realized in performance — anger, resentment, outrage, puzzlement, disgust, vanity, humiliation, scorn, longing, aggression, exultation — puts his body into play as a "visceral protagonist" in a scheme to appropriate his legitimate brother's place. The fraught affects that attend the specters of social illegitimacy, sexual sin, and bodily impurity in the early modern imaginary give us access to how the mechanisms of racialized bastardy might *feel* to an early modern subject. Edmond's articulation of his affective experience as a bastard — as, in effect, a member of a denigrated race — mobilizes a host of contradictory feelings around kinship, sex, and gender as mechanisms of racial meaning. In his famous soliloquy, Edmond casts his older brother as a figure of racial illegitimacy, but this denigration is in part a response to Edmond's deeply felt apprehension and fraught affects of his own racially illegitimate status.

Delivering the first soliloquy of the play, Edmond seizes our attention with an impassioned account of his membership in the race of bastards:

Chakravarty, "Race, Labour, and the Future of the Past: *King Lear*'s 'True Blank,'" *postmedieval: a journal of medieval cultural studies* 11, nos. 2–3 (2020): 204–11, uses the Earl of Kent to "examine the ways in which 'good' service is always already implicated in a racial project" of reproducing whiteness (209).

3. In his wide-ranging survey of bastardy in early modern English drama, Michael Neill explores in colonial/racial terms the attribution to bastards of sexual and bodily impurity: the "type of such adulterate mixing," he notes, is Caliban, who prefigures the fantasy of the "black rapist" ("'In Everything Illegitimate': Imagining the Bastard in Renaissance Drama," in *Putting History to the Question: Power, Politics, and Society in English Renaissance Drama* [New York: Columbia University Press, 2000], 135). Building on Neill's foundational insights, I develop a racial interpretation of bastardy in the case of a non-Black character.
4. Diana Coole and Samantha Frost, eds., "Introducing the New Materialisms," in *New Materialisms: Ontology, Agency, and Politics* (Durham, NC: Duke University Press, 2010) 2, 19.

> Thou, nature, art my goddess. To thy law
> My services are bound. Wherefore should I
> Stand in the plague of custom and permit
> The curiosity of nations to deprive me
> For that I am some twelve or fourteen moonshines
> Lag of a brother? Why "bastard"? wherefore "base",
> When my dimensions are as well compact,
> My mind as generous, and my shape as true,
> As honest madam's issue? Why brand they us
> With "base", with "baseness, bastardy — base, base" —
> Who, in the lusty stealth of nature, take
> More composition and fierce quality
> Than doth, within a dull, stale, tirèd bed,
> Go to th'creating a whole tribe of fops,
> Got 'tween a sleep and wake? Well then,
> Legitimate Edgar, I must have your land.
> Our father's love is to the bastard Edmond
> As to th'legitimate. Fine word, "legitimate".
> Well, my legitimate, if this letter speed,
> And my invention thrive, Edmond the base
> Shall to the legitimate. I grow; I prosper.
> Now gods, stand up for bastards! (2.1.1–22)[5]

My reading of this passage is indebted to Geraldine Heng's influential definition of race as the tendency to "*demarcate human beings through differences among humans that are selectively essentialized as absolute and fundamental, in order to distribute positions and powers differentially to human groups*."[6] Although we are not accustomed to thinking of bastards as a race, Edmond experiences his bastard status as an arbitrary

5. I cite throughout from William Shakespeare, *The Tragedy of King Lear: The Norton Shakespeare*, 3rd ed., ed. Stephen Greenblatt et al. (New York: Norton, 2015).
6. Geraldine Heng, *The Invention of Race in the European Middle Ages* (Cambridge: Cambridge University Press, 2018), 27 original emphasis. To mark my indebtedness to Heng's definition, I will continue to italicize her terms when I cite them.

(*selectively essentialized*) attribution of inborn (*absolute and fundamental*) "baseness" that is used to deprive him of land and title (*powers and positions*). Through his enforced habitation of the "customary" category of bastardy, Edmond experiences the embodied differences signified by illegitimacy as a racial formation.[7]

Although Edmond's anger and resentment are generally acknowledged, previous commentators have overlooked the complexity of Edmond's affective experience of his relegation to a race of bastards, who are *demarcated* from the legitimately born through the "brand" of natural "baseness." Brands were literally used in early modern Europe to mark the fixed *positions and powers* of criminals. In Edmond's metaphor of being branded with baseness, race produces a kind of indelible, always legible, mark of inferiority.[8] As evidence for the medieval racialization of Jews, Heng cites the fact that Jews in thirteenth-century England "were forced by law to wear badges on their chests, to set them apart from the rest of the English population."[9] Edmond bitterly recognizes that in its attribution

7. "Racial formation" refers to "the sociohistorical process by which racial categories are created, inhabited, transformed, and destroyed" (Michael Omi and Howard Winant, *Racial Formation in the United States: From the 1960s to the 1990s*, 2nd ed. [London: Routledge, 1994], 55).
8. Patricia Akhimie, *Shakespeare and the Cultivation of Difference: Race and Conduct in the Early Modern World*, (London: Routledge, 2018), 4–5. Sydnee Wagner, *Outlandish People: Gypsies, Race, and Fantasies of National Identity in Early Modern England* (PhD diss., City University of New York Graduate Center, 2019), discusses sixteenth-century laws that called for the branding of "Egyptians" or gypsies. Neill describes the dramatic bastard as a "member of a hybrid genus," a "creature whose mixed nature is expressed in an idiom that systematically subverts the 'natural' decorums of kind" ("'In Everything Illegitimate,'" 129–30). Neill cites Sir John Fortescue's racializing account of the bastard as one who draws "a certain corruption and stain from the sin of his parents"; thus nature "mark[ed] the natural or bastard children as it were with a certain privy mark in their souls" (Fortescue, qtd. in Neill, "'In Everything Illegitimate,'" 132).
9. Heng, *The Invention of Race in the European Middle Ages*, 15. An echo of this history might be present in Shylock's declaration that "sufferance is the badge of all our tribe." Both the notion of an outward racial mark (brand/badge) and the unusual Shakespearean word "tribe," as I will discuss, connect Edmond's soliloquy to *The Merchant of Venice*. Tellingly, "tribe" appears four times in *The Merchant of Venice*, as well as three

to bastards, "base" functions as both a social status – "low in the social scale; not noble, low-born" – and a moral judgment of natural character – "Of a low or inferior quality or standard; poor, inadequately good."[10] Patricia Akhimie's reading of the "base Indian/Judean" in Othello's final soliloquy imparts a racial significance to "base," which denotes "a faulty state of mind, a low estate, a moral failure, and an adulteration and impurity; it connotes ignorance or naïveté, willful defiance or simple misfor-

times in *Othello*; it appears twice in *Coriolanus*, and once in *King Lear*. Writing of Charles Macklin, the eighteenth-century actor who played Shylock with a red beard, Stephen Orgel describes the beard as the "badge of all our tribe" for stage Shylocks. Orgel's use of Shylock's phrase suggests that red hair functioned theatrically as a physiological marker of the Jewish tribe or race ("Imagining Shylock," in *Imagining Shakespeare: A History of Texts and Visions* [New York: Palgrave Macmillan, 2003], 145). Gabriel Egan also connects Edmond's soliloquy to Shylock: the "belief that what happens to the couple during the act of conception shapes the individual conceived has a long history, from the story of Jacob setting parti-coloured wands before Laban's sheep to make them conceive parti-coloured lambs (Genesis 30.31–40) told in *The Merchant of Venice* (1.3.70–89)" (*Green Shakespeare: From Ecopolitics to Ecocriticism* [London: Routledge, 2006], 135). Carmen Nocentelli claims that in early modern Europe "sexual practices and erotic proclivities became *badges* of identity that could evince the truth of one's racial belonging" (*Empires of Love: Europe, Asia and the Making of Early Modern Identity* [Philadelphia: University of Pennsylvania Press, 2013], 9 emphasis added).

10. Respectively, OED *Online*, s.v., "base," adj. 6.b, adj. 7.a. On degree as a marker of racial difference in the Renaissance, see Lara Bovilsky, *Barbarous Play: Race on the English Renaissance Stage* (Minneapolis: Minnesota University Press, 2008), 14 and (in relation to *Othello*) 45–49. In an influential essay with a titular nod to bastardy, Kim F. Hall, "'These Bastard Signs of Fair': Literary Whiteness in Shakespeare's Sonnets," in *Post-Colonial Shakespeares*, ed. Ania Loomba and Martin Orkin (London: Routledge, 1998), 64–83, also discusses social degree and/as race. According to Jean E. Feerick, during this period "*race* is most frequently used and understood as a mode of social differentiation that naturalizes a rigid social hierarchy within a polity" (*Strangers in Blood: Relocating Race in the Renaissance*, [Toronto: University of Toronto Press, 2010], 6 original emphasis). In arguing that bastardy is figured as race in *King Lear*, I depart from Feerick, who argues that in early modern England "race" signified primarily membership in an elite: "To be of 'base race' was an oxymoron; baseness precluded membership in a race" (8). Nonetheless, it is significant that in Edmond's soliloquy his membership (or not) in an elite lineage is precisely what is at stake.

tune."[11] Conflating "the somatic with the behavioral," Othello assigns the Indian/Judean to a race of "intemperate, savage, and base people without the desire or the ability to improve themselves."[12] "Base" thus figures the somatic and behavioral differences between "temperate, civil, noble, and genteel people"[13] and savage races incapable of moral cultivation. If, as Akhimie shows, the discourse of baseness mobilizes racial categories, then it is no surprise that Edmond decries the mark of baseness that renders his social status an oxymoron. Edmond recognizes that no amount of earnest self-improvement can erase his essentialized status as "Edmond the base." Getting lands "by wit" (1.2.160) will require not slow cultivation, but instead a treacherous and "willful defiance"[14] that would seem to confirm the impurity of mind and body customarily attributed to bastards.

Relegated to an inferior race by the law and "custom" of primogeniture, Edmond takes solace in a different account of the nature of bastards than the one that subtends such laws. Edmond at once exposes as ideological (arbitrary, false, unjust) the national customs that group him with all other bastards as a naturally inferior race and mobilizes his own self-interested account of bastardy that groups him with all other (male) bastards as a naturally superior race. According to Edmond, bastards enjoy a naturally enhanced manhood that derives from their parents' ardent and illegal "stealth of nature" at their conception.[15] Consequently, bastards enjoy more composition (stronger "constitution of body" / "constitution of mind and body combined")[16] and a more fierce ("high-spirited, brave,

11. Akhimie, *Shakespeare and the Cultivation of Difference*, 78.
12. Akhimie, *Shakespeare and the Cultivation of Difference*, 78, 14.
13. Akhimie, *Shakespeare and the Cultivation of Difference*, 14.
14. Akhimie, *Shakespeare and the Cultivation of Difference*, 78.
15. On the early modern view that bastards enjoyed "exceptionally passionate energies" due to the lustful conditions of their birth, see Neill, "'In Everything Illegitimate,'" 131–32; Allison Findlay, *Illegitimate Power: Bastards in Renaissance Drama*, (Manchester: Manchester University Press, 1994), 129–36. Findlay notes of the expression "natural child," a euphemism for bastard, that "'natural' denotes a bastard's metaphorical exclusion from culture, from divine spirit and human law" (129).
16. OED *Online*, s.v., "composition," n. 16.a.–b.

valiant"; "proud, haughty")[17] character than their legitimately conceived counterparts. Edmond's positing of an enhanced masculinity might well serve to compensate for the ugly feelings that attend his forcible debasement as a bastard.

For Edmond, membership in a race or tribe produces a complex affective charge. While his masculine kinship with other bastards might seem to repair his feeling of social and familial alienation, he also chafes about being grouped with men whom he seems to regard as his inferiors in body and character. Edmond explicitly groups himself with other bastards as members of a race characterized both as inferior — "Why brand they us / With 'base'?" — and as superior — those "[w]ho, in the lusty stealth of nature take / More composition and fierce quality" from their birth than the legitimately born. By attributing to bastards "more composition and fierce quality" than legitimate men, Edmond can imagine himself as part of an affective community constituted via membership in the racial category to which the law has assigned them.[18] At the same time, he implicitly distinguishes himself from other bastards as a naturally superior individual, a particularly distinguished bastard who is comparable to any "honest madam's issue."[19] Edmond here turns from identification with

17. OED *Online*, s.v., "fierce," adj. 2., 3.
18. As Patricia Akhimie notes of this speech, "'[q]uality' is a heritable trait related to rank and legitimacy" ("'Qualities of Breeding': Race, Class, and Conduct in *The Merchant of Venice*," in *The Merchant of Venice: The State of Play*, ed. M. Lindsay Kaplan [London: The Arden Shakespeare/Bloomsbury, 2020], 156). The agency of law in creating and sustaining racial inequality is a central tenet of Critical Race Theory; see Kimberlé Crenshaw, Neil Gotanda, Gary Peller, and Kendall Thomas, eds., *Critical Race Theory: The Key Writings That Formed the Movement* (New York: New Press, 1995).
19. According to Emily C. Bartels, "In asking 'why brand they us,' [Edmond] embraces us as his confidantes and supporters, if not his next of kin. In so doing, he also sets us apart from an unappealing 'they' who privilege tribes of fops bred of dull, stale, tired beds over bastards of 'fierce quality.' If we resist, we become 'they.' If we comply, we join the ranks of a victimized and knowing 'us' — just the sort of subject we (especially non-aristocratic spectators) love to love, the sort of subject we might resemble, and the sort of subject who, therefore, resembles us" ("Breaking the Illusion of Being: Shakespeare and the Performance of Self," *Theatre Journal* 46, no. 2 [1994]: 177). Unlike Bar-

other bastards to identification with a hypothetical legitimately conceived man with whom he might compare in excellence of "dimensions," "mind," and "shape." In attributing the source of this counterpart's legitimacy to maternal honesty, however, Edmond evokes the tainted racial origins that unjustly prevent his fine qualities from being legible underneath the blot of bastardy. Recognizing the primary meaning of "issue" as "the action of going, flowing, or coming out," we can more easily hear in Edmond's resentment the undertones of revulsion against the corrupt maternal body from which his own "dimensions," "mind," and "shape" – howsoever since cultivated into a state of manly excellence – first emerged.[20] To be a bastard is to be the "issue" of a base mother and thus always marked as belonging to a base, inferior race.[21]

Although some critics have marked the gendering mechanisms in bastardy, they have not accounted for how gender ideologies intersect with racial ideologies in Edmond's rhetoric. Robert J. Bauer argues that to Edmond, "nature ... means a life force that thrives as long as he strives"; it is a "physical" and "undisciplined nature that blindly seeks to dominate and control".[22] Yet Edmond renders his devotion to nature not "blindly" or in an "undisciplined" fashion but in terms of a masculine "service" that carries courtly and erotic overtones.[23] Neither can Edmond's disciplined

tels, I am arguing that Edmond's "us" functions not to interpellate the audience as his kin, but to recognize other bastards as sharing his "base" racial designation.

20. *OED Online*, s.v., "issue," n. I.1.

21. The *OED Online* cites an example from 1620 as the first illustration of "issue" in the sense of "a race or people" (s.v., "issue," n. II.5.b). The pressure on lineage in Edmond's soliloquy arguably makes his use of "issue" intelligible not only as "offspring," but also as "race." On revulsion at the corrupting maternal body in Shakespearean tragedy, see Janet Adelman, *Suffocating Mothers: Fantasies of Maternal Origin in Shakespeare, Hamlet to The Tempest* (London: Routledge, 1992).

22. Robert J. Bauer, "Despite of Mine Own Nature: Edmund and the Orders, Cosmic and Moral," *Texas Studies in Literature and Language* 10, no. 3 (1968): 359, 360.

23. Along with allusions to Jews in Edmond's soliloquy, there might be the suggestion of paganism in his devotion to the "goddess" Nature. Nocentelli remarks that "in early modern Europe notions of 'nature' were never too far apart from the image of 'Nature' as the goddess of procreative sex" (*Empires of Love*, 21). According to Peter Harrison, *"Religion" and the Religions in the English Enlightenment* (Cambridge: Cambridge Uni-

masculine "service" to nature be explained by Michael Neill's observation that bastards' connection with nature implied a feminizing maternal influence: "For all his supposedly 'unnatural' qualities, the bastard was traditionally described as a 'natural child' because, conceived without benefit of matrimony, his origins lay outside the order of culture (imagined as masculine) in the (typically feminine) domain of nature."[24] Likewise, Alison Findlay explains that the "danger of the unsocialised bastard comes from his origins in a feminine, uncivilised world of nature."[25] As we have seen, Edmond does allude to his origins in a dishonest maternal body. In serving the "law" of nature, however, Edmond seems less to reassert his association with feminine incivility than to demand that his natural (individual, inborn) bodily capacities be publicly recognized despite the customary legal constraints that would sink him into oblivion within the general race of bastards.

In Edmond's experience of his body, then, gender articulates the outlines of race, just as race articulates the outlines of gender. If it is "curiosity" — artificial and overprecise distinctions between "legitimate" and "illegitimate" conceptions — that relegates him to bastard oblivion, then through his masculine service to nature Edmond will bring to bear a counter-curiosity in measuring the refinement of his own natural body, as manifested in his "compact," "generous," and "true" appearance and capa-

versity Press, 1990), English Protestants commonly identified "heathens," "idolaters," and "pagans" with the worship of nature. The Cambridge Platonist Nathaniel Culverwel writes that "Nature's Law" would be more readily found in a "naked Indian," a "rude American," or a "mere Pagan," than in a Greek, Roman, Jew, or Christian" (qtd. in Harrison, *"Religion" and the Religions in the English Enlightenment*, 42). John Drakakis, "Jews, Bastards, and Black Rams (and Women): Representations of 'Otherness' in Shakespearean Texts," *SEDERI* 13 (2003): 55–75, argues that Jews, bastards, and Blacks are structurally similar as "others" in Shakespeare. I thank John Kuhn for referring me to Harrison.

24. Michael Neill, "Bastardy, Counterfeiting, and Misogyny in *The Revenger's Tragedy*," in *Putting History to the Question: Power, Politics, and Society in English Renaissance Drama* (New York: Columbia University Press, 2000), 135.
25. Findlay, *Illegitimate Power*, 40.

bilities.[26] Fittingly, Edmond identifies his mind as "generous" – meaning "noble of spirit, honourable" – despite being barred from claiming the status of "generous" in the sense of coming from "noble or aristocratic lineage; high-born."[27] At once recognizing his brotherhood in a race of bastards and distinguishing himself from this essentialized group, Edmond carefully observes and records his "natural" bodily gifts, thereby opening up the possibility of his difference from other bastards who might possess his natural fierceness but not his distinct superiority of shape, mind, and limbs. Nature's "law" thus counters the race-making logics of nations with an insistence on individual masculine distinction that thwarts any attempts to *selectively essentialize* some differences over others. Hence, the movement in Edmond's soliloquy from first person plural ("why brand they *us*") to a first-person singular stressing his powers of expansion and erection ("I grow; I prosper").[28] Edmond, after all, aims not to alter any laws to advance the interests of all bastards, but merely to work within the present conditions of possibility to "top" his legitimately born brother.[29]

In his project of willful and affectively expansive self-advancement, Edmond, relegated by his birth to a socially disadvantaged race of persons, weaponizes his precarious identity through what Carol Mejia LaPerle describes, in an argument about *Titus Andronicus*'s Aaron, as a

26. OED *Online*, s.v., "curiosity," n. 4.b: "Unduly minute or subtle treatment; nicety, subtlety."
27. OED *Online*, s.v., "generous," adj. 1.a, 2.a.
28. In stressing his prosperity, Edmond seems to claim the respectable status of industrious, profitable provider that was a central tenet of early modern patriarchal manhood. See Alexandra Shepard, *Meanings of Manhood in Early Modern England*, (Oxford: Oxford University Press, 2003), 186–87.
29. If we read this textual crux as "top the legitimate" instead of "to the legitimate," we activate the possible image of racialized male-male sodomy/bestiality that Jeffrey Masten identifies in *Othello*'s language of topping/tupping (*Queer Philologies: Sex, Language, and Affect in Shakespeare's Time* [Philadelphia: University of Pennsylvania Press, 2016], 214–22). Making himself erect ("I grow"), Edmond will screw his brother. Or, to activate a common early modern pun, Edmond, who now "[s]tands in the plague of custom," will "stand" or erect himself, whether or not the gods "stand up" for him.

"racialize[d] will."[30] Aaron's violent will, depicted in the play as an expression of his Black nature, exists in defiant opposition to the "public, social will that underwrites Roman authority."[31] Because Edmond is not Black, he can rewrite his social identity in a way not available to Aaron, a transformative capacity of will that Edmond conveys through a clothing metaphor: "Let me, if not by birth, have lands by wit. / All's with me meet that I can fashion fit" (1.2.160–61). Still, Edmond's willful advancement of his own interests at any cost does correspond with LaPerle's account of Aaron's will as "a perpetual threat" to the dominant social order.[32] Moreover, just as Aaron's "violent volition is explicitly correlated to his physical characteristics" as a Black man,[33] so the repetition of the word "fierce" in regard to Edmond's violent plots underlines how his racial characteristics as a bastard — "fierce quality" and strong constitution — facilitate his treachery against his brother, their father, and the dominant social order they represent. When framing Edgar, Edmond realizes that wounding himself as if in self-defense against his brother's attack would "beget opinion / Of my more fierce endeavour" (2.1.33–4). Edmond's misleading information leads to Gloucester's capture and torture. Just before his blinding, Gloucester, unaware of how his words apply to his own son, condemns the bestial fierceness of children who would physically harm their fathers, thus striking against lineage as the very foundation of social order. He admonishes Regan: "I would not see thy cruel nails / Pluck out [Lear's] poor old eyes, nor thy fierce sister / In his anointed flesh stick boarish fangs" (3.7.54–56). The masculine fierceness that Edmond attributes to his identity as a bastard empowers him to undermine the very social system responsible for that racialized identity.

If Edmond is linked both affectively and sexually with Regan and Goneril as children who violently unmake patriarchal lineage for personal gain,

30. Carol Mejia LaPerle, "'If I Might Have My Will': Aaron's Affect and Race in *Titus Andronicus*," in *Titus Andronicus: The State of Play*, ed. Farah Karim-Cooper (London: The Arden Shakespeare/Bloomsbury, 2019), 138. I thank Carol Mejia LaPerle for sharing with me her work and her thoughts about this project.
31. LaPerle, "'If I Might Have My Will,'" 139.
32. LaPerle, "'If I Might Have My Will,'" 142.
33. LaPerle, "'If I Might Have My Will,'" 142.

then he is also racially stained through his mother's sexual fault. As I have described, Edmond glances at his mother's dishonesty in comparing himself favorably to "honest madam's issue." Edgar more pointedly articulates the intersection of racial and sexual corruption in bastardy. Positioning Edmond as the providential scourge of their father's adultery, Edgar's stunning moral pronouncement places ultimate blame on the embodied darkness of female sexuality:

> The gods are just, and of our pleasant vices
> Make instruments to plague us.
> The dark and vicious place where thee he got
> Cost him his eyes. (5.3.160–63)

Edmond takes his life from the "dark and vicious place" whose blackness signifies both *illegitimate female sexuality* — as in Joyce Green MacDonald's analysis of bastardy in Samuel Daniel's *Letter from Octavia* as a "blemish" worse "than a slavish wipe, or birth hour's blot" — and *female sexuality as illegitimate*, what Janet Adelman calls "the mother's dark place."[34] In "'The Darke and Vicious Place,'" Peter L. Rudnytsky further explores this misogynist rendering of the vagina as the vicious "place" from which both sexual sin and illegitimate birth originate.[35] According to Rudnytsky, "As Kent alleges of Oswald, Edmond is 'the Sonne and Heire of a Mungrill Bitch,' irrevocably doomed by the whore at his origin."[36]

34. Joyce Green MacDonald, *Women and Race in Early Modern Texts* (Cambridge: Cambridge University Press, 2002), 42; Adelman, 107.
35. Peter L. Rudnytsky, "'The Darke and Vicious Place': The Dread of the Vagina in *King Lear*," *Modern Philology* 96, no. 3 (1999): 291–311. See also Adelman: "the female sexual place is necessarily the place of corruption, the 'sulphurous pit' ... that is Lear's equivalent to Edgar's 'dark and vicious place'; present only as a site of illegitimacy, the mother ... transmits her faults to her issue, the children whose corrupt sexuality records their origin" (*Suffocating Mothers*, 108); and Bovilsky: "Patriarchal logics, after all, as frequently take the form of overemphasizing the mother's responsibilities in guaranteeing the reputation and moral inheritance of her children as with common ideologies that attribute a presumed and unalterable immorality of children conceived or born outside of 'wedlock' to their mother's faults" (*Barbarous Play*, 48).
36. Rudnytsky, "'The Darke and Vicious Place,'" 297.

As a "whoreson," Edmond's "virility is tainted"; again, Rudnytsky argues, Edmond is "tainted" by the "darke and vicious place" from which he was born — a prostitute's vagina.[37] Although Rudnytsky does not directly address race, his analysis of the play's imagery of darkness and mongrel hybridity, as well as his own emphasis on Edmond's being "tainted" by his mother's dark sexuality, corroborate the racial implications of bastardy I have been exploring in Edmond's soliloquy.

Of course, although Edgar's point is that *Gloucester* has been justly punished for adultery via Edmond's treachery, his language contrasts the seemingly trivial "pleasant vice" of Gloucester's sexual lapse with an explicit disgust for and condemnation of a "dark and vicious" female sexuality/body. The "instruments" of justice in this passage are, first and foremost, the dark female place in which Gloucester pleasurably begets Edmond; then the bastard son who takes life from this darkness; and finally the implement that Cornwall uses to remove Gloucester's eyes and cast him into darkness. If for Edmond racialized bastardy feels paradoxically both humiliating ("base, base") and empowering ("I grow; I prosper"), then for Edgar it feels unambivalently frightening, disgusting, and worthy of punishment. Given this emphasis on the pleasure offered and the danger posed by this "dark and vicious" woman, what would happen to our reading of this passage (and Edmond) were we to imagine Edmond's mother as, in fact, a Black woman — the kind of figure that Lynda Boose finds unrepresentable on the early modern English stage?[38] Although the play does not explicitly prompt us to imagine Edmond's mother as dark-

37. Rudnytsky, "'The Darke and Vicious Place,'" 303. Rudnytsky seems to assume that Edmond's mother is literally a prostitute, even though "whore" might only signify a promiscuous woman (304).

38. Lynda E. Boose, "'The Getting of a Lawful Race': Racial Discourse in Early Modern England and the Unrepresentable Black Woman," in *Women, "Race," and Writing in the Early Modern Period*, ed. Margo Hendricks and Patricia Parker (London: Routledge, 1994), 35-54. On the representation of Black women as lustful and seductive in medieval and early modern European texts, see Valentin Groebner, "The Carnal Knowing of a Colored Body: Sleeping with Arabs and Blacks in the European Imagination, 1300–1550," in *The Origins of Racism in the West*, ed. Miriam Eliav-Feldon, Benjamin Isaac, and Joseph Ziegler (Cambridge: Cambridge University Press, 2009), 217–31.

skinned — if anything, Gloucester's praise of her as "fair" suggests the inverse (1.1.20) — her "fault" racializes Edmond in that having a "son for her cradle ere she had a husband for her bed" constitutes ocular proof of sexual sin (1.1.13–14).[39] Although Kent graciously compliments the proper "issue" of this maternal fault, Gloucester's identification of his son as a "whoreson" — the issue of a whore — shows how illegitimate sexuality is racialized through fear and disgust at the maternal body's ability to impress its sinful darkness upon its issue (1.1.15, 21).[40]

Suffering public degradation as a "whoreson," Edmond privately degrades Edgar by assigning him to a "tribe of fops," a phrase that deploys racial and gendered meanings to disparage "legitimate" conception. In early modern England, "tribe" was primarily used to refer to the twelve tribes of Israel, not to Native Americans.[41] We have already considered the pertinence to Edmond of Othello's self-comparison to the "base Indian/ Judean" who "threw a pearl away / Richer than all his tribe."[42] Othello's usage suggests the possibility that "tribe" had racial applications aside from Judaism.[43] Whereas Edmond attributes an enhanced masculinity to bastards, he sneers at the legitimately born as "fops" whose natural constitutions have been enervated by the "dull, stale, tired" sex of their married parents. "Fop" in the early seventeenth century generally meant

39. In one of many contradictions structuring Edmond's bastard status, he is doubly untimely: both too early — born "before he was sent for" (1.1.19–20) — and too late — born twelve or fourteen months "[l]ag of a brother" (1.2.6).

40. On fear as an embodied experience, particularly with regard to race, see Sara Ahmed, "The Affective Politics of Fear," in *The Cultural Politics of Emotion*, 2nd ed. (Edinburgh: Edinburgh University Press, 2014), 62–81.

41. OED *Online*, s.v., "tribe," n. 1.a: "A group of people forming a community and claiming descent from a common ancestor; *spec.* each of the twelve divisions of the people of Israel, claiming descent from the twelve sons of Jacob."

42. William Shakespeare, *The Tragedy of Othello the Moor of Venice: The Norton Shakespeare*, 3rd ed., ed. Stephen Greenblatt et al. (New York: Norton, 2015), 5.2.356-7.

43. An extremely capacious religious/geographic/racial term in the early modern period, "Indian" might refer to Native Americans or to East Indians/Moors. See Michael Neill, "'Mulattos,' 'Blacks,' and 'Indian Moors': *Othello* and Early Modern Constructions of Human Difference," in *Putting History to the Question: Power, Politics, and Society in English Renaissance Drama* (New York: Columbia University Press, 2000), 269–84.

"fool" — as in Edmond's mockery of the "excellent foppery" of astrology — but the "effeminate" (mannered, vain) behavioral characteristic of the Restoration fop is already recognizable in the foolish courtiers of Shakespeare and Ben Jonson.[44] In other words, it is possible that "fop" signified in the earlier seventeenth century as a type of gender and erotic transgression.[45] Although the legitimacy of martial sex gives Edgar a social and legal advantage over his younger, bastard brother, that very legitimacy — the product of dutiful and passionless intercourse — generates males of a duller, weaker constitution. Edmond reformulates sexual legitimacy as a form of embodied weakness. In this sense, legitimately conceived men also constitute a "natural" race (or "tribe") that is physiologically inferior to the fierce bastard race over which such men nonetheless enjoy social supremacy.

In exploring the racialization of bastardy, my analysis of *King Lear* has elaborated on the intersecting racial components of lineage, gender, and sexuality. Edmond describes the parental sexuality that produces lineage as a cause of greater or lesser manhood in sons: dull marital sex produces legitimate, foppish sons; ardent adulterous sex produces illegitimate, fierce, bastard sons. Following this logic to its conclusion, we might better understand why Edmond scorns "legitimate" as a "fine word": "fine" signifies not only superiority and purity, but also foppish affectation, fas-

44. According to Jessica Landis, "[t]he unifying characteristics between fop figures, these sometimes seemingly disparate representations of affectation and self-presentation, include excessive tendencies, affected manners, and irrepressible ambition. Fops ape the behaviors of their social superiors in attempts to better their positions among courtiers, gentlemen, soldiers, gallants, and arguably other types of successful men. In their mimicry, however, they get distracted by frivolous aspects of masculine cultural identities" ("Affecting Manhood: Masculinity, Effeminacy, and the Fop Figure in Early Modern English Drama" [PhD diss., University of Massachusetts, 2015], 8).
45. On the type of the effeminate courtier specifically and for the idea of sexual types more generally, see Mario DiGangi, *Sexual Types: Embodiment, Agency, and Dramatic Character from Shakespeare to Shirley* (Philadelphia: University of Pennsylvania Press, 2011), esp. Chapter 3.

tidiousness, and insincerity.[46] If legitimate lineage is reproduced through the generational repetition of the dull marital sex that produces foppish sons, *ad infinitum*, then racial degeneracy is not, as Jean E. Feerick has detailed, merely an ever-present "possibility," but an inevitability.[47] Ironically, a noble family's only salvation from degenerating into a "tribe" of self-replicating fops would seem to rest in the fierceness of an illegitimate son such as Edmond, who might inject a renewed manly spirit into the bloodline. Does the bastard's fierce manliness also suggest his ability to reproduce at once a legitimate and a manly (i.e., non-foppish) bloodline through his capacity for "fierce" or passionate marital sex? Having just decried the "tribe of fops" that Edgar stands poised to sire, Edmond appears to reach an abrupt and overconfident conclusion: "Well then, / Legitimate Edgar, I must have your land. / Our father's love is to the bastard Edmond / As to th'legitimate." Edmond's brutal imperative seems less arbitrary if he imagines himself in this moment as not only a daring opportunist, but also the eventual restorer of patriarchal lineage — the son who will redeem his father's sexual fault and earn his love by displacing his foppish older brother and reinvigorating the family blood. But the bold action that to Edmond feels like a heroic destiny might well be experienced by an early modern audience as a racialized affect: the fear that the undoing of noble lineage could undo the foundations of common good will.

As we know, instead of becoming his father's savior, Edmond will eagerly seize the chance to become one of the "instruments" of his father's demise. In relegating Edmond to the role of fatal instrument, Edgar reminds his base brother that he embodies the indelible racial/gendered/sexual taint of maternal darkness and dark maternity. Once his purposes are realized, Edgar, unlike Edmond, can shed the markers of race and reconstitute his identity as a legitimate son and heir. Edmond can never

46. OED *Online*, s.v., "fine," adj., adv., and n.2 A.I: "Pure, perfect; of the best or very high quality"; II.11: "Characterized by or affecting refinement or elegance; (affectedly) dainty or genteel; fastidious, prim"; II.12.a: "Flattering, complimentary; deceptively or insincerely approbatory; (also) of the nature of empty rhetoric."
47. Feerick, *Strangers in Blood*, 16.

escape the racialized category of bastardy that will ultimately be exposed, punished, and purged from the commonwealth. This is why Edmond's singular attempt at moral self-improvement in the play – the rescinding of the execution warrant for Lear and Cordelia – fails so miserably. Howsoever future-facing and self-authoring Edmond may will himself to be – "I grow; I prosper. / Now gods, stand up for bastards!" – from the perspective of the legitimately born, he can always be shunted back to the "dark and vicious place" of his racial/sexual origins, a place upon which the gods can only be expected to exert their terrible justice.

SECTION III

Feelings and Forms of Anti-Blackness

8. Black Ink, White Feelings: Early Modern Print Technology and Anti-Black Racism

AVERYL DIETERING

What is the influence of early modern English print and print technology on the development of anti-black affects in English culture?[1] Bringing together the fields of book history, premodern critical race studies, embodiment studies, and Afro-pessimism, I argue that the anti-black racism in England that fueled the growth of the transatlantic slave trade and the British Empire was, in part, informed by representations of black figures in print media. I trace this genealogy not to propose a grand narrative of race or racism, but to consider the technology and materiality of print as an under-theorized factor in the growth of white supremacy and global anti-blackness. I examine the materiality of early modern English print, and print illustrations of black bodies in early modern texts, to show how print illustrations of blackness were deployed to foster the growth of a white English identity that defined itself in opposition to blackness. The materiality and technology of print and print illustrations informed English readers to see black bodies as non-human. Further, illustrated black bodies were used to produce anti-black affects essential to English identity, especially as Englishness in the early modern period begins to become more associated with the racial identity of whiteness.

1. Following Matthieu Chapman and many of the other Afro-pessimist philosophers with whom I engage later in this chapter, I use the lowercase *black* to refer to Sub-Saharan Africans and the African Diaspora; I also use *black* to refer to the pigment of ink. In the medium of print, a black figure is often black in both race and pigment, and it is this entanglement that I theorize. On the connection between "black as race and black as pigment" see Miles P. Grier, *Reading Black Characters: Atlantic Encounters with Othello 1604–1855* (Charlottesville: University of Virginia Press, forthcoming).

In early modern England, bodies and texts were imagined as having meaning and being legible in similar ways. The process of reading a text was often used as a metaphor to describe reading a body, such as Thomas Browne's description of physiognomers who could "spy the signatures and marks of mercy: for there are mystically in our faces certain characters which carry in them the motto of our souls, wherein he that cannot read A.B.C. may read our natures."[2] The body was also used as a metaphor for reading texts, such as the popular skin-as-frontispiece trope that Claudia Benthien traces in early modern anatomies.[3] In this visual trope, the frontispiece of an anatomy was designed to look like an anatomized body holding open its skin to reveal the anatomy text underneath, drawing a comparison between turning the pages of the text and peeling back layers of human flesh. With the growth of print in England, the connections between reading texts and reading bodies were informed by the technology of print: bodies were seen as imprinted/pressed with meaning. The metaphors of print technology used in *The Winter's Tale* describe the familial similarities between Leontes and his infant daughter Perdita — "Although the print be little, the whole matter / And copy of the father"[4] — and between Polixenes and his son Florizel:

> Your mother was most true to wedlock, Prince,
> For she did print your royal father off,
> Conceiving you.[5]

In these passages, bodies become texts and texts become bodies. Further, print technology also transformed the illustrations that accompanied printed texts, as the process of illustrating a text through woodcuts or engravings was more similar in form to printing than to painting, drawing,

2. Thomas Browne, *Religio Medici* (London: Printed for Andrew Crooke, 1642), 116.
3. Claudia Benthien, *Skin: On the Cultural Border Between Self and World*, trans. Thomas Dunlap (New York: Columbia University Press, 2002), 43–45.
4. William Shakespeare, "The Winter's Tale," in *The Norton Shakespeare*, 2nd ed., ed. Stephen Greenblatt, Walter Cohen, Jean E. Howard, and Katharine Eisaman Maus (New York: Norton, 2008), 2.3.99–100.
5. Shakespeare, "The Winter's Tale," 5.1.123–25.

or sketching. Thus, when an early modern reader saw an illustration of a person in a text, they were using their body (also imagined as a text) to read a text (also imagined as a body). The illustration of a body, in turn, was metaphorically also a text, while as a printed illustration, it was also literally a text. These close metaphorical connections between physical bodies and printed texts and illustrations helped to shape the early modern English imagination of what bodies could be: legible, meaningful, containing truth and knowledge — but only to those with the skills to read them correctly.

As the body and printed texts and illustrations stood as metaphors for each other and became entangled with each other, racial formations informed this entanglement. With the exception of a few scholars whose works I engage with later in my argument, these connections between print, bodies, and race have gone largely unnoticed in studies of book history and the history of print. And yet, just as the technology of print informed early modern understandings of bodies, the technology of print also informed early modern understandings of raced bodies.

Print Technology and the Transition to Black and White

Prior to the printing press, the vast majority of illustrations in illuminated manuscripts were hand-drawn or hand-painted. With the advent of the printing press, print illustrations were more likely to be printed along with the text, as it was faster to produce many illustrations by pressing the same woodblock or engraved plate repeatedly than by drawing the same illustration over and over. Both printed text and print illustrations are composed of lines that are organized to make meaning. What allows the reader to regard them as different from each other is context. For example, readers use context clues to decide if a short, straight line is part of an alphabetical letter, is one of many hatches and cross-hatches used to make a shadow, or is part of a nose on an illustrated face. Readers distinguish between these different types of lines so quickly that they often fail to acknowledge their material similarity: everything that is represented in early modern print — from the alphabetical letters to all kinds of illustrated images — consists of *organized gatherings of legible lines*. Furthermore, print text and print illustrations both share material similarity as legible lines of dark ink on a lighter page. Illustrators of illuminated manuscripts could portray visual elements such as color, shadow, depth, and texture with a variety of pigments, materials, and artistic techniques. But in print illustration, all visual elements must be represented by dark ink lines on a lighter page.[6]

Metaphorical Text-Bodies: The Invisible White Body, the Inky Black Body

The trope of comparing texts and bodies was not new to the early modern period, but the shift from illuminated manuscripts with polychromatic

6. To be clear, hand-drawn or hand-painted illustrations in early modern texts and prints were still common. Readers could purchase texts and prints with colorized illustrations (albeit likely at a higher price), or they could arrange for illustrations to be colored and painted after purchase. However, my point is that the vast majority of early modern English print illustrations were encountered first as dark ink lines on a light page, even if they were altered and colorized afterwards. I also want to draw attention to my description of print as dark ink on light pages, rather than the more common description of *black* ink on a *white* page. It is true that in the early modern period, printers and paper mills labored to create blacker inks and whiter paper. However, the blackness of ink and the whiteness of paper depended on the quality of materials and the process of combining them. But given that there were so many different recipes for creating ink and paper, it is more accurate to speak of a veritable rainbow of dark inks (some very black, others not) and light pages (some very white, others not), despite the fact that today and in the early modern period, it is common to speak of all dark inks as black and all light pages as white. I will switch to using black ink and white page for the rest of my argument, but only to address their importance as metaphors we live by, metaphors that have, in turn, influenced the creation of racial metaphors about bodies as black and white. For more on this, see Kim F. Hall, "Introduction," in *Things of Darkness: Economies of Race and Gender in Early Modern England* (Ithaca, NY: Cornell University Press, 1995), 1–24, in which she argues that metaphors of dark and light, black and white, do not simply signify European aesthetic standards, but rather are powerfully racialized metaphors that influence how early modern English readers thought of themselves as opposed to racial others. As I will discuss later, Miles P. Grier, "Inkface: The Slave Stigma in England's Early Imperial Imagination," *Scripturalizing the Human: The Written as the Political*, ed. Vincent L. Wimbush (London: Routledge, 2015), 193–220, also explores the early modern context of the black/white dichotomy.

pigments, to printed texts imagined through an oppositional binary of black ink and white page, altered the way texts and bodies were compared to each other. In Act 4, Scene 3 of Shakespeare's *As You Like It*, Rosalind, dressed as the young man Ganymede, receives a letter from Phebe, a shepherdess who has fallen for Rosalind-as-Ganymede, and is angry that the young man does not return her affections. Surprised at the ferocity of Phebe's words, Rosalind declares

> […] Women's gentle brain
> Could not drop forth such giant-rude invention
> Such Ethiope words, blacker in their effect
> Than in their countenance.[7]

Rosalind's description of these "Ethiope words" draws connections between ink, Ethiopian bodies, negative emotions ("giant-rude"), and the color black. Yet, the function of black here is not simply as a pigment, but as an expression of hyperbole: the words are so "giant-rude" that their effect is "blacker" than their "countenance," which alludes to early modern adages that imagined both ink and Ethiopians as the blackest of black. In "Inkface," Miles P. Grier argues that the "black and white idiom of the print-based ink culture through which [Europeans] forged ties, conducted business, and claimed possession" "rewr[o]te the semiotics of servitude."[8] In this new semiotics, to be associated with black ink was to "designate [someone] as one who could never be an insightful reader because [they] were meant *to be read* by a white expert."[9] The roles of literate reader and legible text could not be reversed. Grier notes: "The idea that 'blacks' might have something knowledgeable to say about 'the ways of white folks' became as preposterous as imagining that letters could turn around and offer an interpretation of the page on which they stood."[10]

7. William Shakespeare, "As You Like It," in *The Norton Shakespeare*, 2nd ed., ed. Stephen Greenblatt, Walter Cohen, Jean E. Howard, and Katharine Eisaman Maus (New York: Norton, 2008), 4.3.35–38.
8. Grier, "Inkface," 204.
9. Grier, "Inkface," 195 original emphasis.
10. Grier, "Inkface," 201.

In Grier's formulation, white, unlike black, "was not a color to be analyzed; it was a mere background, a platform serving as a chromatic foil so that signifying black characters could stand out."[11] In this way, the page, associated with the English body in contrast to the ink associated with the Ethiopian body, could both exercise its power of interpretation over inky black characters while also erasing and obscuring its own power when necessary.

This particular kind of anti-blackness grants the white page expansive interpretative freedom, predicated on black ink's inability to interpret itself or signify anything other than rude, negative emotions. For example, the white page can also symbolize potential, as in this description of Belphoebe from Book II of Spenser's *The Faerie Queene*:

> Her yuorie forhead, full of bountie braue,
> Like a broad table did it selfe dispred,
> For Loue his loftie triumphes to engraue,
> And write the battailes of his great godhead:
> All good and honour might therein be red:
> For there their dwelling was.[12]

Belphoebe's ivory forehead is a surface for Love to engrave, yet the poetic syntax — "For Loue his loftie triumphes *to* engraue" (emphasis added) — makes it clear that the engraving has not happened yet. Not to mention that if it had, her forehead would not be ivory. Just as Shakespeare's Rosalind associates blackness with ink, Ethiopian bodies, and negative emotions, this description of Belphoebe associates whiteness with the page, English bodies, and positive emotive words such as *bountie braue*, *Loue*, and *good and honour*. Thus, the English body becomes associated with the whiteness of the page: a page that is imagined not as empty or lacking, but more positively as a blankness that is full of potential. And even if there is no mention of black bodies or black ink in the description of

11. Grier, "Inkface," 201.
12. Edmund Spenser, *The Faerie Queene Disposed into XII Bookes, Fashioning Twelue Morall Vertues*, (London: Printed by H. L. for Mathew Lownes, 1609), II.iii.24.1–6.

Belphoebe, the association between the whiteness of the page and its blankness as a positive potential is not possible without the anti-black reading of black bodies and ink as full of negative emotions and lacking interpretative potential.

What I find interesting about these references, aside from the use of print metaphors to link English bodies to whiteness and African bodies to blackness, is that neither reference acknowledges that legibility is dependent on the high contrast between black ink and white page. Black letters are not legible on just any type or color of background; it is the contrast and interplay between ink and page that makes words legible. Yet in both Rosalind's critique and the description of Belphoebe's forehead, legibility and meaning are imagined as residing within black letters; the white page underneath them seems almost to disappear. I address this to point out that although print technology presented English readers with new opportunities to assign value to skin color, the values that they assigned should not be considered as predetermined by this technology. On the contrary, the associations made between ink, paper, skin, and race in *As You Like It* and *The Faerie Queene* show that the interplay between ink and page to produce legible text — which could have produced many different ways of thinking about the relationship between skin color, meaning, and value — was overdetermined by the anti-blackness of early modern English culture.

Locating Emotions in the Inky Body, or, How to Read for White Feelings

The examples from *As You Like It* and *The Faerie Queene* demonstrate the growing associations between the color black, ink, African bodies, and negative emotions on the one hand, and the connections between the color white, the "blank" page, English bodies, and positive emotions on the other hand. Print illustrations of black bodies and white bodies — illustrations that, by the nature of print technology, must be made up of the binary contrast of black ink and white page, even if the body represented is meant to be represented as ivory white or completely black — show the influence of print technology on early modern English racism. To develop these ideas about the influence of print technology on early modern English racism, I turn to three illustrations from canonical early modern texts.

Figure 1. Illustration from the frontispiece of Thomas Kyd, *The Spanish Tragedy* (London: W. White, 1615), Courtesy of Wikipedia. Public Domain.

The frontispiece of Thomas Kyd's *The Spanish Tragedy* shows how early modern English illustrations that flood skin with black ink often result in faces that appear comparatively rudimentary, difficult to read, and lacking in nuanced emotion (Fig. 1). The woodcut conflates moments from Scenes 4 and 5 of Act 2 to show Hieronimo discovering the murdered body of his son Horatio. On the right, Bel-Imperia, who is Horatio's lover and the daughter of the King of Spain, calls for help while Lorenzo, Bel-Imperia's brother, tries to stop her from crying out, as he fears she will reveal his role in planning and carrying out Horatio's murder. Unlike the other characters, Lorenzo has a black face. Scholars have argued that Lorenzo's black face could refer to many English beliefs about the Spanish, such as the Black Legend genre of anti-Spanish propaganda very popular in England, or associations that the English made between Spaniards and Moors. Given the stage direction in Scene 4 that calls for Lorenzo to be "disguised," it could also be that he is in blackface or wearing a black cloth mask.[13] This possibility introduces the meta-theatrics of portraying race on the early modern stage, as a black cloth mask could be used to signify both a disguise and, as Ian Smith has shown, black skin.[14] My point is not to determine which interpretation is correct, but to show how these possible interpretations repeatedly show growing connections between the color black, ink, dark skin, and negative emotions. I also want to draw attention to the fact that Lorenzo's face, compared to the other characters' faces, lacks a great amount of detail. The other characters have eyes, noses, mouths, eyebrows, and facial hair, with enough detail in these features that it is possible to read a general expression of alarm on Hieronimo's face and anger or fear on Bel-Imperia's face. But Lorenzo only has eyes and a nose; there is a white space near where his mouth should be, but whether that represents his mouth or is just a flaw in the imprint is unclear. His emotions might be guessed from his physical actions or his words, but not from his face.

13. Thomas Kyd, "The Spanish Tragedy," in *English Renaissance Drama*, ed. David Bevington, Lars Engle, Katharine Eisaman Maus, and Eric Rasmussen (New York: Norton, 2002), 2.4.50sd.
14. Ian Smith, "The Textile Black Body: Race and 'shadowed livery' in *The Merchant of Venice*," in *The Oxford Handbook of Shakespeare and Embodiment: Gender, Sexuality, and Race*, ed. Valerie Traub (Oxford: Oxford University Press, 2016), 170–85.

Figure 2. Illustration from the frontispiece of Christopher Marlowe, *Doctor Faustus* (London: John Wright, 1620), Courtesy of Wikipedia. Public Domain.

The frontispiece of Christopher Marlowe's *Doctor Faustus* develops difficult-to-read inky black skin in a new direction through the figure of the devil Mephistopheles, whose emotions are not necessary to read because he is already assumed to be malignant and evil (Fig. 2). A devil is on a different register than a racially othered body, and yet there is an undeniable connection drawn in this image between evil and black skin, as well as the lack of detail in the illustration of the devil. Faustus, for his part, gets detailed facial features, even some hatching on the sides of his face that show shadow and dimensionality. He gazes up and out, his expression serious and determined. Again, the illustration of the devil is comparatively rudimentary. While he has more identifiable facial features than Lorenzo, there is not enough detail to guess his emotions. Like Lorenzo, the black skin stands in for an always already assumed negative affect and evil desire. Like Horatio, Hieronimo, and Bel-Imperia, Faustus's white skin signals a character that readers can identify, or with whom they might empathize.

Lorenzo's face and Mephistopheles's body are illustrated with solid ink, while details are done in white page, in what is known as the white line style of woodcut printing. In this style, lines are carved into a woodblock to create an image, then ink is applied to the woodblock so that when pressed, the ink appears on the page everywhere except for the lines of the image. Despite the crudeness and lack of detail in Lorenzo's face and Mephistopheles's body, the white line style is not an inherently simple or unsophisticated art. The incredible detail possible in the white line style is clear in the *Standard Bearers* series of white line woodcut prints by Urs Graf, who is credited with popularizing the white line style in the early sixteenth century. However, in print illustrations in England, the white line style seems to have been an underdeveloped technique compared to the black line style, in which Horatio, Hieronimo, Bel-Imperia, Faustus, and most of the other objects of the woodcut prints are illustrated. The black line style is a relief printing technique that is essentially the reverse of the white line style: instead of carving lines into the woodblock to form an image, the artist carves away everything but the lines that form the image, so that when pressed, the ink will only appear on the page as the lines of the image. The unequal development of these styles meant that a face portrayed in the white line style did not have as much detail and depth as a face portrayed in the more established black line style. Because faces in the white line style were read as racially black, this meant that black bodies, especially black faces, chronically lacked detail and depth in English print art.

Æthiopem lauare. 57

LEAVE of with paine, the blackamore to ſkowre,
With waſhinge ofte, and wipinge more then due:
For thou ſhalt finde, that Nature is of powre,
Doe what thou canſte, to keepe his former hue:
Thoughe with a forke, wee Nature thruſte awaie,
Shee turnes againe, if wee withdrawe our hande:
And thoughe, wee ofte to conquer her aſſaie,
Yet all in vaine, ſhee turnes if ſtill wee ſtande:
Then euermore, in what thou doeſt aſſaie,
Let reaſon rule, and doe the thinges thou maie.

Eraſmus ex Luciano.
Abluis Æthiopem fruſtra: quin deſinis artē?
Haud unquā efficies nox ſit ut atra, dies.
Horat. 1. Epiſt. 10.
Naturam expellas furca tamen uſque recurret.

Figure 3. "Æthiopem lavare," from Geoffrey Whitney, *A Choice of Emblemes* (Leyden: Christopher Plantyn and Francis Raphelengius, 1586) p. 57.

But even avoiding the white line style as a method to illustrate black skin and returning to the more developed black line style does not address the problems with viewing illustrations of black skin, as is clear in the illustration, "Æthiopem lavare," from Geoffrey Whitney's A *Choice of Emblemes*, which shows the common English proverb about the futility of washing an Ethiope white (Fig. 3). In this case, the Ethiope is illustrated in the black line style, but their skin is represented by abundant hatching across their entire body. Hatching is the closely-drawn parallel lines; cross-hatching is when an artist uses two or more layers of hatching at angles to each other. Whereas hatching shows dimensionality, light, and shadow on the other characters and objects in the illustration, hatching only signifies skin color on the Ethiope, thus making them devoid of the dimensionality allowed to the other humans and even objects. And while the technology of the engraving (the other two illustrations were woodcut prints, which tended to allow for less detail than engraved prints) and black line style create a more sophisticated image, the hatched lines across the entirety of the body make it harder to see the body's details and facial features compared to the bodies whose skin is only partially hatched, and thus lighter-looking.

These three print illustrations – whether woodcut or engraving, in black line or white line style – depict characters with dark skin as defined primarily by their blackness; a blackness that is conflated with lack of dimension and is void of specificity. Such illustrations signal to the white English reader that they need not be concerned about the fact that it is difficult to read detail or emotion in black bodies. After all, these black bodies are not really imagined as individuals: just as they lack visual dimensionality, they also lack affective dimensionality. Because they lack individuality and affective dimensionality, they are not human beings like the white bodies; they do not have access to that ontological status. The black body is difficult to read precisely because it does not really need to be read in detail: it is defined by blackness. White English readers are invited to define themselves, then, in opposition to this blackness; they do not view the illustrated black body to understand or identify with that body, but to distinguish themselves from it so that they can have the dimensionality, individuality, and emotions not afforded to the black body. Whiteness is defined not only by identifying with whites against blackness, but also by identifying with the humanity and ontology of the white individual against the non-humanity and non-ontology of the black body. I borrow the term *white feelings* – a term popularized by protesters and artists in Black Lives Matter movement — to describe the affective process that occurs when viewing and then rejecting the illustrated black body in order to claim dimensionality, individuality, and emotions. Though the English-as-white racial paradigm does not become fully-fledged until the late seventeenth century and into the eighteenth century, I use *white feelings* both to signal the beginnings of English whiteness and the rejection of the black text or black illustration.

Early Modern Afro-pessimism and the White Anatomizing Gaze

Bringing to the fore the technical mechanisms that create this affective register, I turn to a black figure in a seventeenth-century print illustration. Unlike the three previous illustrations, this printed anatomy does not depict the figure's black skin in the white line style or with excessive hatching. However, I argue that this is because the figure's black skin has been artistically lightened to satisfy the inquisitive demands of the scientific white gaze. Because such lightened skin makes it harder for the illustration to signal to English readers to develop white feelings in opposition to the figure, the illustration's accompanying description assists in this racial–affective work. Just as the text that accompanied the illustrations from *The Spanish Tragedy*, *Doctor Faustus*, and *A Choice of Emblemes* informed the reader's interpretation of those illustrations, this same technology of text printed with illustrations maximizes the effect of this double legibility in the anatomy. The interplay between text and illustration teaches the reader first how to identify the figure as non-human, then how to mark oneself as white and English through correctly producing learned emotive responses to the figure, and finally how to erase the provenance of these learned emotive responses by rewriting them as a logical response to the negative emotion that is always already inherent in the non-human black figure.

The Printer to the Reader.

AFter *Michaelmas* Terme in the yeare 1629. A body was brought from the place of Execution to the Physitions Colledge to be Cut vp for an Anatomy, and by Chance, the officer of the Chollidge brought the body of a cruell Wretch, who had murthered the Son of one Master *Scot* a Chyrurgian of goodnote in this City. This Wrech was of a very truculent countenance and aspect, as the Almighty God would therein discover the cruelty of his heart. His haire was black & curled not very long, but thick & bushy, his forehead little aboue an inch high, his browes great and prominent, his eyes set deep in their sockets, his nose crooked with a round knob or batten at the end which also some

wh

Figure 4. Print illustration in "The Printer to the Reader," appearing after the title page of *An Explanation of the Fashion and Use of Three and Fifty Instruments of Chirurgery*, a surgical treatise bound to the end of Helkiah Crooke's *Mikrokosmogr aphia* (1631).

The final pages of the 1631 reprint of Helkiah Crooke's anatomy, *Mikrokosmographia*, contain a treatise on surgical instruments. Between the treatise's title page and preface is an unnumbered section labelled "The Printer to the Reader," illustrated with a three-quarter page woodcut (Fig. 4). The description begins:

> After Michaelmas Term in the year 1629. A body was brought from the place of Execution to the Physicians College to be Cut up for an Anatomy, and by Chance, the officer of the College brought the body of a cruel Wretch, who had murdered the Son of one Master Scot a Chyrurgian of good note in this City. This Wretch was of a very truculent countenance and aspect, as the Almighty God would therein discover the cruelty of his heart.[15]

The passage then goes on to describe the figure's facial features in racist language – "His hair was black & curled not very long, but thick & bushy, his forehead little above an inch high, his brows great and prominent ... his nose crooked with a round knob or button at the end which also somewhat Turned upward ... his nether lip was as big as three lips" – that is similar to how later white Europeans would describe the physical features of sub-Saharan black Africans.[16] Of course, as is clear from the illustration, the figure's skin is not flooded with black ink or covered in hatching to mark it as black. The figure's skin is heavily hatched and,

15. "The Printer to the Reader," in "An Explanation of the Fashion and Use of Three and Fifty Instruments of Chirurgery," in *Mikrokosmographia: A Description of the Body of Man*, ed. Helkiah Crooke (London: Printed by Thomas and Richard Cotes, and are to be sold by Michael Sparke, 1631), sig. F1r. "The Printer to the Reader" does not specify its author aside from the title's claim that this preface is directed to the reader from the printer. There is no printer listed on the title page of surgical treatise, though the title page says that this treatise was printed for Michael Sparke, who was the same bookseller listed on the title page of *Mikrokosmosgraphia*, in which Thomas and Richard Cotes were listed as printers. I believe it is likely that either Thomas or Richard was eponymous printer of "The Printer to the Reader," but I have left this preface without an author as authorship cannot be proven.
16. "The Printer to the Reader," sig. F1r–v.

in some places, cross-hatched. But because in print illustrations, color, shadow, depth, and texture are all represented by black ink lines on a white page, it is difficult to tell whether the hatching and cross-hatching are designed to show dimensionality and detail or whether they are meant to suggest color. One could argue that given the ambiguous hatching in the illustration and the lack of any reference to black skin in the passage, it would be difficult to make a strong case that this is an illustration of a racially *black* figure, especially because, as Anu Korhonen has argued, the English seemed particularly obsessed with black skin as a racial marker.[17] However, I contend that this illustration shows that the technology and craftsmanship of print illustration, combined with the printed text accompanying the illustration, could also signal blackness as a racial formation without the visual cue of flooding a figure's skin with ink. The reason why this figure has such detail — as shown previously, details that are not present in many other depictions of figures with dark skin — is because of the gaze that directs the text, a gaze that requires a high level of detail to carry out its racist, pseudoscientific reading of the figure.

The shift in considering black racial formation beyond blackness as a color is relevant precisely because the illustration appears in an anatomical text, which presumes a scientific, anatomizing gaze. The anatomizing gaze had undergone a seismic shift in the sixteenth century. In *De Fabrica*, Andreas Vesalius had rejected the old Galenic model of anatomy that drew many of its conclusions about the human body from dissections of animal bodies in favor of a new model of anatomy that conducted dissections on human bodies and was interested in the human as a species apart. Although non-human others still appeared sporadically in early modern anatomies, they were increasingly used to emphasize differences, rather than similarities, between humans and non-human others. This means that one of the first moves of the anatomizing gaze is to decide whether to categorize a body as a human or a non-human other. Given the lan-

17. Anu Korhonen, "Washing the Ethiopian White: Conceptualising Black Skin in Renaissance England," in *Black Africans in Renaissance Europe*, ed. T. F. Earle and K. J. P. Lowe (Cambridge: Cambridge University Press, 2005), 94–112.

guage of the passage that describes the figure – "deformity" is mentioned multiple times and later in the passage, the figure is called a "monstrous shape" and "prodigious" – it appears that the anatomizing gaze persuades the reader to doubt the figure's humanity. Rather than categorizing the figure as a human with some distinctive physical features, the anatomy's language of monstrosity categorizes the entire figure as a non-human deformity; a "shape," not a person. In this way, the figure is similar to the three print illustrations of black bodies discussed earlier: in all cases, the reader is encouraged to position themself in opposition to these non-human others not simply to maintain a white English identity against a racial other, but more importantly, to maintain their ontological status as a human in the face of a non-human other.

Because the history of print makes invisible its complicity in the dehumanization of black personhood, its history needs to be interrogated by newer forms of analysis. To theorize these antagonistic encounters between white English readers and print illustrations of black bodies, I turn to Afro-pessimist philosophy. One of the foundational logics of Afro-pessimism is that anti-black violence is not a failure of civil society; rather, civil society depends on and is structured by anti-black violence. This irreconcilable antagonism between civil society and blackness further exposes that the human is not a universal given, but rather an ontological position that defines itself against black sentient flesh. Here I shift my terms from *black body* to use the Afro-pessimistic term *black sentient flesh*, which denotes a shift away from understanding race as a matter of identity and experience to understanding race as ontological and paradigmatic positionality; that is to say, Afro-pessimist claims can be better understood along the axis of human/black rather than the axis of white/non-white. This is not to affirm a kind of scientific or biological essentialism, but to question the human as a universal given, to show how the human is a constructed position and how humanity, in the words of Patrice Douglass, Selamawit D. Terrefe, and Frank B. Wilderson is "made legible through the irreconcilable distinction between humans and blackness."[18] I also want to draw attention to my use of the word *figure* to describe the subject of the illustration, as *figure* simultaneously attends to the ontological positionality of black sentient flesh as not human and not a body, and to the subject as an artistic representation.

Afro-pessimism and early modern studies have not often crossed paths. This is partially because of disciplinary boundaries: Afro-pessimists have often focused on the Middle Passage, the enslaved's journey in slave ships across the Atlantic to the Americas, as the originary rupture between blackness and humanity that positioned the black as an a priori slave and not a human. As a result — and I acknowledge this is a generalization — Afro-pessimist research tends to focus on anti-black racism after the beginning of the transatlantic slave trade, tracing the African diaspora from the African continent to the Americas. Early modernists have typically considered these matters as outside of the purview of their chronological or national and regional bounds. Nonetheless, early modernists such as Kim F. Hall and Matthieu Chapman, as well as historians like Jennifer Morgan, have begun reaching across this disciplinary divide. In *Anti-Black Racism in Early Modern English Drama*, Chapman argues that "anti-black racism existed within the [English] subject based strictly on concepts of blackness before encounters with black Africans. [This] repositions the ontological rupture between blackness and humanity, which Saidiya Hartman originates on the slave ship, to an *a priori*, always already condition."[19] Under Chapman's formulation, it is the growth of anti-blackness based on concepts of blackness, and the fetishization of the human in early modern England, that ruptures blackness from humanity. In other words, it seems unlikely that black Africans would have been subjected to the horrors of slavery and the Middle Passage if Europeans had not already defined them as non-humans and enemies to civil society. This

18. Patrice Douglass, Selamawit D. Terrefe, and Frank B. Wilderson, "Afro-pessimism," *Oxford Bibliographies*, Oxford University Press, last modified 28 August 2018, https://doi.org/10.1093/OBO/9780190280024-0056.
19. Matthieu Chapman, *Anti-Black Racism in Early Modern English Drama: The Other "Other"* (London: Routledge, 2017), 25.

essay traces a portion of this subjection in the growing print industry and its investments in racial formation.

Chapman's work focuses on the interplay between early modern anti-black racism and performances of blackness on the English stage. I extend Chapman's formulation of the Afro-pessimistic early modern to the genres of anatomy and print illustrations. My application of Afro-pessimistic analysis intervenes in two ways. First, insofar as early modern anatomies are preoccupied with defending and defining the boundaries of the human, Afro-pessimistic analysis reveals the ontological precepts that underwrite racial subjection. Likewise, insofar as print illustrations conjure images of black sentient flesh for the English reader to define themselves against in order to assure themselves of their own humanity, Afro-pessimistic analysis reveals the ways the black/white binary of print and print illustrations primes a black vs. human antagonism. How does the printed text and illustration work together to teach the reader to distinguish this figure as something apart from the other humans represented in the anatomy and the chirurgical treatise? First, we may consider that, like the other bodies represented in the anatomy, he appears alive, despite the fact that, according to the description, he had been executed before arriving at the Physician's College. For the other anatomical bodies, liveliness is a way of managing the reader's affects: the otherwise horrifying specter of mutilated, dissected flesh is mitigated through the calm, passively open bodies, who appear to welcome their own anatomizing, gladly giving up their bodies to the pursuit of scientific knowledge. Yet this figure is not in the process of being dissected or marked for dissection like the other bodies in the anatomy, nor is he in the process of being wounded or healed, like the bodies in the chirurgical treatise. What these other bodies have is a divide between interiority and exteriority, the idea that the human body has an interior that can be opened to reveal truth and knowledge about it. The illustration of the figure does not gesture to any kind of interiority; like the other black beings in the previously discussed illustrations, he does not have any kind of personal or individual dimensionality. Rather, he is more akin to the monsters who sometimes appear at the end of early modern anatomies and chirurgical treatises: they are shown un-dissected, suggesting that one does not need to access their interiority to gain knowledge about them; everything necessary to know about them is shown on their surface. Hence the name *monster*, from the Latin *monstrare*, to show or demonstrate. The figure's visual similarity to that of the anatomical monster is also reaffirmed by the categorization of his feet as a major deformity and his face as a lesser deformity in the description: "Such was his face, but the greatest deformity was in his feet."[20] This language encourages the reader to see the figure's flesh not simply as harmless physical anomalies or evidence of a spectrum of human difference, but as a sign to mark him apart from humans.

I have shown that this figure can be categorized with non-human others such as monsters, but can the figure be categorized specifically as non-human black sentient flesh? Part of the Afro-pessimistic definition of the enslaved – and therefore, the black – is the gratuitous violence to which they are subjected, violence that is not contingent on any kind of transgression (perceived or otherwise) but is always present. One might object that the execution and dissection of the black figure is contingent on the murder of *the Son*, yet the passage's intense focus on the figure's flesh as an outward sign of an a priori wicked, evil mind and comparative lack of interest in the actual murder belies this claim (consider the artistic detail of the print and the fact that this print is the largest illustration of a single figure in the entire text; this focus on the visual asks the reader to focus on the figure's flesh, not his actions). The murder of *the Son* is not the event that justifies the violence, it simply proves that the figure was always already an enemy to civil society, proves the danger of letting someone who is so clearly marked with evil roam free. If the violence were contingent on the figure's alleged criminal act, then the process of dissecting the figure would – like the other anatomical specimens in the text, who were likely based on the bodies of dissected criminals – return the figure to society as a representative body whose anonymity has functioned to distance them from their crime. But this is not the case. The figure has not been distanced from his crime, and the details about him – who he murdered, when he was brought from the executioner, etc. – make his namelessness not a sign of protective anonymity, but a sign that he has no individuality as a human, no relationality to civil soci-

20. "The Printer to the Reader," sig. F1v.

ety. The other characters mentioned in the passage enjoy membership in incredibly complex, overlapping networks of family, business, government, friendship, and status — consider the multilayered kinship ties enumerated in the phrase "the Son of one Master Scot a Chyrurgian of good note in this City" — but the figure has no name, no heritage, no family. Due to his lack of heritage or kinship, the figure functions on the level of narrative as a force of anti-kinship; his alleged murder of *the Son* not only appears to threaten the entirety of civil society, but also its futurity.

But showing how the anatomy categorizes the figure as non-human black sentient flesh is incomplete without considering the affective process of reading that trains readers to identify with English whiteness, to develop white feelings. In this case, the illustration and descriptive passage work in concert to discipline the white reader who might see a human here, motivating them to develop white feelings through the shame of misreading. This misreading begins when the white reader is lulled into a sense of calmness and security through the print illustration's visual tropes. The illustration features a pastoral landscape upon which the figure stands in *contrapposto*, with most of his weight on right foot. This classical stance bestows the figure with an air of relaxation and places him in a posture of utmost visibility. His palms face the reader, in a gesture of candor; his face, which serenely gazes out at the reader, repeats these themes of relaxation, calmness, and visual openness. These visual tropes present the reader with a figure open for visual consumption, whose tranquil aura encourages a similarly peaceful response from the reader. But the passage upbraids the reader for this (mis)reading:

> This monstrous shape of a man I have thought good to cut and have added this relation thereto from certain knowledge; (for there were a thousand witnesses of it) that you may know Almighty God doth sometime set his brand and mark upon wicked men: First that we may know and avoid them: Secondly to shew his detestation of a mind which in his eternal wisdom, he foresaw would be so foul and ulcerated, and finally because so wicked a

> mind might have a proportionable habitation, to wit, a prodigious and deformed body.[21]

This part of the passage contains the only direct admonition from the printer to the reader: "This monstrous shape of a man I have thought good to cut … that *you* may know Almighty God doth sometime set his brand and mark upon wicked men."[22] In this moment of direct address, the reader who might have identified with the figure or simply have interpreted him as non-threatening is shamed for being fooled, for misreading, and for being a bad Christian who cannot see God's marks upon the wicked. It is this shame that directs the wayward reader from identifying or empathizing with the figure and towards identifying with civil society, formulated here as the "thousand witnesses." It is this affective process that leads to white feelings; whiteness is confirmed by becoming a witness.

I return to the metaphor at the opening of this essay: bodies are texts and texts are bodies. But if we are to attend seriously to the early modern writers who imagined and reaffirmed the connections between the page, whiteness, and humanness on the one hand, and the connections between ink, blackness, and non-human abject black flesh on the other hand, then we must reread this formulation through an Afro-pessimist lens: bodies are texts and texts are bodies, but black sentient flesh is ink and ink is black sentient flesh. The early modern move to imagine print as an inherently raced material creates a cultural concept of print as always already a technology of race-making, regardless of whether the printed

21. "The Printer to the Reader," sig. F1v.
22. "The Printer to the Reader," sig. F1v emphases added. The cutting that the printer references in the phrase "I have thought good to cut" plays on the similarities between the cutting of a woodblock print and the cutting in an anatomical dissection. However, the kind of cutting that the printer is referring to is not the kind of anatomical cutting that shows a body with interiority and exteriority, but rather the cutting of a woodblock print, in which the figure only exists as an exterior. The passage later hints at the figure's interior, but the interior is never shown because it is too loathsome. In the end, the marks upon the figure's exterior erase any need to explore the figure's interiority or even consider its existence.

text or illustration can be said to address race overtly. Early modern print and print illustrations are ancestors of modern white supremacy and global anti-blackness; theorizing the entanglement of print and race more fully reveals print's material role in developing the white emotions, reading practices, and subjectivity that undergirded anti-blackness in early modern England.[23]

23. This essay is dedicated to the memory of Professor Brandie R. Siegfried. I would like to thank Kim F. Hall, Arthur L. Little Jr., and Matthieu Chapman for their input on this essay as it developed.

9. "Away, You Ethiop!": *A Midsummer Night's Dream* and the Denial of Black Affect—A Song to Underscore the Burning of Police Stations

MATTHIEU CHAPMAN

You so numb you watch the cops choke out a man like me
Until my voice goes from a shriek to a whisper "I can't breathe."
And you sit there in house on couch and watch it on TV
The most you give's a Twitter rant and call it a tragedy
But truly the travesty's you've been robbed of your empathy
~ Run the Jewels, "Walking in the Snow"[1]

♦♦♦

***** Content Warning for My Non-Black Colleagues *****
This essay contains use of the "N-word."

♦♦♦

*****Content Warning for My Black Folx*****
This essay contains descriptions of black (anti)life and the continuum of anti-black violence that coincides with the lack of consideration granted

1. Run the Jewels (RTJ), "Walking in the Snow," MP3 audio, track 6 on RTJ4, Jewel Runners/BMG, 2020.

to black lives in civil society.[2] Niggas die on these pages, just as a nigga died a little writing it.[3]

♦♦♦

"Hey," she said, leaning sheepishly into the doorway of my office, "can we talk about the apparatus?"

Ah, yes, the apparatus.

"Sure," I said, "what's up?"

She crossed the threshold from the main hallway of the theatre building at Central Washington University and into my unseasonably hot, sticky office. The theatre department occupied one of the oldest buildings on a campus originally founded in 1891. Ellensburg, in the central high desert of Washington State, was made the home of a state university as a consolation prize for missing out on being the state capital after a fire destroyed the downtown in the late 1880s.

"Should I close the door?" I asked. I asked everyone who entered my office this question. I never knew what information a student would share when they approached: oftentimes, they would ask about course work or readings; other times, they would vent about microaggressions and slights they had received from faculty and students. On rare occasions,

2. I use "civil society" in the Gramscian sense, as the private or non-state sphere of society that includes structures of filiation (family, home, etc.) as opposed to political society that includes structures of affiliation (police, government, etc.), although the two often overlap. To Antonio Gramsci, political society is the realm of force and civil society is the realm of consent: political society enforces rule; civil society consents to being ruled. For a brief explanation, see: Sassoon, Anne Showstack (1991b). "Civil Society". In Bottomore, Tom; Harris, Laurence; Kiernan, V.G; Miliband, Ralph (eds.). *The Dictionary of Marxist Thought* (Second ed.). Blackwell Publishers Ltd. pp. 83–85. ISBN 0-631-16481-2. For the origin of Gramsci's thought, see: Gramsci, Antonio. Gramsci, Antonio. *Prison Notebooks*. 3 Vol. Columbia University Press, 2011.
3. The point of the essay is that civil society grants recognition to the capacity for anti-black discourse such as nigger to cause damage and offense to non-black bodies, but disregards any notions of progress or pro-blackness or "wokeness" when it comes to actual actions that end black lives and broadcast, without concern, black death.

they would tell me personal secrets of sexual violence or other crimes that universities have an incentive to ignore.

This student's tone led me to believe that this would be closer to the latter than the former.

"I am concerned the apparatus might be transphobic," she said.

The apparatus in question was a ten-inch purple strap-on dildo that was being used as a prop in the production of William Shakespeare's *A Midsummer Night's Dream* that I was directing for the Central Theatre Ensemble, which is the department's name either for the group involved in the production of department plays or for the plays themselves — I was never quite sure. The costume designer, fearful that the students would treat the sex toy as a toy and not as a serious prop, demanded that the entire creative team never refer to the object by any of the colloquial names with which we were familiar, but rather by the sterile, professional term of "the apparatus." As anyone who has ever known a late-adolescent human could probably tell you, this phraseology did not have the desired effect, and instead "apparatus" just became a new slang term for genitalia within the cast.

While I am derisive of and utterly disdain the capital C "Concept" that often covers productions of Shakespeare's texts in layer after layer of aesthetic distractions that assuage the director's ego but do little to enhance or even communicate the text at hand, I do believe that productions of Shakespeare's works, like any production of any play, must have a clear story to tell beyond the narrative contained in Shakespeare's words. In this case, using the various couplings and un-couplings and re-couplings that occur between the lovers — indeed even between species — as foundation and evidence, I wanted the production to question not only the stability, but also the very purpose, of cis-normative, monogamous hegemony in Western culture. To do so, I was very cautious to avoid demeaning or discouraging any specific attractions between beings — whether polyamorous, interracial, or interspecies — and instead presented the varied sexual explorations of the play as a normal part of life, as experiences to embrace rather than to condemn or abstain from.

To further this goal of normalizing varying sexualities, the roles of all of the Mechanicals, that roving troupe of theatrical performers, were filled by women. As such, the "heroic" Bottom's transformation from man to ass became a transformation from woman to ass. Offstage, Bottom would add the donkey head and the apparatus, and reappear with both.

"I'm worried," said the student, "that the audience will think that the Mechanicals are afraid of a person who underwent a gender swap and not only the donkey stuff." My student was concerned that Quince's cry of "O Monstrous! O Strange!"[4] at the sight of the newly transformed Bottom would contain double meanings for the audience: first, the audience would read terror at the sight of a woman turned half-donkey; second, they would read the addition of the apparatus as an anatomical transformation, making the Mechanicals flee in terror at the sight of a woman turned man.

This fear had never occurred to me.

"I never thought of that," I told the student, "but you're right. How do we fix it?"

"Would it be possible," she asked hesitantly, "to maybe have Bottom come back on stage after the transformation with just the ass-head first, and then maybe have him put on the apparatus while onstage?"

It was such an elegant solution to a problem I didn't even recognize, and the solution strengthened the story as a whole, removing the audience's ability to read the apparatus as the source of the Mechanicals' fear and making the moment transphobic. The apparatus would now be given to the ass-headed Bottom as a gift from Titania, thus making the apparatus part and parcel of her desire for Bottom.

It would have been easy in the moment to brush off this student's concerns and continue with the staging we had already blocked; but in truth, I was quite proud. I was not only proud that she saw an issue, presented an argument for why it was an issue, and offered a constructive solution, but I was also proud that my assistant directors, stage managers, and myself had created a rehearsal atmosphere wherein students were comfortable bringing these issues to me.

4. William Shakespeare, A *Midsummer Night's Dream*, ed. Barbara Mowat, Paul Werstine, Michael Poston, and Rebecca Niles (Washington: Folger Shakespeare Library, n.d.), 3.1.105, accessed 9 August 2020, https://shakespeare.folger.edu/shakespeares-works/a-midsummer-nights-dream/.

Which made that night's rehearsal all the more flummoxing.

"Away, you Ethiop!"[5] bellowed Lysander across the stage.

Although Bottom's transformation from man to ass is perhaps one of the most well-known stage moments in Shakespeare's canon, so much so that it is memorialized in woodcuts and statues, it is not the only transformation to occur within the play. Amid lovers switching lovers and a fairy loving a monster, Hermia, at least in the eyes of her love Lysander, undergoes a racial transformation: from fair beloved to Ethiop — from non-black to black.

After the earlier discussion concerning the potential transphobia of the staging, I expected this line to cause some consternation among my multi-ethnic, multi-racial cast. In both instances, the character's transformation causes immediate disgust and revulsion among their cohorts onstage. Yet, in the case of Bottom, he immediately finds new companionship with Titania. Hermia, once transformed, is subject to insults and hate not only from Lysander, who marks her as black, but also from the uncharmed Helena.[6] It is not until the end of the scene, when Puck removes the potion and thus the transformation, that Hermia finds companionship again. The monstrous, half-man, half-animal Bottom receives consideration as an object of desire. The blackened Hermia does not.

Hermia's transformation to black, and the resulting exile by her love, never triggered any remarks from the cast. Instead, "Away, you Ethiop!"[7]

5. Shakespeare, A *Midsummer Night's Dream*, 3.2.265.

6. The following insults are lobbed at Hermia by the rest of the party. Lysander: "Hang off, thou cat, thou burr! Vile thing, let loose" (3.2.270); "Out, loathèd med'cine! O, hated potion, hence!" (3.2.275); "And never did desire to see thee more. / Therefore be out of hope, of question, of doubt. / Be certain, nothing truer, 'tis no jest / That I do hate thee" (3.2.290–95). Helena: "Have you no modesty, no maiden shame, / No touch of bashfulness? What, will you tear / Impatient answers from my gentle tongue? / Fie, fie, you counterfeit, you puppet, you" (3.2.300–303).

7. "Away, you Ethiop!" is not the only racial insult Lysander throws at Hermia. "Out, tawny Tartar, out!" follows a mere six lines later (3.2.274), and also contains racial intent. See Bernadette Andrea, "The Tartar Girl, The Persian Princess, and Early Modern English Women's Authorship from Elizabeth I to Mary Wroth," in *Women Writing Back / Writing Women Back: Traditional Perspectives from the Late Middle Ages to the Dawn of the*

echoed throughout the space, crashed off the ceiling, and cascaded down the walls. The slur never resonated with the minds and flesh occupying the space. In the moment, I was perplexed, but the confusion only rose to a vague, "hmmm?" in the furrowing of my brow and not a question in my mouth. I shook it off as best I could and continued rehearsal uninterrupted. Yet the inarticulable question would not cease bouncing around my preconscious. "These are bright, socially engaged students," I thought. "Why didn't anyone ask about this line? What *should* they ask about this line?"

Modern Era, ed. Anke Gilleir, Alicia C. Montoya, and Suzan van Dijk (Leiden, Netherlands: Brill, 2010), 257–81. But these two insults do not operate on the same register. "Out, tawny Tartar, out!" engages with conflicts between racialized identities of whiteness and Asian and Muslim, such as colonization, religion, and empire, that, while important, operate under the assumption that both sides in the conflict are human. Hate against Asians is a real and important issue. Hate against Muslims is a real and important issue. This essay recognizes the importance of such tragedies and arguments; however, we must also recognize that the suffering of Asians and Muslims is not analogous with the suffering of blacks. While Asians and Muslims are subject to white supremacy, they also are both recognized as human and participate, although as junior partners, in the civil society that is built on anti-blackness. For discussion of the unique grammar of suffering that afflicts blackness, see: Saidiya Hartman, *Scenes of Subjection: Terror, Slavery, and Self-Making in Nineteenth Century America* (Oxford: Oxford University Press, 1997); Frank B. Wilderson III, *Afropessimism* (New York: Liveright Publishing, 2020); "Gramsci's Black Marx: Whither the Slave in Civil Society?" *Social Identities* 9, no. 2 (2003): 225–40; "The Prison Slave as Hegemony's (Silent) Scandal," *Social Justice* 30, no. 2 (2003): 18–27; Zakiyyah Iman Jackson, *Becoming human: Matter and Meaning in an Antiblack World* (New York: New York University Press, 2020). For how this grammar of suffering resonates with blackness in Early Modern English thought, see Matthieu Chapman, *Anti-Black Racism in Early Modern English Drama: The Other "Other"* (London: Routledge, 2017); and "Red, White, and Black: Shakespeare's *The Tempest* and the Structuring of Racial Antagonisms in Early Modern England and the New World," *Theatre History Studies* 39, no. 1 (2020): 7–23. Attempting to analogize Asian and Muslim suffering with that of blacks erases the differences between the human conflicts of broad racism and white supremacy under which Asians and Muslims suffer and the specifics of the irreconcilable antagonism between blacks and humanity that defines anti-blackness.

"It can't be a lack of awareness," I thought. The department was currently embroiled in a controversy over racial representation in the season's previous show, in which Chinese characters were played by white students. The willingness of one student of black and Japanese descent to speak about issues of racial representation led to protests of the production, and this student was currently cast as Oberon.

Was it an issue of power? Was this student, this black student, so used to being unheard, marginalized, and terrorized by the university apparatus (yes, I use the term here intentionally) that he decided it was too much of a risk to raise the ire of the university again, as he had done mere weeks earlier?

"It can't be power," I thought, "or, at least, not *just* power." I am familiar with student/faculty power dynamics, and I do my best to defuse them by openly stating that grades are coercive in nature, an apparatus (again, that word) designed to subdue any radical thoughts the students may have and dismiss any opinions or ideas that are not to the professor's liking. Too often in my own experience, grades were used this way: as a threat, as a marker not of education and learning, but of conformity. As a cudgel to beat a square peg into a round hole.

But regardless of my larger thoughts on academia, just earlier that day a student was comfortable enough to express her concerns with the play's representation of gender and sexuality. Yet, as I stood there hearing the student repeat the line over and over as we worked and re-worked the scene, no one questioned the line's anti-black sentiments. The entire cast seemed completely unaffected (indeed, un-affect-ed) by it.

The differences between these two moments resonated in the publicity for the production. Each poster and program was accompanied by a content warning for sexual content.

No content warning was given for racial violence.

We are so conditioned as human beings to read blackness as undesiring and undeserving of love that the intersection of blackness and desire is unimaginable. The libidinal economy from which desires arise is already coded with anti-black violence to the extent that we are precluded from empathizing with those who are victims of it. As such, civil society's visual and linguistic methods of communication are so dependent on anti-black violence that it goes unheard — even when spoken. The bar for black suffering is so high that unless a nigga is hanging from a tree, we don't think violence is occurring.

This essay ruminates on that moment, using this singular absence of questioning to raise questions about the capacity of black flesh, even imagined black flesh, to resonate with human affect, and to ponder the limits of human imagination in relation to desire, violence, and blackness. Using affect theory and Afro-pessimism as the framework of this interrogation, I offer a reading of this text and this moment that positions *A Midsummer Night's Dream* within a continuum of anti-black imagery that establishes blackness as beyond the bounds of affective resonance with civil society.

♦♦♦

Scholarship on race in early modern England has become a flourishing field. Although studies into the topic date back to the mid-twentieth century,[8] the field began to claim its place in the current zeitgeist in the 1990s with Kim F. Hall's *Things of Darkness* and Margo Hendricks and Patricia Parker's edited collection *Women, "Race" and Writing in the Early Modern Period*, among others.[9] Over the following decades, scholars such as Ayanna Thompson, Arthur L. Little Jr., Ian Smith, and Joyce Green MacDonald each made substantial contributions not only to studies of race in the English Renaissance, but also to the discipline of Renaissance Stud-

8. Examples of earlier texts on race in early modern England include (among others): Anthony Gerard Barthelemy, *Black Face, Maligned Race: The Representation of Blacks in English Drama from Shakespeare to Southerne* (Baton Rouge: University of Louisiana Press, 1987); Eldred D. Jones, *Othello's Countrymen: A Study of the African in Elizabethan and Jacobean Drama* (Oxford: Oxford University Press, 1965); *The Elizabethan Image of Africa* (Charlottesville: University of Virginia Press, 1971); Peter Fryer, *Staying Power: A History of Black People in Britain* (London: Pluto Press, 1984).

9. Kim F. Hall, *Things of Darkness: Economies of Race and Gender in Early Modern England* (Ithaca, NY: Cornell University Press, 1995); Margo Hendricks and Patricia Parker, eds. *Women, "Race" and Writing in the Early Modern Period* (London: Routledge, 1994).

ies.[10] Even so, as the field of scholarship highlights the importance of race in early modern literature, it is important to build on these insights to reach theatre practice and further interrogate the trigger points for theatre practitioners.

While the field has continued to grow over the last twenty-plus years, it is only just beginning to break away from longstanding assumptions of what exactly constitutes race and to whom. Most scholarship on race in early modern England functions under two assumptive logics: first, that race is primarily phenotypical differences between types of humans; and second, that whites compose a normative, non-racialized subject. These assumptive logics help us to understand why, despite the countless advances made in studies of race in English drama, the majority of works that look at race in drama focus on Shakespeare's "race plays": *Othello* and *Titus Andronicus*.[11] Recently, however, scholars such as Little and Noémie Ndiaye have offered new and expanded lenses for analyzing race in the period that extends beyond the obvious and outdated notion of "racialized others" and de-centers English whiteness as the normative subject in favor of more networked analyses.[12]

A *Midsummer Night's Dream* is not untouched by the growth of critical race approaches to Shakespeare. Most notably, Patricia Akhimie focuses

10. Ayanna Thompson, *Performing Race and Torture on the Early Modern Stage* (London: Routledge, 2008); Arthur L. Little Jr., *Shakespeare Jungle Fever: National-Imperial Re-Visions of Race, Rape, and Sacrifice*, (Stanford, CA: Stanford University Press, 2000); Ian Smith, *Race and Rhetoric in the Renaissance: Barbarian Errors* (New York: Palgrave MacMillan, 2009); Joyce Green Macdonald, *Race, Ethnicity, and Power in the Renaissance* (Madison, NJ: Fairleigh Dickinson University Press, 1997); *Women and Race in Early Modern Texts* (Cambridge: Cambridge University Press, 2002).
11. Although these two are not the only Shakespearean works to be discussed in relation to race and its varying intersections with nation, gender, and religion, they do bear the majority of the intellectual labor on the topic.
12. Arthur Little Jr. is the editor of *White People in Shakespeare* (London: The Arden Shakespeare/Bloomsbury, forthcoming), a collection that analyzes whiteness as a category of race in early modern England. Noémie Ndiaye, *Scripts of Blackness: Early Modern Performance Culture and the Making of Race* (Philadelphia: University of Pennsylvania Press, forthcoming), offers a transnational approach to race that seeks uncover networks of difference that transcend nation-state analyses.

on the rude Mechanicals as a site of intersection of class and race in the English project of cultivation.[13] However, most studies that engage with the play's treatment of race center on the little Indian boy, a character who never appears on stage. This "little changeling boy" whose "mother was a vot'ress of [Titania's] order" has been discussed in relation to colonialist desire, the nuclear family, and other topics.[14] But precisely because the little Indian boy is unseen, his racialization resides in the audience's imagination.[15]

But there is another imagined racialized other in the play, one whose presence is the target of immediate disgust and abjection. When Lysander awakens under the spell of Robin Goodfellow, his love for fair Hermia is

13. Patricia Akhimie, *Shakespeare and the Cultivation of Difference: Race and Conduct in the Early Modern World* (London: Routledge, 2018).
14. Shakespeare, *A Midsummer Night's Dream*, 2.1.123, 127. See Margo Hendricks, "'Obscured by Dreams': Race, Empire, and Shakespeare's *A Midsummer Night's Dream*," *Shakespeare Quarterly* 47, no. 1 (1996): 37–60; Thomas R. Frosch, "The Missing Child in *A Midsummer Night's Dream*," *American Imago* 64, no. 4 (2007): 485–511; Maurice Hunt, "Individuation in *A Midsummer Night's Dream*," *South Central Review* 3, no. 2 (1986): 1–13; Ania Loomba, "The Great Indian Vanishing Trick — Colonialism, Property, and the Family in *A Midsummer Night's Dream*," in *A Feminist Companion to Shakespeare*, 2nd ed., ed. Dympna Callaghan (Malden, MA: Wiley Blackwell, 2016), 181–206; Shirley Nelson Garner, "A Midsummer Night's Dream: 'Jack Shall Have Jill; / Nought Shall Go Ill,'" *Women's Studies: An Inter-Disciplinary Journal* 9, no. 1 (1981): 47–63.
15. Although the Indian Boy not appearing onstage in the original text, many productions have staged him. I agree with Hendricks's argument that, "Whether the Indian boy appears onstage at all is generally of little consequence, since he has no lines and would function as little more than a stage prop," in regards to any individual staging ("'Obscured by Dreams,'" 37). But, as Hendricks points out, the Indian Boy was staged at least as early as 1906 and has a long history of being staged, despite the fact that he does not appear in the text. By staging the Indian Boy and giving him presence as an object of desire, these productions place him within the paradigmatic position of the subaltern or the object, both positions that are defined by their relation to the subject. The Ethiope, the abject black, is defined by its incapacity for relations that are recognized by civil society. By staging the Indian Boy, directors throw the revulsion and abjection contained in "Ethiope" into further relief.

transformed, and, in turn, transforms her into a detested Ethiope[16] – an insult that has no other referents within the context of the play, arriving without warning and passing without comment.

What accounts for the distinction between these two racialized others? Why is an imagined Indian boy an object of desire while the imagined Ethiope the abject of desire? Why does the love between a Faerie and an ass receive textual consideration and exploration, while the disgust of black flesh requires neither?

These questions signal the role of affect in the Early Modern English's attempts to articulate and test the bounds not only of human subjectivity, but of human imagination in regards to blackness. With affect theory and Afro-pessimism providing the vocabularies for analysis, Shakespeare's *A Midsummer Night's Dream* becomes part of a centuries-long continuum of anti-black violence that distorts the affective resonance between blackness and humanity.

♦ ♦ ♦

On 25 May 2020, Officer Derek Chauvin, a state-sponsored and taxpayer funded terrorist, kneeled on the neck of George Floyd for eight minutes and forty-six seconds, causing death by strangulation asphyxiation. Three of his terrorist compatriots stood as bystanders while the murder occurred.

I saw the video. Not by choice, necessarily, but when I awoke on the morning of the 26th and logged in to Facebook, I saw the video shared countless times – mostly as autoplay videos that assault the viewer when

16. "Ethiope" has long history within the discourse and culture of early modern England as an abject being whose positionality and race are immutable. For discussions of the immutability of the Ethiope in processes of conversions, see Dennis Austin Britton, *Becoming Christian: Race, Reformation, and Early Modern English Romance* (New York: Fordham University Press 2014); Chapman, *Anti-Black Racism in Early Modern English Drama*. For the deployment of Ethiope as an insult for comic effect, see Patricia Akhimie, "Racist Humor and Shakespearean Comedy" in *The Cambridge Companion to Shakespeare and Race*, ed. Ayanna Thompson (Cambridge: Cambridge University Press, 2021), 47–61.

they click the link for a news article, but occasionally a friend would share the video by itself.

I like my friends. They are generally intelligent, conscientious people. The vast majority believe in social justice and content warnings and burning down police stations. Which made the sharing of the video all the more disturbing. Not that they shared it — I would expect these friends, so involved in racial, social, and gender justice issues, to share this news as a condemnation of police violence and to ask, "How much is enough?" But I was shocked that not once did I see the video shared with a content warning. In clicking "post" or "share," these friends decided that the unbridled sadism and violence of this officer toward this black man needed to be seen, needed to be shared. They did not, however, consider the effect that this video would have on the black lives who were forced to relive this violence on their screens and who live this violence every day. In their zeal to present spectacular violence against black bodies to the world as a call for social justice, these friends committed their own acts of anti-black violence.

Unfortunately, the cycle of black death is the way of our world. George Floyd's death and the visual reminders of black inhumanity are so interwoven in the fabric of our society that it would be easy to assume that the Run the Jewels rhymes serving as the epigraph for this essay are about George Floyd. *RTJ4*, however, was completed before the death of George Floyd. Killer Mike (Michael Render) is in fact rapping about the murder of Eric Garner, another black man whose crime was technically tax-evasion related to selling loose cigarettes without paying taxes, but whose crime was historically and ontologically related to having the gall to assert his humanity as a black man to the slavecatchers.[17]

These murders are just two small dots, two data points in an infinite continuum of anti-black violence that structures black life. This continuum is so inextricable from the American consciousness that Jim Crow

17. The history of police in America begins with the Slave Patrol of South Carolina in 1704, which was organized to apprehend escaped slaves and squash slave rebellions. These slave patrols expanded throughout the thirteen colonies and lasted until over a decade after the Civil War.

and Emmitt Till and MLK and Michael Brown and Trayvon Martin and Eric Garner and Sandra Bland and Breonna Taylor — individual people in unique situations — collapse into one and the same. Black death is so much a part of our consciousness that the names and dates and causes of the dead are erased, replacing their individuality with the redundant and tiresome tropes of "unarmed black man," "unarmed black woman," and "unarmed black child."[18]

The role of black suffering and its incapacity to produce affect is so much a part of our thought that it exists beyond thought, influencing our actions before they occur. The content warnings that begin this essay exist solely to throw into relief how stories and images of black death, black exile, black suffering, and anti-black violence — a combination of phenomena that construct black social death in civil society — are rarely accompanied on news outlets and social media with content warnings.[19]

In fact, it is quite the opposite. The distribution of images of black death have a long history of being thoughtlessly produced and consumed by white culture. When officers beat Rodney King as he cried for help and mercy in 1991, the videotape was broadcast nightly on the news, and the acquittal of his assailants sparked the LA Riots in 1992. School textbooks contain images of civil rights protestors attacked by dogs and suppressed with firehoses.[20] David Marriott writes extensively on the distribution of

18. These phrases are all shockingly racist. Choosing to state "unarmed" reveals that we assume danger, violence, and criminality from black bodies.
19. Orlando Patterson, *Slavery and Social Death: A Comparative Study* (Cambridge, MA: Harvard University Press, 1985), articulates social death as a state that defines the enslaved in various slave-owning societies consisting of three elements: 1. General dishonor; 2. Natal alienation; and 3. Subject to gratuitous violence prior to an act of transgression.
20. The dissemination of black death is not only visual, but textual. Mississippi was praised in 2011 for setting a new standard that all grades must include an in-depth analysis of the Civil Rights Movement in social studies classes. According to a 2017 article by Sierra Mannie, an analysis of textbooks used in the state of Mississippi for grades K–12 showed that all 148 districts in the state still used outdated texts for teaching about the Civil Rights Movement, the most egregious of which only included five pages of Civil Rights content while making sixty-nine mentions of one of the state's former pro-lynching governors ("Mississippi Textbooks Gloss over Civil Rights Struggle," *Education*

lynching photography as a form of identity and cultural formation for white Americans.[21] Uncle Tom's whipping at the hands of Simon Legree in George L. Aiken's 1852 stage adaptation of *Uncle Tom's Cabin* is burdened with the pathos of the play.[22] The assassination of Crispus Attucks that is memorialized in W. L. *Champney's famous* 1856 *print and woodcuts and drawings from even earlier*, sparked the Boston Massacre.[23] This list goes on and on — as long as there has been an America, Americans have produced, distributed, and memorialized images of black death and the destruction of black flesh.

The burgeoning field of Afro-pessimism posits that the paradigmatic structure of the world is predicated on an irreconcilable antagonism between blackness and humanity. As such, black flesh is not recognized as human. Instead, blackness serves as the ontological abject against and through which humanity is able to articulate its existence.[24]

However, Afro-pessimists often focus on America in their analyses of blackness, a slippage that assumes abject blackness as a uniquely American problem — as Frank B. Wilderson III states, "Africans went into the ships and came out as black."[25] Christina Sharpe's *In the Wake* solidifies this conceptualization, articulating black being in relation to four distinct elements of the Middle Passage: the Wake, the Ship, the Hold, and the Weather. Sharpe calls for theorists to engage in "wake work," or work that engages with "the impossibility of [black belonging] by representing the

Week, 4 October 2017, https://www.edweek.org/ew/articles/2017/10/04/why-students-are-ignorant-about-the-civil.html).

21. David Marriott, *On Black Men* (New York: Columbia University Press, 2000).
22. George L. Aiken, *Uncle Tom's Cabin* (New York: Samuel French, 1858).
23. W. L. Chapmney, *The Boston Massacre, March* 5, 1770 (New York: Metropolitan Museum of Art, 1856).
24. Frank B. Wilderson III, *Red, White, and Black: Cinema and the Structure of US Antagonisms* (Durham, NC: Duke University Press, 2010), distinguishes this essential antagonism in subjectivity from important conflicts between identities. See also Chapman, *Anti-Black Racism in Early Modern English Drama.*
25. Wilderson, *Red, White, and Black*, 39.

paradoxes of blackness within and after the legacy of slavery's denial of Black humanity."[26]

In this essay, I have both engaged with the paradoxes of black life in the afterlives of slavery, as well as signaled to the possibility of blackness exceeding and preceding the Wake that Sharpe argues structures black being. While the former certainly falls under Sharpe's rubric of wake work, the latter is wake work of another kind — the kind that questions the afterlives of slavery by questioning whether black slavery had or has a pre-life. Can black slavery have an *after*life if black slavery never begins or ends, but rather exists in an absolute and atemporal *is*? Is there a time of the black human, or are all times of the black slave? What if the hold of the slave ship is a product of a wave of anti-black thought and psychic processes that structured humanity in the early modern period?

If so, then the time of black humanity was not cut short by the Ship. The black was not severed from the human in the Hold. The grotesque pastime of reveling in the destruction of black flesh is not exclusive to America; it predates the American experiment. Black social death did not enter into the paradigmatic structure of the world in the wake of the slave ship. Black inhumanity predates the transatlantic accumulation and displacement of black bodies, as evidenced by the maps and narratives and woodcuts and stories of the early modern English. The American culture of black death contains echoes of and echoes throughout our readings and thinking of a much larger geographical and temporal span. If we look in the art of Restoration England, we see Oroonoko dismembered and flayed both on the page and the stage.[27] This dismemberment of black flesh for audience entertainment is one of the cultural practices that the English re-established after the Interregnum, with Elizabethan plays such as George Peele's *The Battle of Alcazar* containing the destruction of black

26. Christina Sharpe, *In the Wake: On Blackness and Being* (Durham, NC: Duke University Press, 2016), 13.
27. See Aphra Behn, *Oroonoko: Or, the Royal Slave* (London: Printed for Will. Canning, at his Shop in the Temple-Cloysters, 1688) and Thomas Southerne's 1695 stage adaptation, *Oroonoko: A Tragedy*. See also Thompson, *Performing Race and Torture on the Early Modern Stage*, esp. Chapter 3.

flesh, as the only black moor, Muly Muhamet, is flayed for his fratricide.[28] Prior to all of this, Queen Elizabeth bestowed John Hawkyns with a new family crest containing a bound black slave.[29]

The constant and overt distribution of black death, of black suffering and destruction, should have worn down the hardest of hearts by now. According to psychologist Silvan S. Thompkins, who codified and described the nine human affects, thus establishing affect theory as a field of psychology, one of the key components of affect is affective resonance, or a person's tendency to resonate and experience the same affect in response to viewing a display of that affect by another person.[30] In other words, when humans view a human experiencing terror, the affect of the viewed (terror) should impact and cause the viewer to experience a similar affect (terror). This affective resonance is the emotional component of empathy.[31]

The sheer volume of black death that appears in our art and clutters our media, and its representation of fear, humiliation, and terror, should have driven society to either fight for change or unravel into madness. Yet, the proliferation of video and the ease of social media has aided the trend's increase — "I can't breathe" at the click of a button. Black death is such a part of our culture that it is consistently woven into representation; for instance, in the trope of the black man being the first to die

28. Chapman, *Anti-Black Racism in Early Modern English Drama*, 67–105.
29. Hall, *Things of Darkness*, 20.
30. For a complete articulation the theory, the nine affects, and affective resonance, see Silvan S. Thompkins, *Affect, Imagery, Consciousness: Volume 1: The Positive Affects* (London: Tavistock, 1962), as well as the 3 subsequent volumes. While affect theory has been interpreted and expounded on in various analyses in relation to critical theory, perhaps most notably by Gilles Delueze and Félix Guattari, in Deleuze, Gilles, and Félix Guattari. A *thousand plateaus: Capitalism and schizophrenia*. Bloomsbury Publishing, 1988. I intentionally use Thompkins to show how even at its inception, affect theory functions with a humanist assumptive logic that cannot account for the lack of relationality between blackness and humanity.
31. Ana Seara-Cardoso, Catherine L. Sebastian, Essi Viding, and Jonathan P. Roiser, "Affective Resonance in Response to Others' Emotional Faces Varies with Affective Ratings and Psychopathic Traits in Amygdala and Anterior Insula," *Social Neuroscience* 11, no. 2 (2016): 140–52.

in a horror film. Black death is a latent and unacknowledged force, from the film genres of horror and action that allow audiences to take pleasure in the death of black people, to the erasure of black social media personalities and content creators whose talents and products gain popularity once stolen by white social media stars.

But the definition of affective resonance reveals the repeatedly seen but often unspoken scandal of civil society – that civil society does not view the destruction of black flesh, the accumulation of black deaths, empathetically. Black death does not resonate affectively with humanity – blackness distorts affect for humanity. Afro-pessimists have offered many possible interpretations of this affective distortion. In *Scenes of Subjection*, Saidiya Hartman dissects various primary source documents from the pre-bellum South, including personal letters, court cases, and slave narratives, to argue that the Master was incapable of feeling empathy for the Slave – that under the overwhelming gratuitous violence, the line between Slave terror and Slave enjoyment was obliterated.[32] Jared Sexton goes one step further in *Amalgamation Schemes*, arguing that the relationship of pure domination between the Master and the Slave demands that affects – be they love, lust, fear, or terror – be analyzed in relation to scales of coercion, rendering all affects as violent affects.[33] While Hartman argues for a lack of affective resonance and Sexton argues that black affects are always read as violence, Wilderson offers an articulation of the relation between non-black and black affect as one of mutation and distortion. In "Social Death and Narrative Aporia in 12 *Years a Slave*," he argues that the visual signifier that is the destruction of black flesh actually reads as pleasurable to civil society. This disconnect signals to the sadomasochistic underpinnings of a human psyche that gains coherence through the obliteration of non-human, black flesh.[34]

32. Hartman, *Scenes of Subjection*, esp. Chapter 1.

33. Jared Sexton, *Amalgamation Schemes: Antiblackness and the Critique of Multiculturalism* (Minneapolis: University of Minnesota Press, 2008), esp. Chapter 2.

34. Frank B. Wilderson III, "Social Death and Narrative Aporia in 12 *Years a Slave*," *Black Camera: An International Film Journal* 7, no. 1 (2015): 134–49.

Arising from black flesh, "I can't breathe" and a cry for mama – the echoing melody of black suffering – is music to white ears.

♦♦♦

Fetch me that flower; the herb I showed thee once:
The juice of it on sleeping eyelids laid
Will make or man or woman madly dote
Upon the next live creature that it sees.
Fetch me this herb; and be thou here again
Ere the leviathan can swim a league.
...
Having once this juice,
I'll watch Titania when she is asleep
And drop the liquor of it in her eyes.
The next thing then she, waking looks upon
(Be it on lion, bear, or wolf, or bull,
On meddling monkey, or on busy ape)
She shall pursue it with the soul of love.
~ Oberon[35]

"Away, you Ethiop!"

Another verse in the constant song of black death – a rounding chorus with no beginning or end.

While Oberon targets his faerie queen Titania with his charm, the magic also reaches, by way of Puck's mistaking of identities, to the human realm and into the eyes of the mortal lovers, Lysander and Demetrius. Once awakened, Titania shows desire for the transformed Bottom, who now walks the stage as half-man, half-ass.[36] When the mortal lovers awaken,

35. Shakespeare, *A Midsummer Night's Dream*, 2.1.175–80, 2.1.183–89.

36. This interspecies desire is explored in Bruce Boehrer, "Economies of Desire in *A Midsummer Night's Dream*," *Shakespeare Studies* 32 (2004): 99–117; Gabriel Rieger, "'I Woo'd

both Demetrius and Lysander have fallen for the formerly detested Helena,[37] leaving Hermia to receive the ire of her former love Lysander.

But from where does this ire arrive? The text states that the spell only makes someone fall in love with who they first see — the charm creates desire. As in the case of Bottom and Titania, when she falls for the man-made-ass. The charm does not disrupt Titania's other relations — she still treats her faerie servants with, if not kindness, at least some modicum of recognition and respect.

The revulsion of blackness that occurs in the casting out of the imagined Ethiope, newly appearing in the visage of Hermia, arrives without warning and departs without comment. The affect does not arise from the charm, as it produces doting love from the viewer, regardless of the species of the viewed, be it bear, or wolf, or ape. Yet Lysander, without provocation other than pleas of love, produces hatred and violence towards Hermia. This hatred and violence are invoked by blackness. Blackness and revulsion appear together without textual motivation. They are one and the same — always present, always connected in the white psyche, even when blackness is absent in the physical world.

In the examples of Hartman, Sexton, and Wilderson above, the affective distortion between humans and blacks relies on the destruction of, or potential for the destruction of, black flesh. But in A *Midsummer Night's Dream*, black flesh does not appear. The lack of black flesh allows us to rethink the relationship between blackness and affect. For Afro-pessimist scholars, the violence done towards black flesh, specifically the violence of the Middle Passage and chattel slavery, created a rift between blackness and humanity that is the origin of the affective distortion. But here, in this text written in 1595/96 and first performed in 1605 — some fifteen to twenty-five years before Jamestown — Shakespeare deploys black-

Thee with My Sword, / and Won Thy Love Doing Thee Injuries': The Erotic Economies of A *Midsummer Night's Dream*," *The Upstart Crow* 28 (2009): 70–81; Lorna Hutson, "The Shakespearean Unscene: Sexual Phantasies in A *Midsummer Night's Dream*," *Journal of the British Academy* 4 (2016): 169–95.

37. In his pursuit of Hermia, Demetrius tells Helena how much he detests her by stating directly to her, "I am sick when I do look on thee" (2.1.219).

ness concurrently with a reversal of affect. The simultaneity of blackness's appearance with Lysander's loss of love for Hermia positions even the thought of blackness as congruent with disgust and revulsion. The charm that creates doting love for man and beast also produces absolute abjection for blackness. In other words, black flesh is not necessary for affective distortion to occur, but rather, the mere thought of blackness is enough to distort affect. The thought of blackness is inseparable from and is in itself always already a signifier of abjection, exile, and violence.

This affect, this disgust, the inconceivability and unimaginability of black coupling, nay, of even black presence within civil society, is in the text, but is not of the text. Many affects in the play are interwoven into the plot: Titania's love across species has a textual basis and a comedic effect, and both her and Oberon's desire for the non-black other, the Indian boy, serves as catalyst for their turmoil. These interracial relations – one occurring outside the boundaries of the human race and the other occurring between racialized humans – throw into stark relief the English psyche's struggle to categorize blackness into epistemology. Shakespeare imagines affective resonance between woman and beast, or between man, woman, and Indian boy, and in doing so, explores the boundaries of human desire.

But the text positions blackness outside the boundaries of human desire. "Away, you Ethiop!" is understood, so much so that it needs no redress – black desire is unimaginable. This difference serves to articulate black positionality as in the world, but not of the world. A species divide between blacks and non-blacks, as Wilderson posits,[38] is a possibility, but if it is so, it would be fruitful to interrogate the evolution of this divide. These dual transformations offer a glimpse into an English mind attempting to categorize the divide between man and animal simultaneous to the divide between human and black. The former is to be categorized and explored, tested along bounds of empathy and desire. Bottom and Titania exhibit affective resonance with one another, despite

38. Hartman, Saidiya V., and Frank B. Wilderson. "The position of the unthought." *Qui Parle* 13, no. 2 (2003): 183-201, 190. Wilderson first applies the notion of a species divide between blacks and humanity on page 190.

the spell's governing of desire. Hermia, once imagined as black, bears no consideration. Lysander's love is simply cast away. She is unworthy of recognition and discarded – in the world, but not of the world; just as the Ethiope is in the text, but not of the text. Hermia, once imagined black, produces affect that goes unresonated and, in fact, unrecognized. Lysander does not respond to her pleas with reason or understanding, but with insults, rage, and commands.

The violence done to blackness, from Shakespeare's audiences in the 1590s to my own in the 21st century, needs no contextualization, no warning. In fact, it is comedy. For Shakespeare's audience – just like for the audiences of the deaths of George Floyd and Eric Garner and the recipients of lynching photos – the connection between Blackness and abjection, the reaction of disdain and disgust, and the failure to bear witness to the suffering of blackness needs no origin and no explanation. Black suffering, even thoughts of blackness, do not resonate with empathy, but with pleasure, to feed the sadomasochistic psyche of an anti-black civil society. Now, in the age of social media and neoliberal capitalism, black death has become currency for civil society – the sadomasochistic pleasure of affirmations given by white colleagues for virtue signaling Black Lives Matter on the internet while allowing the racism in their jobs, schools, and lives to fester.

Black death is always present, always echoing throughout our thoughts, actions, and reactions. Shakespeare shouts "Away, you Ethiop!" and his words kill. This black death echoes across four-hundred years and four-thousand productions and forty million black deaths and rings in my ears in the present. But my soul and my mind have been desensitized and calloused to the redundant, constant, inescapable suffering and dying of black bodies, of blackness. So much so that I shout it again, my voice ringing through past, history, and present, catching the sound and perpetrating, representing, re-performing black death over and over. There is no beginning; is there no end? When these echoes emanate from Shakespeare's text and find their ways to modern ears, they are rarely accompanied by content warnings. Have you ever seen a production of *A Midsummer Night's Dream* with a content warning for racial violence? Have you ever given one to your students when teaching it in your classes?

Do you even interpret those three words as violence?

I hope you have.

I hope you do.

I, regrettably, have not.

◆◆◆

"Away, you Ethiop!"[39] (echoes ... *I can't breathe.*)

"Out, tawny Tartar, out!"[40] (echoes ... *Momma, I love you.*)

Two lines. Seven words. Three seconds of air within two hours of performance.

They pass without comment or consequence in the text, and often, they pass without comment in modern productions.

But not without consequence.

With those three seconds of air, *A Midsummer Night's Dream* takes its place within a continuum that positions blackness as beyond the bounds of affective resonance and portrays blackness as absolute abjection – deserving of our disgust while never receiving our empathy. Allowing those words to pass without comment alienates the non-white members of our audience and the non-white students in our classrooms. As I think back on the moment now, I feel shame. Shame that I did not consider the feelings of my black and brown brothers and sisters in the audience. Shame that I allowed these moments to occur uncritically, unapologetically. Shame that in all the production's consideration and nuanced representations of gender I still ran roughshod over the topic of race. Shame that I missed a teachable moment for my students.

Shame that in failing to grant affective consideration to blackness, I created another data point on the continuum of anti-black violence and the denial of black suffering.

The sexual content – the explorations of same-sex courtship, bestiality, and polygamy – registered for my university as problematic and controversial enough to warrant content warnings. (*I can't breathe*) But the cast-

39. Shakespeare, *A Midsummer Night's Dream*, 3.2.265.

40. Shakespeare, *A Midsummer Night's Dream*, 3.2.274.

ing out of my history, the history of all of my brothers and sisters – the utter and unexplained disdain for my presence, my existence, my life (do black lives matter?) – those words, those lines, those seconds did not generate a content warning for our production.

I have never seen them generate a content warning.

"Away, you Ethiop!" (*echoes ...*)

"Out, tawny Tartar, out!" (*echoes ...*)

With those two lines. With those seven words. With those three seconds, I told a narrative that continues a history built upon a simple but undeniable doctrine – black lives do not matter. They cannot matter. Black death does.

10. Othello's Unfortunate Happiness

CORA FOX

William Shakespeare's *Othello* opens with a plot to change the color of Othello's joy. After he has informed Roderigo of Othello's secret marriage to Desdemona, Iago famously ignites Roderigo's jealousy and prejudice in a series of slurs that draw attention to Othello's racialized body, provoking the lament: "What a full fortune does the thicklips owe / If he can carry't [his marriage to Desdemona] thus!" (1.1.65–66).[1] Building on this regret over what Roderigo deems Othello's potentially "full fortune," Iago suggests to Roderigo that he manipulate Desdemona's father by informing him publicly of her deception:

> Call up her father,
> Rouse him, make after him, poison his delight,
> Proclaim him in the streets, incense her kinsmen,
> And, though he in a fertile climate dwell,
> Plague him with flies! Though that his joy be joy
> Yet throw such changes of vexation on't
> As it may lose some colour. (1.1.67–72)

Although the ultimate target of this weaponized unhappiness is explicitly Othello, Brabantio's shame is framed first as a means to that end, but the pronouns and the misery already migrate in Iago's speech from Brabantio to Othello. Because Roderigo is focused on Othello's successful and presumably pleasurable marriage to Desdemona, the joyful man (the repeated "him" and "he") in Iago's urgings becomes more likely Othello. After all, who is it who will be proclaimed in the streets and whose dwelling in Venice's fertile climate is more at stake? Iago is referencing the climactic humoral landscape that produced multiple, sometimes competing, early

1. Unless otherwise stated, all references to the play are to William Shakespeare, *Othello*, rev. ed., ed. E. A. J. Honigmann (London: The Arden Shakespeare/Bloomsbury, 2016).

modern stereotypes of character and race based on geographic location, a discourse termed "geohumoralism" by Mary Floyd-Wilson.[2] Geohumoralism informs early notions of race, so it helps to construct the figurations of racial hatred and fear of miscegenation that circulate in this scene. The metaphor comparing sorrow-bringing anxieties or suffering to the flies that can infest a fertile climate draws attention to Othello's embodied geohumoral difference, building upon the assumption that as a Moor, Othello was born in a climate unlike that of Venice and thus is a humoral outsider. Iago is likely fantasizing about how to destroy Othello's embodied person — imagining poisons and plagues and flies that would be associated with decaying flesh. Ultimately, it is Othello's presence in Venice that is more a focus of the play's attention, and not Brabantio's. It is "his joy be joy" that is imagined as somehow quintessential or "unalloyed delight," according to E. A. J. Honigmann's editorial note. Othello's body is imagined as both the site of a core emotion — joy (and sexual pleasure) — and the locus for decay and suffering, as the different location of his birth suggests a vulnerability in his humoral ecology that can be exploited by Iago.[3] Roderigo has already held up Othello as one who might wrongfully achieve a "full fortune," and, as I will discuss, the term for the positive feeling "happy" meant "fortunate" as much as it meant to be joyful in this period in the concept's shifting history. Iago's syntactical slide from what Roderigo should do to Brabantio to what Iago will ultimately do to Othello highlights and forecasts the irregular and doomed circulations of positive feelings that intersect with and help to produce the formations of race and difference in the play. Joy has a color in *Othello*, and Iago and the Venetians repeatedly call attention to the ways it is contingent and threatening when that color is Black.

2. On geohumoral notions of difference and their complex and contradictory intersections with emerging concepts of race, see Mary Floyd-Wilson, *English Ethnicity and Race in Early Modern Drama* (Cambridge: Cambridge University Press, 2003).
3. Floyd-Wilson argues that the play "sustains a conflict between an emerging racial stereotype of African sexuality and an older geohumoral discourse. While Iago and Roderigo characterize Othello as a lascivious beast, the Moor draws attention [in his request to have Desdemona accompany him to Cyprus] to his distinct lack of ardor" (*English Ethnicity and Race in Early Modern Drama*, 147).

Through a focus on the ways *Othello* highlights happiness not just as a good feeling, but also as a structure maintained and constantly reinforced through social practices, this essay examines how the play comments on and challenges happiness as a structuring affective attachment. Addressing the work of Sara Ahmed and Lauren Berlant, as well as other affect theorists participating in what Ahmed has called a "happiness turn" in affect studies, this reading of the play documents the racial politics of Othello's experience of positive emotions and explores the play's stakes in narratives of happiness that underlie social practices. In doing so, it records Othello as a figure in what Ahmed has called a Western "unhappiness archive." According to Ahmed:

> these archives take shape through the circulation of cultural objects that articulate unhappiness with the history of happiness. An unhappy archive is one assembled around the struggle against happiness. We have inherited already so much from authors who have challenged the very appeal of happiness — and yet these authors are never or rarely cited by the literature of happiness. These archives do not simply supplement philosophy and its happiness archive. They challenge it.[4]

Shakespeare's play — created within the representational forms and structures of early modern romance and domestic tragedy — offers just this kind of challenge and struggle against happiness. Beyond reinforcing the tragic decline of its protagonist, it obsessively returns to the promise of happiness that motivates marriage and the forces that pervert and prevent this attachment for the racialized Moor. In its representation of a Black character who is promised a happy inclusion in Venetian life only to have it eroded within a tragic frame, *Othello* is a play that does the work of challenging the appeal of happiness itself.

Othello begins the play as a joyful man, but the plan before Iago actually has a plan, as articulated in this first scene, involves revoking Othello's unlicensed access to happiness. That his state of joy should "lose some

4. Sara Ahmed, *The Promise of Happiness* (Durham, NC: Duke University Press, 2010), 18.

colour" references the humoral associations of positive emotions with the sanguine, or ruddy, body and face. But color here is figuratively connected to Othello's Blackness as well.[5] Iago's plan seems to be to change the humoral intensity of joy's hue on Othello's face or to lessen the positive feelings associated with his darker complexion. The color in this exchange is ambiguously attached to Othello, and in particular his skin and his feelings, suggesting the ways his humoral emotional regulation is tied to his embodied characterization as a Moor in the play. The "changes of vexation" (or "chances" in the Folio) will rob the joyful man of what is deemed his unfortunate good fortune. In fact, the unfortunate happiness circulating here also attaches to Desdemona herself, since once Brabantio discovers that Desdemona has indeed eloped with Othello, he calls her "unhappy girl!" (1.1.161) after declaring that his own pleasurable life has been permanently altered: "what's to come of my despised time / Is naught but bitterness" (1.1.159–160). The biopolitical negotiations and threats to individual happiness that are articulated in the opening minutes of the play highlight the structural and networked nature of joy itself, which shifts and changes and makes human beings vulnerable to the vexations of social life.

In addition to foreshadowing Iago's plot to bring down Othello by manipulating racializing narratives and stereotypes, this opening scene focuses on the way positive affects, as structures of social experience, will be weaponized in the plotting of the play to bring about Othello's

5. The *Oxford English Dictionary* defines "color" in this period in both humoral and racial terms. OED *Online*, s.v., "color," n.1: "the hue of a person's skin, typically of the face, esp. as reflecting or indicating physical health or emotional state; a person's complexion" (I.2.a); "rosiness or ruddiness of the complexion as an indication of health or wellbeing" (I.3.a); "pigmentation of the skin, typically as an indication of someone's race or ethnicity; spec. dark skin, as opposed to white or fair skin" (I.4.a). For a thorough consideration of humoral notions of health and the emotions as marked by signs on the face, see Gail Kern Paster, *Humoring the Body: Emotions and the Shakespearean Stage* (Chicago: University of Chicago Press, 2014); *The Body Embarrassed: Drama and the Disciplines of Shame in Early Modern England* (Ithaca, NY: Cornell University Press, 1993). Addressing the complexities of facial and bodily color in early modern racial formations, see Kim F. Hall, *Things of Darkness: Economies of Race and Gender in Early Modern England* (Ithaca, NY: Cornell University Press, 1996).

unhappiness. Articulated within the form of tragedy, the play reveals the structural contingency of Othello's joy and his sense of belonging. Affect theorists have called attention to the ways happiness as a structure draws boundaries that include and exclude individuals or groups.[6] As Ahmed explains, "ideas of happiness involve social as well as moral distinctions insofar as they rest on who is worthy as well as capable of being happy 'in the right way.'"[7] The play, and Othello as a character himself, question whether he can be happy in that "right way." Happiness, according to Ahmed, is at the center of philosophy and ethics because it is "what we want, whatever it is."[8] It is an affective structure related to optimism, which — as Lauren Berlant points out in her analysis of contemporary life — can operate to create unhealthy attachments, unethical social practices, and biopolitical exclusions, particularly when it obscures social conditions.[9] Although the appeal of happiness, like desire itself, is an empty structure, the content filling that form — the values and formations of individual and communal identity that constitute social life — are neither politically neutral nor culturally timeless. Instead, they reflect and construct new social conditions in each iteration, in each representation of what joy looks like and who experiences it. To place the play in an archive of unhappiness — on a timeline of how happiness is used to define the conditions of life for racialized others — is to suggest the power of this particular drama as a precursor to the racialization of happiness in the present. It is an attempt to speak of Othello as he is now, as Ian Smith has suggested, to meet what he calls the play's "intellectual demand" on its literary critics to engage the play as a source for racial formations in the

6. In reading this opening exchange and the play overall as they represent the ways happiness affectively constructs racial identities, I am responding broadly to Ahmed's work in *The Promise of Happiness* and *Willful Subjects* (Durham, NC: Duke University Press, 2015).In my focus on unhealthy or unproductive affective attachments, I am inspired by Lauren Berlant, *Cruel Optimism* (Durham, NC: Duke University Press, 2011).
7. Ahmed, *The Promise of Happiness*, 13.
8. Ahmed, *The Promise of Happiness*, 14.
9. Berlant, *Cruel Optimism*.

present.[10] As Ahmed points out, "through narrative, the promise of happiness is located as well as distributed,"[11] and *Othello* both reinforces and extends Ahmed's analysis of the dangers of the promise of happiness.

Reading *Othello*'s refiguring and theorizations of happiness is made more urgent by the fact that joy expressed by a Black person is still a threat to central cultural formations that reinscribe white privilege in the present. Witness, for instance, the aggressive white policing of joyful events attended by Black people, such as the incident in McKinney, TX, in 2015, in which a happily boisterous teenage pool party prompted emergency calls from white neighbors. In that instance, video of a white police officer tackling a teenage girl in a swimsuit and drawing his weapon on her friends who tried to intervene prompted some outrage, but also further disciplined and traumatized its viewers.[12] Joy was also policed in the 2018 "Barbecue Becky" incident, in which a white woman in Oakland, CA, called the police to break up a happy barbecue, citing an inappropriate use of public park space as a cover for her privileged aggression.[13] Ahmed's work helps to shed light on how white supremacy and other embedded structures shut out certain bodies from happiness' promise, and these events reveal the physical manifestations of that cultural logic – shutting them out of literal spaces of joyful gathering. Furthermore, these examples are indicative of how certain cultural practices of happiness themselves can offer an affective structure of desire that excludes racialized subjects from the experience of joy.

To investigate the history of positive feelings that are challenged by *Othello* is to draw attention to the ways happiness, considered structurally, can reinforce unjust or inequitable structures of power. Both his-

10. Ian Smith, "We Are Othello: Speaking of Race in Early Modern Studies," *Shakespeare Quarterly* 67, no. 1 (2016): 112.
11. Ahmed, *The Promise of Happiness*, 45.
12. See NAACP, "NAACP Statement on McKinney Police Department Incident," 8 June 2015, Common Dreams, https://www.commondreams.org/newswire/2015/06/08/naacp-statement-mckinney-police-department-incident.
13. Yesha Callahan, "#CookingOutWhileBlack: White Woman Calls Cops on Black People Cooking Out in Oakland, Calif., Park," 10 May 2018, The Root, https://www.theroot.com/cookingoutwhileblack-white-woman-calls-cops-on-black-1825920347.

torically and especially in this moment, numerous scholars and theater practitioners have pointed out that *Othello* is a provoking and dangerous play: so dangerous, in fact, that Ayanna Thompson and some Black actors – notably Harry Lennix – argue that it should not be staged in the United States in order to avoid the racist stereotypes it reinforces through repetition.[14] The play also has the potential to do harm because it can reproduce on the stage a politics of happiness amenable to white supremacy. As a tragedy, however, and an entry in the "unhappiness archive," the play can highlight, and possibly resist, the unjust attachments and practices in this fictionalized social world that are both the promise and condition of a certain kind of happiness. Community and belonging are stolen from Othello; expressions of joy that accompany community and belonging are policed today. But recognizing the biopolitics of these structures in the tragedy might suggest ways to make present day happiness less unhealthy and unjust. If happiness is, as Ahmed describes it philosophically, "what we want, whatever it is,"[15] then recognizing the historical social practices and values shaping Othello's unhappiness might allow for new attachments and new social practices that are more open to including all persons.

However, Othello's happiness, as it would have been understood in Shakespeare's theater, is both "what we want, whatever it is," *and* a historically specific, early modern, and particularly shifting emotion. This period in English history witnessed a cultural transition from residual notions of happiness as good fortune to emergent ones that defined it primarily as an elevated individual mood or state of joy.[16] Although I have used "joy" and "happiness" interchangeably in discussing the biopolitics of positive affect more generally, further distinctions could be made between moments in the play when the emotion is described as "happi-

14. See Ayanna Thompson, *Passing Strange: Shakespeare, Race and Contemporary America* (Oxford: Oxford University Press, 2011).
15. Ahmed, *The Promise of Happiness*, 14.
16. On culture as a complex of residual, dominant, and emergent processes and values, see Raymond Williams, *Marxism and Literature* (Oxford: Oxford University Press, 1977), Chapter 8. For a short history of happiness as an idea, see Darrin M. McMahon, *Happiness: A History* (New York: Atlantic Monthly Press, 2005).

ness" and when it is referred to by other terms. The importance of the early modern period as marking a transition in ideas and evaluations of positive emotions can be traced in the word "happiness" itself, which traveled from meaning "lucky" or "fortunate" (with "hap" at its root) to the more modern sense of a pleasurable feeling or mood attached to words like "joy."[17] The words "happiness," "delight," "content" and "joy," in fact, reverberate in this play, and although I will point to some of the repetitions of these terms, I am more concerned with Othello's investment and attachment to positive emotions more generally than to a particular category of pleasurable feeling.[18]

In fact, the play navigates competing conceptions of happiness as it is constructed through various models of the body and self that determine Othello's identity as a Moor. The work of many scholars has uncovered the history of "Moor" as a category that was slippery in the period, used to signify differences of race (primarily Black), location (primarily African), and religion (primarily Muslim).[19] As Dennis Britton has argued, when Oth-

17. For an analysis of "hap," see Richard Chamberlain, "What's Happiness in *Hamlet*?" in *The Renaissance of Emotion: Understanding Affect in Shakespeare and His Contemporaries*, ed. Richard Meek and Erin Sullivan (Manchester: Manchester University Press, 2015), 153–74.
18. "Joy" occurs 5 times and not after Act 2, "happiness" 3 times, words derived from "hap" 18 times, "content" 15 times, "delight" 5 times, "merry" 3 times, and "bliss" 2 times. By contrast, words containing "honest" occur 45 times, and "jealous" 16 times. Happiness as an idea, then, is subject to some of the same scrutiny that these other feelings or elements of human character have been. And if the play is about jealousy, as much previous criticism maintains, then it is equally about happiness. One moment not discussed here but important in reading happiness more broadly is Desdemona's insistence that she is pretending to be merry when bantering with Iago to disguise her anxiety while waiting for Othello in act 2 scene 1, for example. In that scene, as in those enabling Othello's tragedy, positive feelings are constructed as both natural and humoral, but they can also be deployed and feigned. Data collected through Open-Source Shakespeare, http://www.opensourceshakespeare.org/, accessed 17 June 2017.
19. There has been excellent work historicizing "the Moor," often launched by investigations into this play. Multiple essays in Margo Hendricks and Patricia Parker, eds., *Women, "Race," and Writing in the Early Modern Period* (London: Routledge 1994) are important entries in this scholarship; Ania Loomba *Shakespeare, Race, and Colonialism*

ello is called an "erring barbarian," his characterization reflects a conception of Moors associated with the growth of the African slave trade, but it also situates him within the romance tradition from which Shakespeare takes his central narrative. Within that tradition, Britton argues, Othello is at least provisionally framed as a heroic character of Christian conversion, although his self-division in the final moments of the play suggests that its tragic structure forecloses the possibility of a structuring happiness based on those romance narratives.[20] Many of these stereotypical narratives surrounding Othello's character that insist upon his difference are excellent examples of what Giovanni Tarantino has called "emotional orientalism." As Tarantino points out, Moors and Black people in the period are often referred to as an "unhappy race," suggesting both their lack of good fortune and their melancholy.[21] As I have suggested, a historicist focus on this geohumoral formation, however central, only captures some of the complexity of how emotion is linked to color and race in this play and the culture if reflects.

Othello's famous expression of joy when he meets Desdemona in Cyprus – "If it were now to die, / T'were now to be most happy" (2.1.174–75) – most insistently calls him out as a character in Ahmed's unhappiness

(Oxford: Oxford University Press, 2002), is foundational. For a discussion and theorization of various works and approaches to this research spanning the last three decades, see Kim F. Hall, "*Othello* and the Problem of Blackness," in *A Companion to Shakespeare's Works, Volume 1: The Tragedies*, ed. Richard Dutton and Jean E. Howard (Malden, MA: Blackwell, 2003), 357–71; Ayanna Thompson, "Introduction," in *Othello*, by William Shakespeare, rev. ed., ed. E. A. J. Honigmann (London: The Arden Shakespeare/ Bloomsbury, 2016). On Moors, early modern race, and the question of how to grapple with charges of anachronism and still engage the history of present racial formations, see Vanessa Corredera, "'Not a Moor Exactly': Shakespeare, *Serial*, and Modern Constructions of Race," *Shakespeare Quarterly* 67, no. 1 (2016): 30–50.

20. Dennis Britton, "Re-'Turning' *Othello*: Transformative and Restorative Romance," *ELH* 78, no. 1 (2011): 27–50.
21. Giovanni Tarantini, "The Colour of Fear in Early Modern Europe: From Sexual Shock to Affective Encompassment" (paper, Powerful Emotions/Emotions and Power c.400–1800 conference, Humanities Research Centre, University of York, UK, 28–29 June 2017).

archive. His articulation of a contingent, temporary, and qualified kind of happiness receives a strong normative response from Desdemona:

> Othello: It gives me wonder great as *my soul's content*
> To see you here before me. O! *my soul's joy,*
> If after every tempest come such calms,
> May the winds blow till they have wakened death,
> And let the laboring bark climb hills of seas,
> Olympus-high, and duck again as low
> As hell's from heaven! *If it were now to die,*
> *'Twere now to be most happy; for I fear*
> *My soul hath her content* so absolute
> That not another comfort like to this
> Succeeds in unknown fate.
>
> Desdemona: The heavens forbid!
> But that our *loves and comforts should increase*
> Even as our days do grow.
>
> Othello: Amen to that, sweet powers!
> I cannot speak enough of this *content;*
> *It stops me here; it is too much of joy*: (2.1.181–95 emphases added)

This scene has sometimes been read — following Carol Thomas-Neely's characterization of Othello as foolishly idealistic in his understandings of women and Stephen Greenblatt's focus on his sexual anxiety — as evidence that Othello is sexually immature, inexperienced, or anxious because he does not understand the true nature of happiness to be found in heterosexual sex and marriage.[22] This reading is supported if, as the text

22. Carol Thomas-Neely argues that this scene cements Othello's representation as dispassionate and controlled, since "Othello feels utterly content with a simple embrace" in meeting her ("Women and Men in *Othello*: 'What Should Such a Fool / Do With so Good a Woman?'" *Shakespeare Studies* 10 [1977]: 138). Stephen Greenblatt examines Othello's sexual anxiety partly in Lacanian terms, and also recognizes that it sets him up as an outsider to narratives preserving orthodox Christian marriage in the play. He

of the play leaves open, Othello has delayed his sexual union with Desdemona until after they have arrived in Cyprus. Desdemona's definition of happiness in marriage, in contrast, reflects a more central cultural formation and ideal of heterosexual union, one that promises an increase in comfort (but interestingly, not joy) over time. Othello's response to Desdemona's correction ("Amen to that!") however, is not naïve, and suggests instead that Othello is characterized as knowing precisely the promise of happiness that is being offered in his marriage to Desdemona. He loses speech when trying to articulate the difference between the satisfaction ("content"), "comfort," and "joy" he feels in Desdemona's presence and the structural and affective investments and risks of marriage, since he says he fears it cannot be guaranteed that he will feel such happiness again. Emphatically — at lines 181, 182, and 189 — he invests his soul, which he feminizes, with these positive affects, distancing them from his body as if aware of the physical dangers of this attachment. Because sexual consummation was also figured in the period as a little death (i.e., ejaculation was sometimes considered a release of the body's vital forces in Galenic medicine), Othello might also be expressing in his sexual desire for Desdemona a simultaneous worry about the vulnerability of his body in this marriage. His fear, it turns out, is well-founded and prophetic, as the tragedy narrativizes not just the failure of his interracial marriage, but also the descent of his characterization into some of the most violent stereotypes attached to Moors in the period. As Ania Loomba and others have pointed out, he becomes the "turbaned Turk" that he memorializes killing in the final moments of the play, and he murders that racialized other within himself as his final act.[23] Othello's articulate insistence on his fear signals his distrust for and alienation from Christian marriage as assurance of happiness. His character recognizes, in other words, that marriage with Des-

notes that "The rich, disturbing pathos of the lovers' passionate reunion in Othello derives then not only from our awareness that Othello's premonition is tragically accurate, but from a rent, a moving ambivalence, in his experience of the ecstatic moment itself" (*Renaissance Self-Fashioning: From More to Shakespeare* [Chicago: University of Chicago Press, 1980], 243).

23. Loomba, *Shakespeare, Race, and Colonialism*, 97.

demona is a potentially unhealthy and unhappy attachment. Rather than a moment in which Othello misunderstands married love, this is a profound moment in which the play marks, through his character, the split between the performance of joy and the forecasted affective state of comfortable happiness. It is the promise of married happiness that Othello recognizes as future-oriented and that the play gives and then takes from its central character. Othello's incoherence in the face of this joy reflects an awareness of the likelihood that this yet-unlived life will be impossible, positioning *Othello* in the archives of unhappiness.

Before the play reaches its tragic conclusion, Othello's character is further excluded from the affective structures of community and the promise of contentment in marriage by the intensity of his emotional reactions to Iago's manipulations, which invoke other painful emotional scripts attached to adultery. As Justin Shaw argues, Othello is increasingly constructed in the play through the intersecting systems of both racism and ableism, and he is excluded from any network of communal care and belonging that might have mitigated these social forces.[24] Instead, his body is displayed to the audience as unsound, most notably when he is given "ocular proof" in the form of the handkerchief he gave to Desdemona. The handkerchief, a symbolic object of attachment for Othello and Desdemona that is circulated as a result of Iago's plotting, becomes the catalyst for Othello's literal fall on the stage, where the manifestations of his anger and despair in his body help to convince him of her treachery: [25]

> Othello: Handkerchief! confessions! handkerchief! — To confess,
> and be hanged for his labor! First to be hanged,
> and then to confess: I tremble at it. Nature would not
> invest herself in such shadowing passion without some
> instruction. It is not words that shakes me thus. Pish!

24. Justin Shaw, "'Rub Him About the Temples': *Othello*, Disability and the Failures of Care," *Early Theatre* 22, no. 2 (2019): 171–84, doi https://doi.org/10.12745/et.22.2.3997.

25. For one particularly relevant investigation of the significance of this famous handkerchief, see Ian Smith, "Othello's Black Handkerchief," *Shakespeare Quarterly* 64, no. 1 (2013): 1–25.

> Noses, ears and lips! Is't possible? Confess! handkerchief!
> O devil! *Falls in a trance.*
>
> Iago: Work on,
> My medicine, work! (4.1.37–45)

Iago labels Othello's trance an "epilepsy" a few lines later (4.1.50), and this scene establishes the weakness of Othello's affective bodily resistance to Iago's ironic medicine, as Othello notes "it is not words that [shake him]."[26] This "fit" is interpreted and framed by Iago and Cassio in this scene, so Othello is indeed shaken by words. Once detached from happiness and its promise, Othello's body registers his suffering and the play thrusts him into a new structure in which what he wants – which is, structurally, his happiness – is tragically only revenge and death.

Othello's alienation from the happy Venetian community becomes the theme of the play's tragic conclusion when he attempts and fails to kill Iago in revenge. Iago announces that he bleeds but is "not killed," and Othello replies: "I am not sorry neither; I'd have thee live, / For in my sense 'tis happiness to die" (5.2.286–87). This is a final ironic turn in the play's meditation on happiness, as Othello recognizes that the only happiness promised to him in the play's realigned racial formations is death. As Ahmed points out, citing the seventeenth-century philosopher Blaise Pascal, "Even suicide is an expression of the will to happiness ... happiness should be thought of not as content but form: if in tending toward something, we tend toward happiness, then happiness provides a container for tendency. Happiness must be emptied of content if it can be filled by 'whatever' it is that we are tending toward."[27] What is this suicidal happiness that Othello is tending toward? Here is where literary representation

26. Shaw reads this moment as analogous to the exhibition of an anatomist's theater: "In five short lines, Iago provides three different diagnoses for Othello's condition – epilepsy, lethargy, and the potential for madness" ("'Rub Him About the Temples,'" 176). It is a failure of medicine that is linked to the overall failure of networks of care in the play, a lack represented by Cassio's weakness and self-centeredness as a friend to Othello and enabled by underlying systems of white supremacy.
27. Ahmed, *Willful Subjects*, 4.

and the embodied stage represent a challenge to structures of happiness beyond the fiction that might make suicide a happy goal, attachment, or conclusion. The "emptied container" of happiness that ends in suicide is strikingly similar, and in this case identical, to the form of tragedy. Since the play repeatedly reveals in its own representations that happiness is both a structuring force and an amorphous container for tendencies and attachments, the final moments stage the full biocultural politics and the ethical stakes of happiness. Therefore, the cathartic satisfaction of witnessing Othello exert his own will to suicide implicates spectators in the politics of happiness that leads to this tragic conclusion. This might be one reason why the play is so difficult to watch.

Additionally, the happiness that has death as its object removes the living body of the actor playing Othello from the social world of the play. After Othello murders Desdemona and Iago's instigation has come to light, Lodovico arrives as the voice of the Venetian state and asks: "Where is this rash and unfortunate man?" (5.2.280). Othello replies: "That's he that was Othello. Here I am" (5.2.281). Othello is described as rash because he has committed the murder, but he is also read as unfortunate by the onstage witness of the play's tragedy. Othello's reply, however, suggests that he recognizes himself in the present to be no longer rash or unfortunate, as he replaces his tendency toward marriage to Desdemona with suicide. His death speaks back to the traditional scripts of happiness that circulate in the play — particularly those attached to marriage and Venetian tolerance — and calls attention to happiness' potential for harm and tragic consequences.

Othello finally refers to the murder of Desdemona as an "unlucky deed" in his famous farewell: "I pray you in your letters, / When you shall these unlucky deeds relate, / Speak of me as I am" (5.2.338–40). He does not, notably, refer to it as an "unhappy" deed, because the affective structure of happiness has become suicidal and disciplinary. As Smith has argued: "His act of self-slaughter, an attack on his own body, is designed to punish a racialized self who, like the 'turbaned Turk,' has committed the heinous assault on Venice in the person of Desdemona."[28] The promise of happiness in married love is replaced with a tending toward suicide, removing Othello's body from Venice but allowing his physical death to be replaced by a brief social glorification in the Venetian state. This structure of desiring his own death is also deeply intertwined and embedded in the generic representational structure of tragedy. The play stages the violence that weaponized and failed narratives of happiness can inflict, just as it develops Othello's narrativized recognition of Venice's contingent and unjust distribution of joy, and it represents his suicide as a final consolatory act of will. In doing so, it draws attention to Othello's tragic and unfortunate happiness, recognizing the irony of tending toward death as the fulfillment of tragedy's formal expectations, giving both the onstage and playgoing audience "what they want, whatever it is." For Othello as a character, happiness emptied of joy is death. For the spectator, that structure is tragedy, which both narrativizes and repeats the racist logic of exclusion that is unleashed when Iago sets out to manipulate the very color of Othello's joy.

Although not generally considered a play about happiness, and in fact, one of the most painful tragedies to watch by many accounts, *Othello* is deeply invested in exploring the social attachments, consequences, and practices of happiness.[29] This might be the case because *Othello* is written at a transitional moment in European history, during which the meaning of "happiness" as a word and an idea shifts from a residual sense of "good fortune" to the more emergent and modern sense of "pleasure." The linguistic shift marks larger cultural transformations that might explain the

28. Smith, "We Are Othello,"111. For a reading of Othello's divided subjectivity, especially at this moment of his suicide, theorized by postcolonial playwrights and through the work of Frantz Fanon and Homi K. Bhabha, see Jyotsna Singh, "Othello's Identity, Postcolonial Theory, and Contemporary African Rewritings of *Othello*," in *Women, "Race," and Writing in the Early Modern Period*, ed. Margo Hendricks and Patricia Parker (London: Routledge, 1994), 287–99.

29. Walter Cohen remarks that *Othello* "has always been popular in performance, although — or perhaps, paradoxically, because — it is excruciating to watch" ("Introduction to *Othello*," in *The Norton Shakespeare: Essential Plays, The Sonnets*, 3rd ed., ed. Stephen Greenblatt et al. [New York: Norton, 2016], 2073).

play's focus on the structures of a happy married life. In this sense *Othello* functions as a primary document in the prehistory of contemporary happiness, operating as a lens for examining the intersecting and intertwined representational investments of social forces influenced by shifting notions of race and gender. At the same time, as a literary work in the unhappiness archive, the play questions joy itself and what it means to want to be happy, especially for those who are made aliens in and to the structures that produce happiness itself, either in the literary form of tragedy or the social world.

Finally, considering Othello's stolen happiness might provide historical insight into the particular disciplinary tendencies of present-day extreme reactions to expressions of Black joy in its recent encounters with white privilege in the United States. When I set out to follow the ways notions of happiness, joy, and comfort circulated in the play, I did not expect to reconsider Othello's suicide as a kind of extreme happiness, and that tragic lesson reverberates beyond the historical situation of the play's writing. If happiness is at the center of philosophy and undergirds human will and desire in these complex structural ways, then acts of joy can indeed be subversive and a form of resistance. Joys that celebrate embodied differences or previously disenfranchised groups rather than structuring exclusions might be further entries in the unhappiness archive, speaking back to past attachments and their false promises. Although this essay can only begin this conversation, this reading of the play clearly supports various political and activist movements that theorize, structure, and celebrate Black joy in the present.[30] Recognizing *Othello*'s place in the archive of unhappiness might also let it reflect on recent attempts to call out toxic positivity, allowing the play's doomed representation of happiness' promise to challenge unhealthy attachments to "what we

30. See, for example, Kleaver Cruz, "The Black Joy Project," https://kleavercruz.com/the-black-joy-project, https://www.instagram.com/theblackjoyproject/; Andrea Walls, "Museum of Black Joy," https://www.museumofblackjoy.com/; Neda Ulaby, "At the 'Museum of Black Joy,' It's the Everyday Moments that Go on Display," NPR, 14 August 2021, https://www.npr.org/2021/08/14/1026447517/museum-of-black-joy-andrea-walls); adrienne maree brown, *Pleasure Activism: The Politics of Feeling Good* (Chico, CA: AK Press, 2019).

want, whatever it is." Although to be happy is no longer synonymous with being lucky, historical awareness of the social situatedness, precarity, and structural nature of positive feelings might generate the conscious practice of a better, more just, and more inclusive happiness.

11. The Racialized Affects of Ill-Will in the Dark Lady Sonnets

CAROL MEJIA LAPERLE

Restricted in form and moored to precedent, sonnets nonetheless explore a wide range of affective experiences. They are not only *about* feelings, but to an extent manufactured what is recognizable even today as the basic diagnostics of erotic attachment: longing, despair, exuberance, arousal, and, if the couplet permits, relief. But critics have rightfully considered the uneven treatment and representation of these erotic attachments, these affective experiences. Bruce R. Smith outlines the power structures of the genre: "The poet, not the mistress, is the *subject* in every sense of the word. Seen in its rhetorical context, a Petrarchan sonnet is a power ploy of speaker over listener; seen in its social context, it is a power-ploy of man over a woman; seen in its sexual context, it is a power-ploy of male over female."[1] Nancy Vickers locates this dominance in the blazon's dismemberment of the beloved muse, in which the poet "cannot allow her to dismember his body; instead he repeatedly, although reverently, scatters hers throughout his scattered rhymes."[2] These influential readings of domination implicit in the form, however, gloss over what has been called the "scandal of Shakespeare's sonnets"[3]; that is, the dark lady's promiscuous and unruly provocations. Kim F. Hall's groundbreaking analysis of the dichotomy of dark and fair has linked it to the cod-

1. Bruce R. Smith, *Homosexual Desire in Shakespeare's England: A Cultural Poetics* (Chicago: University of Chicago Press, 1994), 260 original emphasis.
2. Nancy Vickers, "Diana Described: Scattered Women and Scattered Rhyme," in *Writing and Sexual Difference*, ed. Elizabeth Abel (Chicago: University of Chicago Press, 1982), 109.
3. Margareta de Grazia shifts attention away from the homoerotic scandals of the sequence to remind readers that "the readings of dark mistress sonnets have been blank to the shocking social peril they promulgate" ("The Scandal of Shakespeare's Sonnets," *Shakespeare Survey* 46 [1993]: 49).

ification and exploitation of racial difference.[4] As foil to the fair male friend, the female beloved's darkness is thus a useful resource for William Shakespeare's exploration of the genre's obsession with this dichotomy. But while her function in literary representations of this trope is established, the dark mistress's disruption of male dominance and resistance to passive objectification, and the ways these negative affects shape racial attitudes, require further investigation. To return to the epigraph of this collection, the lady coloured ill (im)poses the problem of feeling.

The dark lady poems, identified with relative consensus as sonnets 127 to 154 of Shakespeare's sequence,[5] departs from the conventional depiction of the unattainable, virtuous, and fair beauty by attributing to the beloved some rather unflattering attributes: dun breasts, wiry black hair, reeking breath, a heavy tread, and an unrestrained sexual appeal that distempers men to distraction. These descriptions are culled from the much-cited sonnet 130 that argues the beloved's eyes are not, as it turns out, like the sun. In her departure from the improbably perfect characteristics of a typical sonnet muse, the dark lady inspires critical attention from those seeking to confirm a historical counterpart.[6] A popular contender as the dark lady is Emilia Lanier, who published the poem *Salve Dues Rex* in 1611 after having been embroiled in a few sexual scandals of her day, such as being the known mistress of Shakespeare's theatre patron, Lord

4. Kim F. Hall, *Things of Darkness: Economies of Race and Gender in Early Modern England* (Ithaca, NY: Cornell University Press, 1995).
5. For discussion of the historical reception of the text and how it affects the sequencing and ordering of the sonnets, see Robert Matz, "The Scandals of Shakespeare's Sonnets," ELH 77, no. 2 (2010): 477–508. Matz proposes that the attention given to the dark lady sonnets shifts depending upon each era's construction of sexuality. He notes that the sequential ordering of the sonnets is not authorized by any direct access to author intention or production consistency.
6. As Dympna Callaghan notices, the "complex constellation of relationships between three principal characters and the degree of emotional reality with which they are rendered. . . makes it impossible to regard the sonnets as entirely fictional, at least in any simple or straightforward sense" (*Shakespeare's Sonnets* [Malden, MA: Blackwell, 2007], 3).

Chamberlain Henry Carey.[7] Even more controversially, "Lucy Negro" or Lucy Morgan, who was a brothel keeper with ties to the court of Queen Elizabeth I, was identified as having connections with Shakespeare and his thespian ilk, such as theatre owner Philip Henslowe.[8] But apart from providing intriguing connections and prurient speculations, these historical accounts cannot fully capture the beloved lady's embodiment of desire, defiance, and darkness.

Instead, I would like to consider the problem of feeling as a disturbance of the sonnet sequence's default investments in white futurity and racial insularity. The poet's emphasis on his male friend's genealogy of fairness is articulated through the elevation of a kin/kind attachment — elevated precisely by the volitional rather than consanguine bond of male friendship.[9] Their idealized attachment is disrupted by the woman "coloured ill" (sonnet 144, line 4). [10]As Dympna Callaghan observes, the dark lady is never actually called the dark lady in the sequence but is, rather, referred to as the woman coloured ill, linking hue to something ominous or harmful.[11] I put pressure on "ill" as simultaneously an attribution of her characterization and a hue that racializes her corruption of desire — both aspects I develop as constitutive of *ill-will*. Volition emerges as an index for the affective experience of racial formation.

7. A. L. Rowse, *Shakespeare's Sonnets: A Modern Edition, with Prose Versions, Introduction and Notes*, 3rd ed. (London: Macmillan Press, 1984), xix.
8. See Duncan Salkeld, *Shakespeare among the Courtesans: Prostitution, Literature, and Drama, 1500–1650* (London: Routledge, 2012). For Luce Negro's presence in the court of Elizabeth, and more importantly the inspiring effects of her historical memory for artistic adaptations, see Joyce Green MacDonald, "Dark Ladies, Black Women: Animating Lucy Negro in Caroline Randall Williams' *Lucy Negro, Redux*," in *GWU Annual Shakespeare Lecture*, posted 19 September 2020 on YouTube, https://www.youtube.com/watch?v=p41IFoBWK_A.
9. This is a distinction productively investigated by Urvashi Chakravarty, "More than Kin, Less than Kind: Similitude, Strangeness, and Early Modern English Homonationalism," *Shakespeare Quarterly* 67, no. 1 (2016): 14–29.
10. Shakespeare, William, et al. The Norton Shakespeare. Third edition. New York: W. W. Norton & Company, 2015. All in-text sonnet citations are from this edition.
11. "She has come to be known as the 'dark lady,' even though Shakespeare himself never calls her that" (Callaghan, *Shakespeare's Sonnets*, 2).

The mistress's denunciation of long-standing Petrarchan ideals challenges poetic form and disrupts male authority even as her departure from sonnet expectations is the hallmark of Shakespeare's innovations in the genre. Like many previous beloveds, Shakespeare's mistress starts as a silent and detached addressee. But in its particular brand of unreciprocated attentions, the sequence rejects the genre's conventions and subverts male desire in ways that depend upon the sexualization and racialization of the beloved's darkness along a spectrum of will: willing submission to a heteronormative, classed hierarchy on the one hand, and on the other, willful, non-compliance that threatens social identities as they are determined by a dominant, shared, idealized, good will. As Sara Ahmed elaborates in *Willful Subjects*, the "idea of willfulness as self-agreement can be related to how *willful subjects* do not will in agreement with others. I would suggest that the diagnosis of willfulness allows the good will to appear *as if it is a universal will*, as a will that has eliminated signs of itself from moral agreement."[12] Thus, "universal will," embedded in the imperatives of the genre's aesthetic demands and gendered desires, is undermined by the dark lady who manifests a willfulness that is "agreeable *to* [her]self."[13] In Ahmed's attempt to offer an "account of the sociality of will," she observes that "to be identified as willful is to become a problem."[14] Within the sonnet sequence's overabundance of wills, amidst a profusion of desires, the sonneteer's will is not thwarted by a chaste and unattainable beloved of the sonnet tradition, a rejection that is at least aligned with the conventions of the genre. Wanton, harsh, formidable — the very opposite of Francesco Petrarch's unsullied Laura or Philip Sidney's distant Stella — the dark lady withholds, subverts, and challenges prevailing notions of her appropriate role in the love triangle. In her refusal to be a passive object of desire or an agreeable participant in its pacification, she calls attention to the sonnet sequence's sociality of will. Unlike the suffering poet whose will — *his* wishes, *his* testaments, *his* gen-

12. Sara Ahmed, *Willful Subjects* (Durham, NC: Duke University Press, 2014), 95 emphases added.

13. Ahmed, *Willful Subjects*, 95 original emphasis.

14. Ahmed, *Willful Subjects*, 19, 3.

itals (since the word was a euphemism for sexual acts and apparatuses) – is frustrated but not problematic, the dark lady's willfulness is coded as abnormal, excessive, and dangerous. This characterization is a form of racialization that evokes, but is not limited to, the markers of somatic Blackness. It is the dark lady's affective performance of ill-will that demarcates the villainizations and exclusions of an indelible racial difference.

Her deviant difference is in stark contrast to the benevolent identicality of male friendship, which provides the throughline for much of the sequence. The dark lady poems depart from the topic of male friendship by shifting attention from amity to promiscuity, from counsel to corruption, from selflessness to the mockery of such sentiments. In doing so, they disrupt the poet's preoccupation with the beauty, virtue, and procreative potential of his fair, young, male friend.[15] Laurie Shannon has established the ways hierarchy haunts the discourse of parity in friendship doctrines: "the insistent emphasis on sexual and social sameness is a systematic response to that most acute form of early modern difference: the hierarchical difference of degree."[16] But the point of this discourse is to imagine a commonweal grounded in the elevation of sameness across and despite hierarchy: "Likeness in both sex and status *is* (the only) political equality in period terms; on the basis of this likeness, writers stress the making of a consensual social bond or body that is not inherently subordinating."[17] Although Shannon does not evoke volition per se, mutual parity is underwritten by mutual wills, enacting a paradigm that not only aligns two male friends' wills with each other, but also replicates a broader social

15. The relationship between the men can be categorized under the early modern understanding of "amity": "While the notion of an exclusive, intimate, affective bond of friendship emerges during this period, early modern amity incorporates a wider range of human interactions than this, including concepts of benevolence, gratitude, humanitarianism, political and social bonds, epistolary exchange and textual gift-giving, loving friendship, ethical union and relationships connected by the soul and by God" (Bronwen Price and Páraic Finnerty, eds., "Amity in Early Modern Literature and Culture: Introduction," special issue, *Literature & History* 20, no. 1 [2011]: 1).
16. Laurie Shannon, *Sovereign Amity: Figures of Friendship in Shakespearean Contexts* (Chicago: University of Chicago Press, 2001), 2.
17. Shannon, *Sovereign Amity*, 3 original emphasis.

understanding of common, good will. Specifically conjoining male friendship to social good, Páraic Finnerty observes that early modern society "celebrat[ed] ideal male friendship as the most perfect human relationship and stress[ed] its importance in the public world of social mobility, patronage and civic virtue, and in the private one of intimacy, affection and companionship."[18] But scholars of early modern friendship have not addressed how intimacy, affection, and companionship — the private basis of a public commonweal — are not only classed and gendered as the purview of male aristocrats but are, furthermore, racially insular.

In the sonnets, good will is coded, reiterated, and ultimately policed as white, in the way that Richard Dyer articulates the machinations of this racial category: "There is a specificity to white representation, but it does not reside in a set of stereotypes so much as in narrative structural positions, rhetorical tropes and habits of perception."[19] Hall has proven that the rhetorical trope of fairness is a fundamental component of English self-fashioning in the eve of colonial exploitation.[20] I build on Hall's influential analysis by considering representation and positionality along a spectrum of will. The dark lady destabilizes the normative structural position of good will as belonging to the male friends' enjoyment and replication of white privilege, even as these aesthetic and social advantages are presumed and thus covert in the genre's policing of desire. Thus, the fair friend's reluctance to marry elicits an accusation of being a "profitless usurer" (sonnet 4, line 7) and a "niggard" (sonnet 4, line 5). Racial slurs that evoke anti-Semitism and anti-Blackness are deployed to emphasize that the fair friend is neither of these identities. Rather, his pale beauty and kind virtue establish fairness/whiteness as the template for humanism's highest aspirations. Furthermore, racial slurs put to relief an idealization of whiteness that does not need to be named as such, for it functions as an invisible but ever-present ideal underwriting and insulating a commonweal of kind kinship. But this ideological assumption requires the appro-

18. Páraic Finnerty, "'Both are Alike, and Both Alike We Like': Sovereignty and Amity in Shakespeare's *King John*," *Literature & History* 20, no. 1 (2011): 39.
19. Richard Dyer, *White: Essays on Race and Culture*, (London: Routledge, 1997), 12.
20. Hall, *Things of Darkness*.

priate expression and inculcation of wills; that is, the fair male friend and the poet demonstrate a concerted alignment of wills even as their desires are in conflict, since both have erotic interests in a promiscuous woman.

In sonnet 134, the persona transforms the conceit of imprisonment into a debilitating debt that thwarts the credit and compromises the well-being of two male friends, shaping the contours of kin/kind in market terms to demonstrate that these binding obligations are *not* commercial exchanges.[21] As a benevolent and generous friend to his male competition, the poet makes an offer: he submits himself to the unscrupulous woman who comes between him and his fair friend.

> And I myself am mortgaged to thy will,
> Myself I'll forfeit, so that other mine
> Thou wilt restore, to be my comfort still: (sonnet 134, lines 2–4)

The "other mine" echoes what Jeffrey Masten has identified as an existential bond accompanying idealized friendships: "the rhetoric of these relationships is centrally concerned with describing ideally persons of absolute identicality, indistinguishability, and interchangeability."[22] Michel de Montaigne's treatment of will is central to this form of idealism. In "On Friendship," he claims that friendship "is I wot not what kinde of quintessence of all this commixture, which having seized all my will, induced the same to plunge and loose it selfe in his, which likewise having seized all his will, brought it to loose and plunge it selfe in mine, with a mutual greediness, and with a semblable concurrence."[23] And so Shakespeare's elaboration of the poet and his male friend's interchangeability is a manifestation of merging and binding; indeed, in Montaigne's words, "plunging" of con-

21. For an astute reading of the ways the language of enterprise and commerce are mystified, see Hall, *Things of Darkness*, esp. Chapter 3. For a reading of friendship and the language of the market, see Lorna Hutson, *The Usurer's Daughter: Male Friendship and Fictions of Women in Sixteenth-Century England* (London: Routledge, 1994).
22. Jeffrey Masten, *Queer Philologies: Sex, Language, and Affect in Shakespeare's Time* (Philadelphia: University of Pennsylvania Press, 2016), 73–74.
23. Michel de Montaigne, "Of Friendship," in *Essays: or Morall, Politike, and Millitarie Discourses*, trans. John Florio (London: Printed by Val. Sims for Edward Blount, 1603), 93.

senting wills with each other. The poet's sacrifice, therefore, hinges on the profundity of their connection, bolsters the foundation of their common will, and becomes a substitution that "betters" the self. Throughout the sonnets, an argument of kin/kind compassion and social obligation runs through the stylized, erotic persuasions that delineate the poet's virtuous but captivated fair friend from the ruthless mistress who seduces both men. In her refusal to concede to the superiority of "fair, kind, and true" (sonnet 105, lines 9–10), the dark lady exerts the affective power of her physical darkness as social disobedience and sexual deviance. Thus, through her disturbance of order, the dark lady performs an exclusion — social and ontological — from the racial logic that mobilizes male friendship as insulating and celebrating whiteness as the default kin/kind.

In doing so, the dark lady challenges the racial insularity implicit in kinship and mobilized by discourses of friendship. Sonnet 134's depiction of a negotiation with the dark lady's will is meant first, to free a friend from promiscuous enticements and second, to restore order by saving a young man who, in other instances, the poet has called "that other mine" (line 3), "my sweet'st friend" (sonnet 133, line 4), and "my next self" (sonnet 133, line 6). Through this sacrifice, friendship can serve as "comfort still" (sonnet 134, line 4). The poet begins sonnet 134 by asking to be mortgaged to *her* will, but the gist is that she will *not* yield to their refinance offer. Part of the mistress's ill-will is in her refusal to put value in their comfortable compromise. Economic language emerges as nothing other than what it is — the traffic of bodies to secure white aristocratic male privilege without acknowledgment of the racial and gendered insularity operating through and afforded by male friendship. Economic terms like "mortgaged" and "forfeit" populate the sonnet's extended conceit of commerce. The dark lady denies the proposition, opting instead to take from both as both lose more. Lamenting "Him have I lost; thou hast both him and me" (line 13), the poet elaborates:

> But thou wilt not, nor he will not be free,
> For thou art covetous and he is kind;
> [...]
> The statute of thy beauty thou wilt take,
> Thou usurer, that put'st forth all to use,

> And sue a friend came debtor for my sake;
> So him I lose through my unkind abuse. (sonnet 134, lines 5–6, 9–12)

The closeness and alignment of male friends' wills is kind — thus the repetition of this pun on the concept of kin/kind is multiply provocative when put to relief by the unkind dark lady. The dark mistress's rejection of the sacrificial offer ensuring the devotion of one lover instead of the contested suffering of two lovers, proves her to be *unfair* (unvirtuous, unchaste, unjust) and *unkind* (cruel, covetous, and refusing to heed the significance of kin). Her refusal of a measured, mutually beneficial exchange between fair participants, and the way this refusal disrupts an idealized kinship that rises above economic interest, renders her a "covetous. . . usurer," an outsider. While this might seem an obvious point — she is the ruthless temptress whose seduction distresses both men and compromises their friendship — I am delineating a more elusive disparity, one in which exclusion from and rejection of moral and social conventions give shape to ill-will. This exclusion from male fairness and kindness hinges on all of the ways the sonnet compels the concession of her will to the desires of the men, two friends who are reciprocally good to, and good for, each other. The dark mistress's power over them, and her exclusion from the economy that values the kinship between friends, depends entirely on her willful rejection of the role they desire her will to play.

And so sonnet 135's super amplification of the word will — 14 instances in a 14-line poem — alerts to the inherent dangers of will as the site of excess, ungovernability, and confusion. "Will" indicates a range of denotative meanings: intentional agency; a hopeful wish; an authoritative decree; a successful persuasion; and of course, an official declaration of the distribution of one's wealth upon death. Other uses for the word are more specific to the period: a euphemism for genitals if not a reference to sexual intercourse and, in this case, a reminder of the author's first name. This last point is much the topic of sonnet 136 that ends: "And then thou lov'st me for my name is Will" (line 14). But prior to this heavy-handed self-promotion, the central argument of sonnet 135 is more subtle: "Wilt thou, whose will is large and spacious, / Not once vouchsafe to hide my will in thine?" (lines 5–6) might be paraphrased as: you are such a slut, what difference does one more lover make? If this seems crass, consider all of the ways that the sonnet evokes notions of accepting, absorbing, and adding the poet's will *into* the dark lady's will, all argued within the context of excess: "And Will to boot, and Will in overplus" (sonnet 135, line 2). The central conceit is that the sea's expansive ability to take in water is like the dark mistress's unlimited capacity to have and to fulfill desires.

> And in my will no fair acceptance shine?
> The sea, all water, yet receives rain still,
> And in abundance addeth to his store;
> So thou, being rich in Will, add to thy Will
> One will of mine, to make thy large Will more. (sonnet 135, lines 8–12)

But unlike the sea that is forever receptive, the beloved does not allow Will's will into *her* large and spacious will (as a euphemism for genitals, this is basically a rejection of penetration). Alas, she will not concede to accommodate just one more will "to make [her] large Will more" or, it seems, to make *his* Will large. The point is that sonnet 135's unruly and dizzy profusions of the word not only build on the sonnet tradition's abiding interest in expressions of desire, sex, power, and wordplay, but they also represent the female beloved's positionality as bound up in her refusal to concede to male projections of sexual compliance or virtuous restraint, rendering her wilfulness ill indeed. And it is not just about procreation per se, for she is already wallowing in the abundant largess of her sexual capacity. Rather, it is her refusal to "vouchsafe" that is reprimanded. Even if sexual consummation ensues, it does not result in "fair acceptance." Thus, ill-will is not so much an affront to moral imperatives undergirding chastity, but rather a disruptive positionality that frustrates Will's will. She embodies not just departure from Petrarchan ideals but, furthermore, a rejection of normative, patriarchal, white heterodox and its attendant expressions of desire, as these expressions are produced for and circulated between male friends. The problem isn't sex — she's having lots of that — the problem of feeling is the refusal to comply, pacify, and ultimately, submit.

This integral aspect of ill-will, the refusal to submit, is bound up in the genre's inherent anti-Blackness, even as the sequence's rhetorical flourishes proclaim otherwise. Part of Shakespeare's innovation in the genre is a confrontation of the disparagements against Black femininity and the poet's insistence that "now is black beauty's successive heir" (sonnet 127, line 3), indicating the dark features of the mistress as superior to light-skinned beauty; indeed, "Thy black is fairest in my judgment's place" (sonnet 131, line 12). Winthrop D. Jordan has established that, in the early modern period, "Englishmen found in the idea of blackness a way of expressing some of their most ingrained values ... Black was an emotionally partisan color, the handmaid and symbol of baseness and evil, a sign of danger and repulsion."[24] Thus, Shakespeare's revision of Blackness is notable as a literary device. Yet Hall's influential analysis of the dominant but volatile polarity of dark and light in English sonnet sequences reveals that "descriptions of dark and light, rather than being mere indications of Elizabethan beauty standards or markers of moral categories, became in the early modern period the conduit through which the English began to formulate the notions of 'self' and 'other.'"[25] Notably, Shakespeare sonnets' praise of Blackness are essentially expressions of the persona's insistent valuation. Statements like "In *my* judgement's place" (sonnet 131, line 12 emphasis added), and "Then will I swear beauty herself is black, / And all they foul that thy complexion lack" (sonnet 132, lines 13–14) rely entirely on self-referential perceptions of the lover. If he is nearly polemical about the beauty of Blackness, then it is to call attention to the value and innovation of his endorsement as much as to any actual aspect of the beloved's features. It belies, in Hall's terms, a way of evoking Blackness to sanction a compulsion to whiten: "Positing a mistress as dark allows the poet to turn her white, to refashion her into an acceptable object of Platonic love and admiration. The loveliness of the Petrarchan beauties, despite their color, represents not *their seductive power* but the *poet*'s power in bringing them

24. Winthrop D. Jordan, *White over Black: American Attitudes toward the Negro, 1550–1812*, 2nd ed. (Chapel Hill: University of North Carolina Press, 2013), 7.
25. Hall, *Things of Darkness*, 2.

to light."[26] Shakespeare's insistence on "bringing to light" his mistress's dark beauty is proof of *his* literary superiority. The assertion of authorial power also signals the poet's unease about the mistress's exertion of sovereignty, one that cannot be compelled either to abide by tradition or to submit to the lovers' demands. When the beloved refuses to concede to the poet's wishes, the sonnets project onto her Blackness moral deviance and social disruption equal to the devil's. It is in response to the mistress's overpowering ill-will, rather than to her somatic darkness, that the poet later retracts his praise by stating "For I have sworn thee fair, and thought thee bright, / Who art as black as hell, as dark as night" (sonnet 147, lines 13–14).

This damning couplet evokes a long tradition of assigning to the black hue the ocular proof of evil. Sonnet 144 deploys a psychomachia trope to depict the struggle for the poet's heart and soul. The good angel is the youthful, fair, and righteous male friend and the ill-coloured mistress is the devil incarnate.

> The better angel is a man right fair:
> The worser spirit a woman coloured ill.
> To win me soon to hell my female evil,
> Tempteth my better angel from my side,
> And would corrupt my saint to be a devil:
> Wooing his purity with her foul pride. (sonnet 144, lines 3–8)

Rather than the recipient of courtship rituals, the "woman coloured ill" woos to corrupt, converting both men by compromising the virtue of the "man right fair." Male friendship that provides comfort, fairness, and kinship (all signs of general good will) is now entirely at her disposal to bring to hellish destruction. Fred Moten reads the love triangle as deviant sexuality: "heteroerotic and necessarily illegitimate procreativity that exists as such only as a function of the racialization of sexual difference."[27] I tarry

26. Hall, *Things of Darkness*, 67 emphases added.
27. Fred Moten, "The Dark Lady and the Sexual Cut: Sonnet Record Frame / Shakespeare Jones Eisenstein," *Women & Performance: a journal of feminist theory* 9, no. 2 (1997): 150.

over Moten's observation of this illegitimate procreativity, which I argue is the dark lady's other threat to whiteness — that of disrupting idealized white futurity couched in the language of purity assigned to the fair young man. The veneration and call for replication of the beloved male friend (via the cultural work of the poems' textual longevity and the biological reproduction via an appropriate white wife) attest to the sequence's preoccupation with the genealogy of fairness. The poet articulates his friend's pure, fair lineage as the natural and inviolable ideal of physical beauty and aspirational virtues, announced in the first two lines of the first sonnet: "From fairest creatures we desire increase, / That thereby beauty's rose might never die." Repeatedly iterating some version of "eternal lines" (sonnet 18, line 12) of "beauty by succession thine" (sonnet 2, line 12), the poet sustains pressure on his fair friend's biological and cultural reproduction. The dark lady's refusal to perform male projections of compliance and virtue go beyond the villainization of her illicit sexuality. She threatens the sequence's original thesis of an ideal young man's beautiful and fair "increase." The dark lady's ill-will is deployed to "win," "tempteth," "corrupt," and "woo" and is thus racialized in that Blackness threatens the genealogy of whiteness. This affective racialization is expressed in the language of sexual corruption, whereby ill-will turns what is pure and angelic into a devil.[28] According to the sonnets' anti-Black rhetoric, she not only menaces the wills she evokes (corrupting the desires of desperate male suitors), she also, as a harbinger of the devil's damnation, fundamentally counters a moral imperative implied in the male friends' constant though tested alliance as that alliance is to be cemented over reproductive white bodies. This is about miscegenation of the male friend's line, certainly, but the anxiety also reveals the fragilities of white futurity. Kind

28. In this way the sonnet echoes Othello's racialization of Desdemona's perceived adultery: "Her name, that was as fresh / As Dian's visage, is now begrimed and black / As mine own face" (3.3.386–388). I would like to thank Ambereen Dadabhoy for pointing out how the corruption anticipated by female promiscuity threatens to racialize all partners. See also Lara Bovilsky, *Barbarous Play: Race on the English Renaissance Stage* (Minneapolis: Minnesota University Press, 2008), Chapter 1.

progeny must be actively protected from the sexual corruptions of a dark beloved's ill-will. The future of fair is at stake.

As a woman of ill-will, the dark lady disrupts the kind friendship of men, undermines authority's investments in kinship, and challenges a white hegemony that presents itself *as* universal good will while underwriting the privileges of male alliances erected over racially unmarked, socially compliant, white female bodies. It is worth noting that the dark lady's villainization as an expression of anti-Black racialization does not ultimately hinge on any specific physical marker.[29] Ian Smith postulates important considerations when limiting race to the "semiotics and politics of skin color":

> More pointedly, what happens when we limit race to the prevalent semiotics and politics of skin color, a view conditioned largely in the American context by the intervening histories of slavery and colonialism, as well as the emergence of biological racism as pseudo-scientific fact? Quite simply, we run the risk of failing to disturb the distinct modern predispositions to equate race and color and so surrender to a reductive, chromal, and somatic phenomenology.[30]

29. Marvin Hunt highlights the relevance of the dark lady's physical markers and claims that "the overpowering contrary beauty of Shakespeare's dark lady and the corrosive effects of desire for her are, in part, direct consequences of her color" ("'Be Dark but not Too Dark': Shakespeare's Dark Lady as a Sign of Color," in *Shakespeare's Sonnets: Critical Essays*, ed. James Schiffer [New York: Garland, 1999], 370). Hunt's close analysis leads him to claim that the sonnet outlines "the liminal sign of a slave woman who, unbaptized, was also unnamed" (384). The analogue located in a historical figure deserves closer inspection in light of research on the existence and participation of Black citizens in London, especially heeding the work of Imtiaz Habib, *Black Lives in the English Archives, 1500–1677: Imprints of the Invisible* (London: Routledge, 2016). However, this chapter's findings do not hinge on a historical analogue to trace the racialized affects of the dark lady.
30. Ian Smith, *Race and Rhetoric in the Renaissance: Barbarian Errors* (New York: Palgrave MacMillan, 2009), 12.

Indeed, the reliance on physical difference as the sole indicator of race with little attention to how darkness intersects with "other means of racialization" has stalled the theorization of race with regards to the sonnets.[31] The ill-will of the dark lady is represented as an aberrant, ungovernable, and dangerous affect. She is firmly designated on the wrong end of the spectrum of compliance and incorporation. As the antagonistic, disruptive, racialized outsider, she fundamentally threatens the sonnets' traditional representations of gendered desire and social identity. In their representation of Black sexuality as fundamentally unkind, Shakespeare's sonnets provide a precedent for excusing, indeed aestheticizing, racial insularity and the future of fair.

It is precisely through her embodiment of ill-will that the dark lady shows the harrying coercion, mercenary self-promotion, and racial insularity of erotic persuasions. The sonnets cultivate a sexual politics marshalled around the affect of her racialized ill-will, rendering the dark lady a threat to the future of fair and categorically excluded from the insularity of kind. In other words, her racialized affect is not a foil to, but rather the foundation for, white male friends' kind kinship. By refusing and undermining kind kin, she is represented as unkind and kinless. Such attributions are fodder for what white supremacists tell themselves about themselves. Readers are compelled to worry over the fair angel's reproductive future — a future threatened by the dark lady's ill-will. To this, habits of perception that support white supremacy obscure the dire outcomes for those who suffer from exclusion and objectification.

For the Black mistress, what are the implications of casting her as a threat to legitimate procreation? What would it entail, and what would it reveal, to reject the premise of her villainization? How would an analysis

31. Representative of a brand of historicism resistant to critical readings of race in the early modern period, David Schalkwyk dismisses as anachronistically inaccurate the critical attention to the dark lady as dark, stating critics are "projecting matrices of ideological signification upon them [the dark lady's descriptions]. How dark we allow her to be will be a mark of her 'otherness', her scandalousness, both of which arise out of our own, twenty-first century history and preoccupations rather than the sonnet's pseudo-descriptions" ("Race, Body, and Language in Shakespeare's Sonnets and Plays," *English Studies in Africa* 47, no. 2 [2009]: 16).

of ill-will, as something other than an expression of evil, bring into relief the racism embroiled in the formation of the commonweal's good will? To break away from the habits inculcated by white hegemony in early modern English studies, it is time to ask a different set of questions. If not in friendship, where is *her* comfort? If not in succession, what is *her* lineage? If not in kind, who is *her* kin?

The unkind kinlessness projected onto the dark mistress's ill-will is not separate from, but rather elemental to, the commodification of Black femininity. As critics and historians have proven about the carnage of slavery, kinlessness is a racialized condition enforced through the commodification of flesh, the abduction of personal volition, and the erasure of a Black genealogy.[32] Achille Mbembe explains that

> For Blacks confronted with the reality of slavery, loss is first of a genealogical order. In the New World, the Black slave is legally stripped of all kinship. Slaves are, in consequence, "without parents." The condition of *kinlessness* is imposed on them through law and power. And eviction from the world of legal kinship is an inherited condition. Birth and descent afford them no right to any form of social relationship or belonging as such.[33]

In the words of Frederick Douglass's painful lament: "My poor mother, like many other slave-women, had many children but NO FAMILY."[34] Jennifer L.

32. Hauntingly, Hortense J. Spillers has theorized kinlessness as "an extension of the boundaries of proliferating properties" and asks us to "sharpen our own sense of the African female's reproductive uses within the diasporic enterprise of Enslavement and the genetic reproduction of the enslaved" ("Mama's Baby, Papa's Maybe: An American Grammar Book," *Diacritics* 17, no. 2 [1987]: 75, 74.
33. Achille Mbembe, *Critique of Black Reason*, trans. Laurent Dubois (Durham, NC: Duke University Press, 2017), 33 original emphasis.
34. Frederick Douglass, *My Bondage and My Freedom* (1855), in *Autobiographies*, ed. Henry Louis Gates, Jr. (New York: Praetorian Books, 1994), 149. Saidiya Hartman reckons with the irretrievability of her African lineage when an ancestor's identity is reduced to marks on flesh: "no one wants to identify her kin by the cipher of slave-trading companies, or by the brand, which supplanted identity and left only a scar in its place" (*Lose*

Morgan investigates the economic, sociological, and historical networks contributing to the formation of Black motherhood in the context of the African diaspora. The denial of kinship and thus the assumption of an inability to be kind was central to the dispossession of the enslaved. Morgan explains this "concept of perpetual and hereditary racial slavery" as dependent upon "a strategic dislodging of Africans from the family of Man would become crucial to rendering them as commodities"[35] Rendered unkind and kinless and thus excluded "from the family of Man," the rhetorical violence unleashed upon the dark lady sanctions, and hauntingly anticipates, the inhumane exploitation of other dark ladies.

The sonnets played a role in the justification for enslavability because they participated in the project of severing kind kinship from Blackness. Black women's abduction and violation for the accumulation of human capital under slavery was justified by and reinforced through the racist attribution of them as unkind (paradoxically drawing from the allegation of lacking feeling and anticipation of active maliciousness) and kinless (paradoxically a source of reproductive power yet unmoored from family, lineage, and community). The dark lady sequence's investment in the future of fair is dependent upon its depiction of a Black woman's incapacity for kindness and refutation of kinship. This foundational fiction, this racist lie, has consequences beyond the page.

Your Mother: A Journey along the Atlantic Slave Route [New York: Farrar, Straus and Giroux, 2007], 80).

35. Jennifer L. Morgan, *Reckoning with Slavery: Gender, Kinship, and Capitalism in the Early Black Atlantic* (Durham, NC: Duke University Press, 2021), 83. Morgan also discusses how "as slaveowners contemplated women's reproductive potential with greed and opportunism, they utilized both outrageous images and callously indifferent strategies to ultimately inscribe enslaved women as racially and culturally different while creating an economic and moral environment in which the appropriation of a woman's children as well as her childbearing potential became rational and, indeed, natural" (*Laboring Women: Reproduction and Gender in New World Slavery* [Philadelphia: University of Pennsylvania Press, 2004], 7).